Discursive Practice in Language Learning and Teaching

Language Learning Monograph Series

Lourdes Ortega, Series Editor
Nick C. Ellis, General Editor

Discursive Practice
in Language Learning and Teaching

Richard F. Young
University of Wisconsin-Madison

WILEY-
BLACKWELL

Blackwell Publishing was acquired by John Wiley & Sons in February 2007. Blackwell's publishing program has been merged with Wiley's global Scientific, Technical, and Medical business to form Wiley-Blackwell.

Registered Office
John Wiley & Sons Ltd, The Atrium, Southern Gate, Chichester, West Sussex, PO19 8SQ, United Kingdom

Editorial Offices
350 Main Street, Malden, MA 02148-5020, USA
9600 Garsington Road, Oxford, OX4 2DQ, UK
The Atrium, Southern Gate, Chichester, West Sussex, PO19 8SQ, UK

For details of our global editorial offices, for customer services, and for information about how to apply for permission to reuse the copyright material in this book please see our website at www.wiley.com/wiley-blackwell.

The right of Richard F. Young to be identified as the author of the editorial material in this work has been asserted in accordance with the Copyright, Designs and Patents Act 1988.

Wiley also publishes its books in a variety of electronic formats. Some content that appears in print may not be available in electronic books.

Designations used by companies to distinguish their products are often claimed as trademarks. All brand names and product names used in this book are trade names, service marks, trademarks or registered trademarks of their respective owners. The publisher is not associated with any product or vendor mentioned in this book. This publication is designed to provide accurate and authoritative information in regard to the subject matter covered. It is sold on the understanding that the publisher is not engaged in rendering professional services. If professional advice or other expert assistance is required, the services of a competent professional should be sought.

Library of Congress Cataloging-in-Publication Data

Young, Richard, 1948-
    Discursive practice in language learning and teaching / Richard F. Young.
        p. cm.
Includes bibliographical references and index.
ISBN 978-1-4051-8444-1
1. Language and languages–Study and teaching–Social aspects. I. Title.
P53.8.Y68 2009
418.0071–dc22

2009000988

A catalogue record for this book is available from the British Library.

Set in 10/13 pt TimesNRPS by Aptara
Printed in the U.S.A. by The Sheridan Press

01—2009

**Discursive Practice in Language
Learning and Teaching**

Contents

Language Learning   ISSN 0023-8333

Series Editor's Foreword

The field of second language acquisition (SLA) has been transformed in the last 10 years by what has been seen by many as a social turn. Increasingly more SLA researchers feel they can no longer afford to ignore the social context of second language learning, and some have directly engaged with the need to appropriately theorize the two notions of "social" and "context." However, multiple understandings of social context coexist across language-related fields, and exactly which one each SLA scholar may be willing to adopt matters deeply in terms of the discipline's ability to offer satisfactory explanations for the learning of additional languages. The matter of crafting a viable ontological and epistemological substance for "social context" can also have dire consequences for the potential for SLA knowledge to be of use to educators who wish to support additional language users in their lifelong development of linguistic, academic, social, cultural, and personal competencies in several languages, rather than only one. This volume by Richard Young in the *Language Learning* Monograph Series presents a highly personal, deeply synthetic, and remarkably organic treatment of the social context of additional language learning. His proposed framework of Discursive Practice serves well the study of additional language learning as a fundamentally and inexorably social phenomenon and is one in which theory and application naturally nourish each other.

Young has himself been at the center of research on context and SLA. For over two decades, he has been committed to examining the social context of second language learning. In his influential early publications, he investigated interaction and attributes of interlocutors from a sociolinguistic perspective, placing systematic variation at the heart of SLA. This was a time in the mid- and late 1980s when SLA researchers reaped the fruits of initial forays into sociolinguistic theories. Nevertheless, for a while during the early 1990s it looked as if SLA's decided engagement with interdisciplinarity would channel most efforts toward making connections with theories developed in a range of cognitive fields. Instead of losing sight of the importance of the social for explaining additional language learning, Young recast his interest in systematic variation into keen attention to the context-bound nature of communication. He began to lay the empirical foundations of a research program whose goal was to elucidate talk in context and context in talk, examining real-world situations of language use such as oral proficiency interviews, college writing conferences, and high school science classrooms. This research program was also strengthened subsequently by attention to written discourse in context. In his present book, Young explicates the approach to studying second language learning that he calls Discursive Practice and which is a culmination of all this previous work. In doing so, he leads readers through an interdisciplinary tour de force in which he offers powerful tools for understanding verbal, nonverbal, and interactional resources that second language users develop as they engage with various communities and contexts.

One important contribution of the book is that it expands the intellectual landscape of SLA. It does so by synthesizing knowledge about language, action, and interaction that has been crafted by diverse positions within semiotics, philosophy, linguistic anthropology, ethnography, and sociology. Young heeds the teachings of classic ethnography of communication in its descriptions of talk in context. He also finds important insights in the political lens afforded by educational ethnography and its revealing scrutiny of local-global complementary tensions. At the same time, he details the value of the emotional standpoint summoned by self-story and narrative methodologies. And he is sympathetic to, as much as he is critical of, the sociological study of social action in the traditions of ethnomethodology and Conversation Analysis. In addition to this epistemological balancing act of syncretism, Young's novel synthesis enables a cogent treatment of useful tools inherited from the Prague School of Functional Linguistics and Systemic Functional Grammar and which remain severely underutilized by SLA researchers. He glues arguments and analyses in the book through a staged, multiple successive exegesis of discourse data that provides readers with a sense of incremental and cyclical enlightment.

Another major contribution of the book is that Young does not shy away from worldly questions about the utility of Discursive Practice for education and social transformation. He is interested in the value that his Discursive Practice framework may have to inform teaching and testing of additional languages across diverse contexts. Consequently, he does not eschew the conundrum of locating *learning* in a theory that posits everything humans learn is context-grounded and in an ontology where knowledge is not a substance that can transfer across individuals or contexts but a process that is always emergent and situated. How can knowledge of a discursive practice carry across contextual boundaries, and how can it aid learners across new contexts? Young engages with this problem of *portability of knowledge*, a felicitous term he coins in this book. His solution is to propose that what is learned are situated configurations of verbal, nonverbal, and interactional resources associated with each practice.

The same resources, once learned through use in context, can be realigned creatively and ported to new contexts, facilitating participation in new and increasingly varied practices over time. Participation in the new practice will be key to new learning, but previously acquired configuration of resources may be ported and make the learning easier.

Finally, *power* does not get forgotten in Young's account either. Throughout the book, Young's forceful argument is that "practices are the everyday pivot between societal structure and the individual" (p. 150). Thus, through his analysis of actual discourse data, he makes a convincing case for the centrality in all language learning of what he repeatedly calls "the battle for subjectivity," a term he takes from feminist poststructuralist Chris Weedon. Furthermore, he cogently draws on the current burgeoning work on community and identity in SLA, but also on Foucauldian views of power and Althusser's notion of *interpellation*, in order to argue that second language learning is only a (small?) part of a wider social ecology in which identities are negotiated, resisted, and appropriated as individuals struggle to position themselves as subjects and as they are constructed and positioned by others through dominant discourses and ideologies—that is, through situated language use itself.

This book is the sixth volume in the *Language Learning* Monograph Series, and the first under my editorship. The goal of this series is to advance knowledge in the language sciences with volumes that review recent findings and current theoretical positions, present new data and interpretations, and sketch interdisciplinary research programs. Volumes are authoritative statements by scholars who have led in the development of a particular line of interdisciplinary research and are intended to serve as a benchmark for interdisciplinary research in the years to come. In *Discursive Practice in Language Learning and Teaching*, Richard Young, who has spearheaded the Series for five volumes and 10 years, offers the field a paradigm of forward-looking interdisciplinarity. Through Young's unique blend of authority and intellectual honesty, the book conjures a rich space for thinking of novel ways forward in future SLA theorizing about the social context.

Lourdes Ortega
University of Hawai'i at Mānoa

Acknowledgments

All books are jointly constructed by an author and those with whom he has had the good fortune to interact, and this book is no exception. Those whose contributions have greatly enriched my thinking and writing include Dell Hymes, Frederick Erickson, Joan Kelly Hall, Numa Markee, Peter Fries, and Chris Candlin. Dell Hymes started it all, but I have been principally inspired by Frederick Erickson's insights into the pivotal relationship between talk and social context, and he will recognize his influence throughout the book. When I began to apply those insights to language learning and teaching, Joan Kelly Hall's trailblazing work on interactional competence was an inspiration. Numa Markee has always been a friend and a foil in arguments about talk-in-interaction, and although he may not agree with the positions that I have taken in this book, I first found them in discussions with him. Peter Fries was a great help when, several years ago, I first began the study of Systemic Functional Grammar and, more recently, Chris Candlin nudged me into a productive new way of presenting SFG.

Many of the ideas that I present in this book were first floated in a seminar on discursive practice that I taught at the University of Wisconsin-Madison, and I recognize the brilliant contributions to that seminar by Hanh Nguyen and Liz Miller, both of whom have since gone on to become independent researchers and whose work I have cited extensively in this book. Many other students, colleagues, and friends have provided useful insights on specific issues with which I struggled while writing this book, and I thank them for their help. They are, in alphabetical order, Hassan Belhiah, Micheline Chalhoub-Deville, Dustin Cowell, Peter De Costa, Cecilia Ford, Celeste Kinginger, Dale Koike, Veronika Lehner, Sally Magnan, Aree Manosuthikit, Junko Mori, Cynthia Nelson, Hyu-Yong Park, François Tochon, Paul Toth, and Robin Worth. For bibliographic help, I am grateful for the services of Brian Knight and the excellent resources provided by the University of Wisconsin-Madison libraries.

This book would never have been written without the enthusiasm and patient encouragement over many months of my editor, Lourdes Ortega. Whenever I sent a draft of a chapter to her, Lourdes always replied promptly with insightful comments and suggestions. It is a better book thanks to her.

Writing is a solitary occupation, but I have enjoyed the company through many long days at the keyboard of Lord Byron, Creamy, and Oreo. At the end of a hard day's writing, I was always refreshed by the company and the cooking of my wife Lingling Ho. During the 25 years of study that led up to the first words that I wrote and then throughout the long months of writing, Lingling has been constant in her love and support for me. I am a lucky man.

Language Learning   ISSN 0023-8333

CHAPTER ONE

What Is Discursive Practice?

In the title of this book *Discursive Practice in Language Learning and Teaching*, most of the words will be familiar to applied linguists and second language (L2) researchers, but the sense of two terms may be unfamiliar. As for "learning" and "teaching"—well, L2 researchers and applied linguists spend much time and effort using these two terms so perhaps they do not stand out. "Practice," too. Although applied linguists may use the term "practice" in slightly different senses, again it is a term used frequently in discussions of learning and teaching. For instance, in his introduction to a recent collection of research articles on *practice* in an L2, DeKeyser (2007) explained what he and the other contributors to his book mean by the term. Practice is not meant to be understood as the opposite of theory, DeKeyser wrote; instead, practice involves specific activities in an L2 that learners engage in, deliberately, with the goal of developing knowledge of and skills in the L2. He adds that for cognitive psychologists, most of the activities included in practice involve repetition of the same or closely similar performance in routines.

In this book, by "practice" I mean something very different from the way the term is defined by DeKeyser. In the sense that I use the word, practice is the construction and reflection of social realities through actions that invoke identity, ideology, belief, and power. How does practice in this sense differ from DeKeyser's definition? First, "practice" as used in this book is not a term of art in L2 studies and it can be applied to all human activities. Second, although practice is goal-oriented, the goal of people who participate in practice is not necessarily L2 learning; in fact, participants' orientation to some goal in a practice may not be deliberate at all, often because the goal is not available to their conscious introspection. Third, yes, the term "practice" as used in this book involves repetition, but what participants do in a practice is not necessarily to repeat their own performance; instead, a person may perform a practice for the first time in their life but, through direct or indirect observation, the person has knowledge of the history of a practice in their community, and it is that history that is extended in practice.

What is fundamentally different about the way that I use the term "practice" in this book is that practice is performance in context. By context, I mean the network of physical, spatial, temporal, social, interactional, institutional, political, and historical circumstances in which participants do a practice. This sense derives from vigorous recent scholarship by anthropologists, philosophers, social theorists, and French poststructuralists. In this tradition, I have used the term "Practice Theory" as an overarching term to include work in closely related fields, including community of practice, literacy practice, social practice, and communicative practice.

Research in Practice Theory has focused on what people do in practices. In this book, I have focused on that part of what people do that involves language and, for this reason, I have called it *discursive* practice. The word "discursive" also needs some explanation because "discourse" has accumulated many senses in recent years. In its original sense in applied linguistics, "discourse" refers to stretches of language above the level of the sentence in conversations or written texts. More recently, "discourse" has also taken on an extended meaning that differs from its use in applied linguistics in at least two ways. First, in the extended meaning of the word, language is not the sole system of signs to be studied as discourse; other semiotic systems are included, such as habits of dress, the built environment, and, of course, gesture. Second, the meaning of "discourse" has been further extended to include societal meaning-making systems such as institutional power, social differentiation of groups, and cultural beliefs that create identities for individuals and position them in social relationships. This sense of "discursive" in "discursive practice" is accurately advertised in the description of the program in discursive practice that I quote from the Web site of the Department of Anthropology at the University of Hawai'i: "The discursive practice approach is grounded in four insights concerning discourse. One is the affirmation that social realities are linguistically/discursively constructed. The second is the appreciation of the context-bound nature of discourse. The third is the idea of discourse as social action. The fourth is the understanding that meaning is negotiated in interaction, rather than being present once-and-for-all in our utterances."

Studying discursive practices involves paying attention not only to the production of meanings by participants as they employ in local actions the verbal, nonverbal, and interactional resources that they command, but it also requires attention to how employment of such resources reflects and creates the processes and meanings of the community in which the local action occurs. As Erickson (2004) wrote, although the conduct of talk in local social interaction is unique and crafted by local social actors for the specific situation of its use at the moment of its uttering, it is at the same time profoundly influenced by processes that occur beyond the temporal and spatial horizon of the immediate occasion of interaction. The aim of discursive practice is to describe both the global context of action and the communicative resources that participants employ in local action. When the context of a practice is known and the configuration of communicative resources is described, the ultimate aim of Practice Theory is to explain the ways in which the global context affects the local employment of resources and vice versa.

What does discursive practice have to do with the second half of the title of this book—language learning and teaching? A prior question is: What does discursive practice have to do with language? With few exceptions, language and linguistic knowledge have been the focus of attention of applied linguists and second language acquisition (SLA) researchers since the earliest studies of second language acquisition. This is not surprising, given the long and distinguished history of the field of linguistics going back to ancient India. The discipline and methodology of linguistics developed to the point that the founders of modern linguistics (von Humboldt, Saussure, and Chomsky) were able to separate a theoretically fixed notion from the mass and heterogeneous activity of production and interpretation of utterances that form a part of our lived experience. The clean and fixed abstraction was called langue, competence, or I-language and was carefully distinguished from the lived reality of parole, performance, or E-language. Lacking a theory of context, linguists did the best they could to isolate a phenomenon believed to underlie actual use. Separating language from context is easy because ever since the invention of writing, language has been easy to isolate. For the modern linguist, the technology of audio and video recording has made the physical and spatial context of language available for analysis, but the technology provides only a blinkered view of the extended context of language. It provides the illusion that language in its physical and spatial context is a real slice of life, but it is a very thin slice indeed, in which language is still isolated from its social, interactional, institutional, political, and historical circumstances.

In a cross-cultural endeavor like L2 learning and teaching, the question of extended context becomes pressing. When we experience life in an L2 community, we become immediately aware that context influences language in the new community in different ways than the influence of our home context on our native language. People living in cross-cultural relationships are brought to a daily realization of the importance of understanding another person's context in order to understand that person's language. One such cross-cultural relationship was described by Veronica Ye (2003), a Chinese woman born in

Shanghai who migrated to live in Australia with her Australian husband. She contrasted the context of linguistic expressions of feeling like "I love you" in the two communities that she knew:

> I was brought up with the Confucian code of behaviour that *nannü shoushou buqin* ('man and woman do not touch each other's hands'). Any intimate behaviour in public would make me extremely uncomfortable. Any expression of emotion should be controlled and subtle. Chinese couples do not say "I love you" to each other, as people in Australia do over the phone, when seeing each other off, and before going to work. We do not place so much emphasis on verbal expressions of love and affection, because they can evaporate quickly. For a Chinese, love and affection are embodied in care and concern, in doing what we believe are good things for the other party. We "force" our husbands to eat in the belief that it is good for them. We criticise them directly as a way of showing endearment and true concern. We do not need to compliment our husbands, saying "I am proud of you," because "honeyed" words are niceties for social purposes. As long as we know this in our hearts, we do not have to say them out aloud, and the other party would know this. When we say our innermost thoughts to our partner and point out their "bad sides" for improvement, we are thinking truly and purely in the interest of the other; it is the ultimate care. It took a few years for my husband to get accustomed to this Chinese "logic" of love, and for me to be more communicative in expressing my love and affection. (p. 5)

Some of the complexities of meanings in cultural context have become apparent through the work of Mey (2001) and Kasper and Rose (2002) in discourse pragmatics. Beyond discourse pragmatics and cross-cultural communication, however, the advantage that Practice Theory brings is that it provides a general interpretive framework for understanding moments of interaction by people in a new community and among people in different communities. Practice Theory explains how the extended context of interaction—the network of social, interactional, institutional, political, and historical circumstances—affects the verbal and nonverbal resources that people employ. In other words, it is not enough to learn a new language in order to understand and appreciate an unfamiliar discursive practice. There is a danger, if we ignore the extended context of language, that learning a new language becomes simply knowing how to express, in a new language, familiar ideas from an old cultural context.

A discursive practice approach to language learning is, then, an approach that engages first with the learning of practices—which means that language learning involves far more than learning a language. Language learning is understood to include not only the acquisition of knowledge about language but also the development of ways in which language and other semiotic systems are put to use in the service of adaptation to a new culture and participation in a new community. What is focused on is the participation of people in practices, how their participation changes, how learners' communicative resources are adapted in the recurrent performance of a practice with different participants, and how they reconfigure those resources to meet the demands and affordances of unfamiliar practices. Because the investigation of language learning begins with practice, the discursive practice approach to language learning is happily epitomized in the Hawaiian expression "ma ka hana ka 'ike" (while working, you learn).

Language teaching also happens in social contexts, and Practice Theory focuses attention on the contexts in which the practices of teaching occur. Language teaching is thus the teaching of discursive practices, and the pedagogy of discursive practices in an L2 has been approached in different ways. One way is to analyze the resources that participants employ in practices in a foreign community and then to teach those resources by attempting to reproduce that practice as a pedagogical exercise. The problem with this pedagogy of practice is that it ignores the function of practice as a pivot between society and the individual and it disregards the fact that the political context of a pedagogical practice is not the same as the context of a practice in the community. As studies of classroom practices have shown, what students learn in a classroom is the classroom practice. Although the language presented in a pedagogical practice may resemble the language used in the discursive practice in the community, it is not the language by itself that creates the social and political context in which the practice occurs in the community. Ways out of this dilemma are suggested throughout this book.

A Look Ahead

In the remaining chapters of this book, I show the origins of Practice Theory and recount how the relationship between language learning and context has been analyzed by researchers. I then provide in some detail a methodology for investigating how participants configure verbal, nonverbal, and interactional resources in a practice. This is followed by two chapters in which I lay out the implications of Practice Theory for language learning, teaching, and testing. In the final chapter, I discuss what further research needs to be done in order to identify what contributions Practice Theory can bring to cognitive-psychological approaches to language learning.

In chapter 2, "Foundations for the Study of Practice," the historical roots of contemporary Practice Theory are unearthed in the work of semioticians, philosophers, and anthropologists. Saussure's semiotic theory is contrasted with that of Peirce, and the importance of Peirce's work for understanding the context of signs is stressed. The philosophy of language in the writings of Wittgenstein, Austin, and Searle is plumbed for a theory of the relationship between language and context. Contemporary writings by linguistic anthropologists Malinowski, Firth, and Mitchell are reviewed to establish the concept of "context of situation," and Hymes's application of the methods of ethnography to communicative events is discussed in detail. The foundations of modern Practice Theory in anthropology as an attempt to explain cultural reproduction in the minutiae of social interaction are located in the work of Bourdieu and Sahlins, and an example of the application of Practice Theory is provided.

Chapter 3, "Investigating Context," begins with the statement that all talk happens somewhere, somehow, at some time and is produced by somebody for some purpose, and the approach that practice theorists have taken is that talk and its context are inseparable. The challenges that face an analyst of practice are then to describe the context, describe the talk, and explain the relationship between talk and context. Four ways of approaching that challenge are reviewed in recent work by a number of researchers. Liu's (2000) analysis of one child's acquisition of English with different interlocutors is presented as an instance of an applied linguistic approach to practice. Toohey's (2000) longitudinal ethnographic analysis of a class of minority-language children in English-medium classrooms in Canada moves the focus of attention from language to context. Garrett and Young's (2009) study is of a single learner and her emotional responses to her language learning experience and extends the notion of context to include learners' emotions. Finally, studies by Baquedano-López (1997/2001), Conteh (2007), Gebhard (2002/2004), and Shameem (2007) describe clearly how ethnic cultural ideologies are transmitted through language instruction.

In chapter 4, "Discursive Resources," the focus of attention moves from the contexts described in chapter 3 to the verbal, nonverbal, and interactional resources that participants employ in discursive practices. These resources are discussed within the frame of participation status and participation framework proposed by Goffman. Verbal resources employed by participants in interaction are analyzed within Systemic Functional Grammar because SFG, as developed originally by Halliday, is the only analytical system that makes explicit connections between language form and context. The way that systemic functional analysis applies in the analysis of practice is exemplified in an analysis of an interaction between a high school teacher and his class. A systemic functional analysis reveals the relationship between language form and language function, but a different approach is needed to show how participants create social meanings and identities in interaction. Conversation Analysis (CA) is the approach used to describe how participants use interactional resources in a practice and an example is provided of a CA analysis of the same classroom interaction that was analyzed systemically earlier in the chapter. Finally, Charles Goodwin's extension of CA methodology to the explication of nonverbal resources is applied to the same classroom interaction.

In chapters 3 and 4, I hope to have laid the foundations for a practice approach to language learning, teaching, and testing, which are the topics of chapters Five and Six. Chapter Five, "Language Learning and Discursive Practice," is framed by three questions: What is learned? Who is learning? Who is participating in the learning? These questions are addressed in two learning theories: Language Socialization and Situated Learning theory. In Language Socialization, the answer to the question of what is learned includes not only language but also ways of acting, ways of feeling, and beliefs. When these are acknowledged as what is learned, the challenges for L2 learners are seen in a new light because using an L2 involves a battle for subjectivity in a new community. Learning a new language involves becoming part of a new community, either a classroom community or a community outside the classroom. The concept of community of practice is introduced in this chapter to show how what is shared in communities is not only a language but a repertoire of styles of communicating. How newcomers approach participation in a community is aptly described in the studies of Situated Learning or legitimate peripheral participation that are reviewed in chapter 5. The chapter concludes with analyses of two examples of situated learning.

Chapter 6, "Contexts of Teaching and Testing," continues the focus on learning, but now in the context of schooling. How does a practice approach explain language learning in relationship to language teaching and language testing? In Practice Theory, a foreign language classroom is a site for pedagogical practices and what students learn is how to participate in those practices. In some cases, pedagogical practices are designed to reproduce practices from the foreign language community in the classroom, but even when the language of pedagogical practice resembles the language used in the discursive practice in the community, the language does not create the same identities as the community practice. In this chapter, the role of ideology, societal politics, and institutional power are identified as important influences on pedagogical practice. In language testing, too, the societal and political consequences of the testing process and test results are brought to the forefront by a practice approach. The question of how far an individual's test results can be generalized to that person's performance in a nontesting context can also be answered in Practice Theory by a comparison of the configuration of resources employed by participants in a testing practice with their configuration in a community practice.

The final chapter, "Prospects for Practice," is forward-looking. In it, I suggest further ways that Practice Theory can be applied to understanding language teaching and learning. In particular, more work is needed to describe the configuration of discursive resources in practices in foreign language communities in order to design effective pedagogies and assessments. A critical approach to identifying and understanding the power relations inherent in practices is also needed. Finally, work is needed to connect theories of L2 cognition and theories of context.

Language Learning   ISSN 0023-8333

CHAPTER TWO

Foundations for the Study of Practice

The fields of language learning and applied linguistics are currently strewn with dichotomies. Inevitably for a multidisciplinary field, the ways in which applied linguists work differ according to our training and our cognitive styles. What applied linguists should study, how to study it, the colleagues to whom our results are communicated, and the eventual impact of our work differ according to our intellectual interests and affiliations. The diversity within the field is enriched by current debates in the humanities and social sciences among those who take very different views about what constitutes knowledge of society, ideas, and even the physical world. The principal fault lines lie between those who hold to modernist views of universality, homogeneity, and the possibility of consensual agreement among diverging points of view and postmodernists who, by contrast, see plurality, variety, and change underlying all knowledge and belief systems and who, in Z. Bauman's (1992) words, therefore see order and agreement among competing world views as only "randomly emerging, shifting and evanescent" (p. 189).

The field of second language acquisition (SLA) has been defined by a dichotomy that has received much attention since a symposium organized at the World Congress of Applied Linguistics in Jyväsklyä, Finland, in 1996. Alan Firth and Johannes Wagner opened the symposium with a paper titled "On Discourse, Communication, and (Some) Fundamental Concepts in SLA Research," and several scholars responded to their paper. The Firth and Wagner paper, the original responses, and one new contribution were published in 1997 in their entirety in *The Modern Language Journal*. The debate that Firth and Wagner started drew in sharp relief for the field of SLA the distinction between modernist and postmodernist views of knowledge, learning, and society. For SLA, the dichotomy was between those researchers who see SLA as a cognitive process located in the mind-brain of a single learner and other researchers who conceive of SLA as an essentially social process distributed among participants in social interaction, some of whom are not native speakers of a language. Ten years later, the major issues in that debate and their impact on the field of SLA were revisited in a special issue of *The Modern Language Journal* edited by Lafford (2007). Lafford summarized the five main points raised by the original Firth and Wagner (1997) paper:

1. [...] F&W (1997) called for a reconceptualization of SLA "as a more theoretically and methodologically balanced enterprise that endeavours to attend to, explicate, and explore, in more equal measures and, where possible, in integrated ways, both the *social* and *cognitive* dimensions of S/FL use and acquisition" (p. 286).
2. F&W (1997, 1998) asserted that the segregation of the concepts of language acquisition and use, typical of work carried out by linguists working within the mainstream cognitive paradigm was an untenable dichotomy [...].
3. [...] The cognitivist conduit model of language learning as the transmission of linguistic elements from one mind to the other needed to be complemented by a model of co-construction in which meaning was negotiated and co-created by the interlocutors themselves.
4. In a cognitive view of SLA, the only identities of interest to language researchers are those of the language learner and the native speaker (NS). [However, ...] multiple identities [...] play a part in the types of interactions that he or she experiences with other interlocutors [...].
5. In light of the socio-political effects of globalization and the increased number of new multilingual communities [...], the SLA database needed to be expanded to allow the investigation of the acquisition and use of L2s in natural contexts outside the classroom.

(Lafford, 2007, pp. 736–736)

These five dichotomies—SLA as a cognitive or social process, learning as acquisition or use, meaning as transmitted or co-constructed, a learner's identity as single or multiple, and language learning occurring inside and outside the classroom—are all issues that will be addressed throughout this work. Each of them establishes two mutually exclusive concepts or concepts opposed by contradiction and, since Hegel, dichotomies have been accepted ways of broaching complex topics. Take, for example, dichotomies that Erickson (2004) used to frame talk and social theory or Linell (2005) acknowledged in his introduction to dialogism: language as an inventory of forms or talk-in-interaction as a process, top-down or bottom-up, local or global, knowing or acting, fact or value, and cognition or emotion. The dichotomies in SLA result from differing interpretations of social and cognitive phenomena in other areas of human studies. In theories of meaning put forward by semioticians, in theories of language put forward by philosophers, and in theories of cultural reproduction advanced by anthropologists are found the foundations of the dichotomies in SLA identified by Firth and Wagner. In this chapter, I review those foundational theories and in later chapters I show how those theories have impacted methodologies of investigating second language (L2) learning, teaching, testing, and use.

Two Theories of Semiotics

The essential difference in studies of language and other systems of human communication that some of these dichotomies reflect is perhaps best captured in the two major 20th-century theories of semiotics: one associated with Ferdinand de Saussure and the other with Charles Sanders Peirce. In Saussure's theory (Saussure, Bally, Sechehaye, Riedlinger, & Baskin, 1966), a sign has two components: the signifier and the signified. The signifier is the form of the sign that we use in perception and communication; for example, a red traffic light, the direction of a weather vane, and a word like "house" all have visual or auditory forms that function as *signifiers*. The complements of these signifiers are their *signifieds*, or what we commonly term their meanings. So, if you are in a car, a red traffic light "means" stop; the direction that a weather vane is pointing "means" the direction that the wind is blowing; and the word "house" signifies a building for human habitation. Saussure believed that the relationship between the signifier and the signified is purely arbitrary, and he illustrated his point with examples of the relationship between signifier and signified in different languages. The signifier of "a building for human habitation" in English is *house*, but in French it is *maison*, in Italian it is *casa*, and in Chinese it is 房子 (fángzi), so there is no way to predict the form of the signifier by looking at what it signifies. In just the same way, if we look at a particular signifier, there is no way to predict what it signifies; for example, when the sound [liy] is spelled *Lee* in English, it is a family name, and when it is spelled *lea*, it means grassland or pasture, but a very similar sound is written *lit* in French and means "bed," and in Chinese, a very similar sound is written 里 (lǐ), which means "in" or "inside." Given that the relationship between signifier and signified (between word and meaning) is arbitrary, Saussure proposed that members of the same speech community share a kind of social contract and one clause, if you like, in that social contract is that the members of the community all accept a particular arbitrary relationship between signifier and signified—between word and meaning. The relationship cannot be changed for, as Saussure said, "No individual, even if he willed it, could modify in any way at all the choice [to associate a signifier with its signified] that has been made; and what is more, the community itself cannot control so much as a single word; it is bound to the existing language" (Saussure et al., 1966, p. 71).

Saussure's social contract theory of meaning solves the problem of how people communicate by using signifiers that bear only an arbitrary relationship to meaning, but it creates an immutable relationship that is independent of any particular moment of communication; yet we know from our daily experience of the hurly-burly of talk-in-interaction that ideas do not always proceed smoothly from one mind to another in spoken and written communication. This is not simply because the individuals with whom we communicate have not, so to speak, signed the same social contract as we have (e.g., young children and foreigners) but because the same physical form of a signifier may create different meanings in the minds of different people at different times and at different places. Take, for example, the utterance "Terry is a Republican." If we know that Terry is a Republican, we know in the context of discussions of politics in the United States that if Terry votes in elections, he most likely votes for Republican candidates. However, do we know Terry's views on specific political issues such as taxation? The role of the federal government in people's lives? The Christian Church? Homosexuality? Workers' rights? If the signifier "Republican" had the same meaning for everyone in the speech community, then the discipline and unanimity in the Republican Party would be truly remarkable, and the answer must be yes, but in reality that is not the case. You may object that a political affiliation is too broad a signifier to mean the same thing in all instances of its use. However, what about a word like "sister"? As a signifier, "sister" has multiple meanings. The entry for "sister" in *Webster's Third New International Dictionary, Unabridged* lists 5 meanings, whereas the entry in the online Urban Dictionary (http://www.urbandictionary.com) contains 14 separate definitions. The number of different definitions of a word is not simply a question of multiple relations between a single signifier and many signifieds, all of which are shared by members of the speech community. No, the meaning of "sister" depends on who uses the word in what circumstances and to whom; for example, the word has very different meanings when a parent says to a child "Be nice to your sister" or when one young woman says to another "You better stay away from my man, sister."

The dyadic relationship between signifier and signified in Saussure's semiotic theory implies that all members of the same community share the same way of making meaning from language, but it is in this respect that Peirce's theory of the sign differs fundamentally from Saussure's theory. Unlike the two components of the sign that Saussure envisioned, Peirce recognized three: object, representamen, and interpretant. The *object* is the referent of the sign, or what is represented as such by the sign (the *signified* in Saussure's terms). The concrete physical form that represents the object Peirce termed *representamen*, and in many ways, the representamen is similar to Saussure's signifier.[1] However, where Peircean semiotics diverges consequentially from Saussure is in the *interpretant* of the sign. The interpretant is not the person who interprets the sign but another sign that produces some effect on that person. The relationship between representamen and interpretant Peirce often described as translation; so "a sign is not a sign unless it translates itself into another sign in which it is more fully developed" (Peirce, Hartshorne, & Weiss, 1933, vol. 5, p. 594). I interpret Peirce's sign language to mean that the relationship between representamen and its object differs from the relationship between interpretant and the object.[2] Because the meaning of every sign lies in this relationship, in talk-in-interaction the meaning of a sign produced by a speaker may differ from the meaning interpreted by the receiver, and in written communication, the meaning of a text intended by the author may differ from the reader's response to the text or, as Peirce put it concisely: "Nothing is a sign unless it is interpreted as a sign" (Peirce et al., 1933, vol. 2, p. 172).

When Saussure's and Peirce's semiotics are compared, one difference that appears immediately is that, to Saussure, a sign is a dyadic relationship of signifier and signified, whereas Peirce theorized a triadic relationship among object, representamen, and interpretant. The difference that concerns us here, however, will be the difference between the immutability of the Saussurean sign and the interpretability of Peirce's conception. Because of the immutability of the Saussurean sign, communication by means of signs happens independently of who is talking, where the interaction occurs, or when the participants interact. In the Peircean system, since the speaker's sign generates a new sign for the hearer, the "Who?" the "Where?" and the "When?" of the interaction are crucial in semiotic communication. Somewhere, somewhen, and somebody are thus indispensable features of communication, and they contrast with the nowhere, nowhen, and nobody of the Saussurean theory. When language is considered a system in its own right and the way language functions is specified in terms of regularities, rules, and relationships that obtain among linguistic elements, then linguistic signs have exactly the kind of immutability, the independence of context, that Saussure maintained. However, as soon as we consider talk in local social interaction as occurring in real time, crafted by local social actors for the specific situation of its use in the moment of uttering (Erickson 2004, p, viii), then we identify the "Where?" "When?" and "Who?" of talk (not language) as indispensable in understanding what talk does.

This is a good argument for the importance of context, perhaps, but we must nonetheless recognize that the methodological strength and the enthusiastic labor of so many in the language sciences have created a deep understanding of how linguistic systems function independently of context while work on the relationship of communication and context is not so well advanced. Aspects of communication that, until recently, have not received much attention are semiotic systems other than language. Because of the primacy of interest in language, other meaning-making systems have been called simply "nonverbal," but work over the past few decades on bodily gesture, facial expression, clothing, spatial positioning, ritual practices, and expressive systems such as the visual arts has helped us to see language as only one among many ways of making meaning and has excited interest about how different semiotic systems combine and interact in communication.

Ways of integrating language with other semiotic systems in order to understand the context-bound nature of communication, talk-in-interaction, and literacy have been the outcome of work in the past 50 years by philosophers such as Wittgenstein, Austin, and Searle, by linguistic anthropologists such as Malinowski, J. R. Firth, Hymes, and Levinson, and by sociologists and ethnographers, including Bourdieu and Sahlins. Although I think that many of these scholars would resist identifying themselves with a single school of thought, they have all contributed to the development of a contemporary conception of the context-bound nature of communication called Practice Theory, and it is to a review of their contributions that I now turn.

Language Games and Activity Types

Some of the earliest investigations of the "Where?" "When?" and "Who?" of talk were carried out by philosophers of ordinary language, especially Wittgenstein, Austin, and Searle. Wittgenstein in his later thinking, first sketched in English in *The Blue and Brown Books* (1969) and then summarized and expanded in German in his *Philosophical Investigations* (2001), suggested that every utterance is a move in a language game. In contrast to earlier theories of utterances as logical propositions, Wittgenstein maintained that understanding the meaning of a speaker's words in talk-in-interaction does not involve knowing the objects to which the speaker's words refer or establishing whether the relationship among those objects asserted by the speaker is true. Instead, meaning involves understanding the function of the utterance in context. Wittgenstein used the term *language game* to emphasize that every moment of speaking is part of a social activity and that the meaning of any utterance cannot be established unless one knows the language game that is being played and the function of the utterance in the game. Knowing the meaning of an utterance thus involves knowing what move the speaker is making in a language game (although one such move in one particular game may indeed be asserting that a proposition is true). Wittgenstein gave an example of the necessity of understanding the language game in which a specific utterance is spoken in order to understand the utterance when he said, "If I hear someone say 'it's raining' but do not know whether I have heard the beginning and end of the period, so far this sentence does not serve to tell me anything" (Wittgenstein, 2001, vol. 1, p. 22).

What are language games? Wittgenstein gave copious examples, including giving orders and obeying them, making up a story and reading it, requesting, thanking, cursing, greeting, praying, constructing an object from a drawing, telling a joke, guessing a riddle, and many more. In most of these games (requesting, thanking, etc.), language plays a central role, but, in some (e.g., constructing an object from a drawing), other semiotic systems are involved. The meaning of a word in a language game depends on the nature of the game and, therefore, a word cannot have a fixed meaning outside of the context of the game. To this, you might object that some elements of meaning adhere to words no matter how they are used in language games and this may be the case, but it is not hard to imagine a language game in which a word has exactly the opposite meaning from its meaning in most games. Wittgenstein's example is "*Say* 'It's cold in here' and *mean* 'It's warm in here.' Can you do it?—And what are you doing as you do it? And is there only one way of doing it?" (Wittgenstein, 2001, vol. 1, p. 510).[3]

Some of Wittgenstein's language games became better known as illocutionary acts (Austin, 1962) or speech acts (Searle, 1969)—social acts, the doing of which does not necessarily entail the assertion of the truth of a proposition; for example, the statement "It's raining" can be considered as a logical proposition when it is a reply to a question about the weather in Madison at 11 o'clock on the morning of March 21, 2007, because the proposition has a truth value that can be established by looking out the window. Speech acts, however, do not have truth value because they are not assertions about states of affairs, the truth of which can be tested. Among the speech acts from Wittgenstein's list of language games, we find "giving orders" and "requesting." The way in which these language games work can be seen in examples of these two speech acts taken from ordinary language. The following examples can be found in the transcript of the famous Scopes Monkey Trial, in which John Scopes, a high school biology teacher, was charged with illegally teaching the theory of evolution (*Tennessee v. John Scopes*, 1925).

Mr. Darrow—Your honor, I am going to ask to have anybody excluded that applauds.

Court—Yes, if you repeat that, ladies and gentlemen, you will be excluded. We cannot have applause. If you have any feeling in this case you must not express it in the courthouse, so don't repeat the applause. If you do, I will have to exclude you.

In this exchange during the jury selection phase of the trial, Clarence Darrow, the defense counsel for John Scopes, requested the judge to silence applause from members of the public in the courtroom, and the judge made the requested order. It makes no sense to say that Darrow's request was true or false or that the judge's order was true or false; one can only say that those speech acts were performed and that they had a certain effect. At the end of the trial after the jury had delivered their guilty verdict, speech acts of requesting and thanking are also notable in the closing exchange between the defense counsel and the judge.

Darrow—May I say a word?

The Court—Colonel, be glad to hear from you.

Darrow—I want to say a word. I want to say in thorough sincerity that I appreciate the courtesy of the counsel on the other side from the beginning of this case, at least the Tennessee counsel, that I appreciated the hospitality of the citizens here. I shall go away with a feeling of respect and gratitude toward them for their courtesy and their liberality toward us persons; and that I appreciate the kind, and I think I may say, general treatment of this court, who might have sent me to jail, but did not. (Laughter in the courtroom.)

Darrow (Continuing)—And on the side of the controversy between the court and my self I have already ruled that the court was right, so I do not need to go further.

The Court—Thank you.

Darrow—But, I mean it.

The Court—Yes.

After making a request to the judge to speak, in this exchange Clarence Darrow thanked the opposing counsel, the citizens of Dayton, Tennessee, where the trail was held, and he also thanked the judge. The judge responded by thanking Darrow. Again, it makes no sense to say that the acts of thanking by Darrow and the judge were true or false. One can say that the speech act of "thanking"—which the judge performed with the utterance "Thank you" and which Darrow performed at much greater length—has certain rules, and

it is participants' observance of these rules that make these utterances acts of
thanking. These rules have very little to do with the actual words uttered; in fact,
Clarence Darrow does not once use the word "thank" and the judge avoids using
the word "appreciate," but both utterances can be considered thanking because
certain contextual conditions are met. These conditions include the copresence
of the person doing the thanking and the person(s) to whom the thanking is
addressed and the sincerity of the person doing the thanking. These conditions
were met on the occasion transcribed from the Scopes Monkey Trial, and so
the speech acts of thanking would be considered by Austin to be "felicitous"
or, less precisely, successful.

The organization of talk in a courtroom is subject to explicit rules that
determine what may or may not be said and who may or may not say it. Because
of these established rules, courtroom language provides many examples of
speech acts, but speech acts were not the only kind of language game that
Wittgenstein intended. In an exploration of the empirical basis for embedding
language within human activities, Levinson (1992) criticized Wittgenstein for
failing to make a distinction between speech acts and speech activities, and
Levinson provided a clear definition of a term "activity types" that includes
and exceeds all of what Wittgenstein called language games. For Levinson,
"activity type":

> refers to any culturally recognized activity, whether or not that activity is
> coextensive with a period of speech or indeed whether any talk takes
> places in it at all. [. . .] In particular, I take the notion of activity type to
> refer to a fuzzy category whose focal members are goal-defined, socially
> constituted, bounded, events with *constraints* on participants, setting and
> so on, but above all on the kinds of allowable contributions. Paradigm
> examples would be teaching, a job interview, a jural [courtroom]
> interrogation, a football game, a task in a workshop, a dinner party, and so
> on. (p. 69)

The first important extension of Wittgenstein's theory in this definition is
Levinson's (1992) recognition that human activities are mediated by language
as well as by and with other semiotic systems. In this respect, activity types can
be considered more general than language games because activity types do not
need to include or be bounded by language activities. Levinson's second addition to Wittgenstein's concept is that activity types are "culturally recognized";
that is, they are not simply activities that people do but they are recognized to
be activities within a cultural framework and, in consequence, may have names

within the culture. The cultural status of activity types and the "constraints on participants, setting, and so on" that Levinson mentioned mean that certain activities can be categorized within a certain type and not within another type. Levinson also mentioned that activity types may be bounded, although they need not be bounded by language.

Activity types thus seem to be quite large, time-consuming undertakings. A dinner party might last a couple of hours, but the Scopes Monkey trial meets Levinson's (1992) definition of an activity type and that lasted 15 days. Activity types seem to lie at the opposite end of a temporal cline from speech acts, which may extend over just one turn-at-talk by a single speaker. Despite their differences, however, activity types serve the purpose for which Wittgenstein coined language games; that is, the meaning of an utterance can only be understood by knowing what activity type it is part of.

An example of how the meaning of an utterance is dependent on the activity type in which the utterance occurs is how questions vary in function in three activity types: ordinary conversation, a courtroom cross-examination, and a foreign language lesson. One dictionary definition of *question* is "an interrogative expression" and *interrogative* is defined as "requiring or seeming to require an answer from the hearer or reader" (*Webster's Third New International Dictionary, Unabridged*. Merriam-Webster, 2002; http://unabridged.merriam-webster.com). This definition of question as part of a sequence of acts is also found in the treatment of "Question-answer" as an adjacency pair in Conversation Analysis: "Given the recognizable production of a first pair part, on its first possible completion its speaker should stop and a next speaker should start and produce a second pair part from the pair type the first is recognizably a member of" (Schegloff & Sacks, 1973, p. 295). These sequential definitions of a question do not, however, specify the function of questions, because that function is subject to the activity type in which it occurs. Consider, first, the question in this mundane conversational exchange from Hanks (1996b, p. 1):

> It is 7:28 A.M. on September 19, 1993. Chicago. Jack has just walked into the kitchen. He is standing at the counter by the sink, pouring a cup of coffee.
> Natalia is wiping off the dining room table. Gazing vacantly at his coffee cup, still drowsy, Jack says,
> "D'the paper come today, sweetheart?"
> She says,
> "It's right on the table."

Is Jack's question "D'the paper come today, sweetheart?" a simple request for information about newspaper delivery? If so, then Natalia could reply simply "yes" or "no," but Hanks gives us some further context for the exchange that shows the function of Jack's question to be somewhat different. Natalia knows that Jack reads the paper with breakfast every day and she does not believe that he has an interest in newspaper delivery; with this knowledge, Natalia hears Jack's question as a request to locate the paper for him, and it is to this unspoken request that she responds. The "rules" of the language game that Natalia and Jack are playing are well known to both of them because they have learned the rules by regular participation in shared early morning moments.

The function of questions in the context of a courtroom examination is very different. Returning for a moment to the Scopes Monkey Trial, one of the most famous episodes in the trial was defense attorney Clarence Darrow's questioning of a well-known opponent of the theory of evolution—William Jennings Bryan. The following is an extract from the trial transcript:

Examination of **W. J. Bryan** by **Clarence Darrow**, of counsel for the defense:

Q–You have given considerable study to the Bible, haven't you, Mr. Bryan?

A–Yes, sir, I have tried to.

Q–Then you have made a general study of it?

A–Yes, I have; I have studied the Bible for about fifty years, or sometime more than that, but, of course, I have studied it more as I have become older than when I was but a boy.

Q–You claim that everything in the Bible should be literally interpreted?

A–I believe everything in the Bible should be accepted as it is given there: some of the Bible is given illustratively. For instance: "Ye are the salt of the earth." I would not insist that man was actually salt, or that he had flesh of salt, but it is used in the sense of salt as saving God's people.

Q–But when you read that Jonah swallowed the whale—or that the whale swallowed Jonah—excuse me please—how do you literally interpret that?

A–When I read that a big fish swallowed Jonah—it does not say whale. . . . That is my recollection of it. A big fish, and I believe it, and I believe in a God who can make a whale and can make a man and make both what He pleases.

Q–Now, you say, the big fish swallowed Jonah, and he there remained how long—three days—and then he spewed him upon the land. You believe that the big fish was made to swallow Jonah?

A–I am not prepared to say that; the Bible merely says it was done.

Q–You don't know whether it was the ordinary run of fish, or made for that purpose?

A–You may guess; you evolutionists guess. . . . .

Q–You are not prepared to say whether that fish was made especially to swallow a man or not?

A–The Bible doesn't say, so I am not prepared to say.

Q–But do you believe He made them—that He made such a fish and that it was big enough to swallow Jonah?

A–Yes, sir. Let me add: One miracle is just as easy to believe as another

Q–Just as hard?

A–It is hard to believe for you, but easy for me. A miracle is a thing performed beyond what man can perform. When you get within the realm of miracles; and it is just as easy to believe the miracle of Jonah as any other miracle in the Bible.

Q–Perfectly easy to believe that Jonah swallowed the whale?

A–If the Bible said so; the Bible doesn't make as extreme statements as evolutionists do. . . .

What was the function of Darrow's questions? Bryan's hostile view of evolution was well known and yet it was Darrow, the defense counsel, who called Bryan to testify. If Darrow had simply wanted information about Bryan's opinions (which were adamantly opposed to those of his client), why would he have called him to testify? Darrow's questioning of Bryan about the literal interpretation of stories in the Bible began with questions about Bryan's acceptance of the story about Jonah being swallowed by a whale and continued with questions about Joshua commanding the Sun to stand still, about the date of the Great Flood, about the creation of the Earth in 6 days, and about the creation of Eve out of Adam's rib. It ended in testy exchanges between the two men. The function of Darrow's questioning was reported by the press the following day as a defeat for Bryan. According to one historian, "As a man and as a legend, Bryan was destroyed by his testimony that day." His performance was described as that of "a pitiable, punch drunk warrior" (Linder, 2007). The question-answer sequence in this activity, as in many instances of examination of a hostile witness by counsel (Levinson, 1992), is adversarial, and the function of the questions is to portray the witness in an unfavorable light to the jury. This is certainly what Clarence Darrow achieved through the sequential rules of question-and-answer that are an acknowledged part of courtroom proceedings, but Darrow used those rules for the institutionally defined goal of defending his client and making the claims of those who interpret the Bible literally appear to be ridiculous and portraying the claimants as foolish.

One final example of a language game in which questions have yet a different function is the foreign language classroom. Seedhouse (2004, pp. 102–103) reported the following sequence of three exchanges in an English lesson in a Norwegian elementary school[4]:

```
1       T:   now I want everybody (.) to listen to me. (1.8)
2            and when I say you are going to say after me, (.)
3            you are going to say what I say. (.) °we can try.°
4            I've got a lamp. a lamp. <say after me> I've got
5            a lamp.
6       LL:  I've got a lamp.
7       T:   (.) I've got a glass, a glass, <say after me>
8            I've got a glass
9       LL:  I've got a glass
10      T:   I've got a vase, a vase <say after me> I've got
11           a vase
12      LL:  I've got a vase.
             ((39 lines omitted))
52→     T:   I've got a hammer. what have you got (Tjartan)?
53      L6:  I have got a hammer.
54      T:   can everybody say I've got.
55      LL:  (whole class) I've got.
56→     T:   fine. I've got a belt. what have you got? (1.0)
57           Kjersti?
58      L7:  (.) hmm I've got a telephone
             ((24 lines omitted))
83      T:   and listen to me again. (.) and look at what I've
84           written. (.) I've got a hammer, <just listen now>
85→          have you got a hammer?
86      L:   (1.0) yes
87      T:   raise your hand up now Bjorn =
88      L13: =yes
89      T:   I've =
90      L13: =I've got a hammer.
91      T:   you've got a hammer and then you answer (1.2) yes
92           I have (1.0) yes I have. <I've got a belt>.
93→          have you got a belt Vegard?
94      L14: er:: (.) erm no
95      T:   (.) you are going to answer only with yes. =
```

```
96    L14: = yes =
97      T: = yes
98    L14: (.) I:: (.) I have
99→     T: I have. fine. I've got a trumpet. <have you got
100         a trumpet Anna?>
101   L15: ah er erm °yes I have°
```

In these teaching exchanges, the teacher begins by stating the rules of the language game explicitly in lines 1–12. The teacher first models a sentence with "I've got . . ." and requires students to produce sentences of this form. The function of the teacher's questions in lines 52 and 56 is to elicit statements of the required linguistic form from students. In the third part of the exchange, the teacher wishes students to respond to yes/no questions with the appropriate short answer "Yes, I have," and the function of the teacher's questions in lines 93 and 99 is again to prompt the students to produce the appropriate linguistic form. As Seedhouse (2004) remarked, establishing the truth value of the students' statements is not at issue in these question-answer pairs because it is apparent from the videotape of the lesson that Vegard does not have a belt and therefore his negative reply in line 94 is true, but this is irrelevant to the rule of the language game, which requires him to respond "Yes, I have."

In these three examples, I want to show that the functions of questions vary according to the activity in which the questions are uttered. In the exchange between Jack and Natalia, Jack's question was apparently about the fact of newspaper delivery but was interpreted by Natalia as a request to locate the newspaper. The superficial function of Clarence Darrow's interrogation of W. J. Bryan in the Scopes Monkey Trial was to establish Bryan's beliefs about the literal truth of the Bible, but his questions were interpreted by the participants in the courthouse as expressions of ridicule. Finally, the teacher's questions in English to the Norwegian children were intended to elicit, from the children, utterances conforming to a particular grammatical structure; the truth of their responses was irrelevant to the goal of the activity. These examples of language used by participants in social activities show that although the same linguistic form is used in different activities, the meaning of that form is subject to the goals of the activity.

Wittgenstein's intuition about the inseparability between meaning and activity is what led him to speculate about language games, but a very similar conclusion was reached empirically by ethnographers who began to examine how oral languages of peoples from distant cultural backgrounds could be translated into a European language and understood within the context of a literate culture. The first to make such an attempt was Bronislaw Malinowsi in his ethnographic research among the Melanesian peoples of the eastern islands of what is now Papua New Guinea.

Context of Situation

Malinowski (1923) wrote his first discussion of the inseparability of meaning and activity as a contribution to a volume of essays that introduced the semiotics of American philosopher C. S. Peirce to a British readership. As I commented earlier, in Peirce's semiotic theory, the speaker's sign generates a new sign for the hearer and, thus, the "Who?" "Where?" and "When?" of the interaction are crucial in semiotic communication. A similar point was made by Malinowski when he wrote that "language is essentially rooted in the reality of the culture, the tribal life and customs of a people, and [. . .] it cannot be explained without reference to these broader contexts of verbal utterance" (p. 305). The necessity of situating language in a broader context in order to understand meaning becomes particularly evident when studies move beyond the analysis of the written (and sometimes dead) languages of the past, especially those of ancient Greece and Rome, which share a common cultural heritage with most modern European languages. Because the study of classical languages is done with little knowledge of the contexts in which inscriptions and texts were produced, the Saussurean theory of language spoken nowhere, nowhen, and by nobody is plausible. However, as soon as an ethnographer tries to explain the spoken language activities of peoples in exotic contexts, it becomes necessary to recognize that the meaning of an utterance can only be understood by considering who produced the utterance and where, when, and why the utterance was produced. Malinowski drew linguists' attention to broader contexts of verbal utterance with the concept of *context of situation*, "which indicates on the one hand that the conception of *context* has to be broadened and on the other that the *situation* in which words are uttered can never be passed over as irrelevant to the linguistic expression" (p. 306).

Although Malinowski first conceived his approach as applying to communication among preliterate peoples, he later recognized his "ethnographic theory of language" as equally applicable to literate European languages (Malinowski, 1935). This important step outside our everyday assumptions in order to identify and appreciate them can only be done by close examination of communication in situations and in languages that are exotic for us, and this is perhaps the main reason why contemporary theories of semiotics owe so much to linguistic anthropology.

Malinowski arrived at the notion of the context of situation because of the difficulty that he experienced in translating into English speech activities performed in Melanesian by inhabitants of the Trobriand Islands (a group of islands in the Solomon Sea to the east of Papua New Guinea). He did little, however, to investigate which features of the context of situation (who participated in an activity, where the activity took place, the goal of the activity, participants' beliefs and shared history) needed to be specified in order to understand the activity. The concept of context of situation was later taken over and expanded by J. R. Firth, who, in a number of publications (J. R. Firth, 1935, 1957), attempted to systematize exactly which features of context of situation were relevant. His list was short and included the following:

A. The participants: persons, personalities, and relevant features of these.
   (i) The verbal action of the participants.
   (ii) The non-verbal action of the participants.
B. The relevant objects and non-verbal and non-personal events.
C. The effect of the verbal action.

(J. R. Firth, 1957, p. 9)

Firth did, however, recognize that this taxonomy of features of the context of situation of a communicative activity must be related to more general contexts, including (a) economic, religious, and other social structures, (b) discourse types such as monologue, choral production, narrative, recitation, explanation, and so on, (c) the number, age, and sex of the participants, and (d) the types of speech acts involved. Although Firth's treatment of context of situation is more specific than Malinowski's, as his colleague Robins (1971, p. 37) noted, Firth did little to fill in the details. The work of showing how to apply Firth's categories to actual talk-in-interaction was left to Mitchell (1957/1975) in his description of the relationship between language and context of situation in commercial activities in towns on the northeastern Mediterranean coast of Libya. Mitchell's research is important because his analysis presages many of the contextual features that later writers, such as Goffman, Hymes, and Gumperz, identified as influential in the analysis of talk-in-interaction.

Mitchell (1957/1975) audio-recorded interactions performed by speakers of Bedouin Arabic in markets and shops where animals, grain, and furniture were bought and sold. Mitchell first described the participants in the interactions and distinguished between *personalities* (the major players in buying and selling, including buyer, seller, auctioneer, and owner) and *persons* (women who sift the grain in preparation for purchase, bystanders, the official who measures the grain, and other municipal officials). Individuals in these different participant roles also participated differently in the commercial interaction, both in terms of what they said and the amount of their verbal contributions. Another element of context that Mitchell noted was "a technical language of buying and selling," or lexical items that are found with high frequency in these transactions and not in other contexts, some of which are "buyer elements" and others are "seller elements"—linguistic actions that help to create identities for participants in the interaction. An example is فَتَحَ أَلله [yaftuħa'lla] "May God bring you fortune," which is only used by a seller to imply a refusal of a bid made by a buyer. In noting differences between the language of commercial interactions in shops and markets, Mitchell was also among the first to recognize the effect of setting and built environment. He also recognized that buying and selling are complex activities and may be broken down into several temporally sequential stages, each of which includes specific language indicating opening and closing of the stage. Four stages can be recognized in an auction, for example: the auctioneer's opening, investigation of the object for sale (including description by the auctioneer), bidding, and conclusion. In a nonauction transaction in a market or shop, the five stages include salutation, inquiry as to the object of sale, investigation of the object of sale, bargaining, and conclusion. Although it is not necessary that every transaction include all stages, the stages are sequential and "there is a mutual expectancy between stages" (Mitchell, p. 176).

Perhaps most relevant to the Wittgensteinian proposal that the meaning of a word in a language activity depends on the nature of the activity and that, therefore, a word cannot have a fixed meaning outside of that context of situation is Mitchell's (1957/1975) frequent recourse to the context of situation in order to interpret the meaning of some expressions in Bedouin Arabic that he translates literally into English.[5] One example from Mitchell's data is a buyer's inquiry as to ownership of goods:

Buyer: ها أَلنَّعْجِيتْ لَكْ؟

han nʕajíet lák?

Are these sheep yours?

Seller: لله كِلّ شِي

lálla kílli ʃíi

Everything belongs to God.

The seller's reply is a characteristically Bedouin way to avoid saying literally "The sheep are mine," but the literal meaning is inferred by both buyer and seller. Another conversational inference is made by a buyer who is feeling sheep that a seller has brought to market. The seller responds with اِسْمِينْ، أَمْغَيْر شَدَّدْ عَزْمَكْ! [ismíen, umɣáyr ʃáddid ʕázmak!] (*They are fat. Just pluck up your courage!*). By asking a potential buyer to pluck up his courage, the seller implies that he wants the buyer to give him the price that he is asking for the sheep, and the buyer infers the same meaning.

Mitchell's explication of context of situation in buying and selling has been acclaimed, but his analysis deals with a specific interaction and he makes no claims to extend his correlation of language with context of situation to a general theory of talk-in-interaction. The more general theory was developed later by Hymes (1962/1974) in his proposal for an ethnography of speaking. Hymes's innovative proposal was that just as anthropologists studied people and cultures with the tools of ethnography, so understanding of language use and social context could be achieved by an ethnography of speaking.

Ethnography of Speaking

Ethnography involves fieldwork with people, often in exotic societies, that results in qualitative descriptions of human social phenomena, and ethnographers stress that social phenomena cannot be understood independently of one another. Hymes had done fieldwork with Native American peoples and, like American ethnographers and linguists Franz Boas, Edward Sapir, and Leonard Bloomfield before him, Hymes observed that Native American ways of speaking are very different from the ways of speaking in the Anglo-American mainstream. Not only are the grammars of Native American languages different from those of European languages, but the ways that Native Americans use their languages are also very different. In Native American communities, who can say what to whom, under what circumstances, and how people value different kinds of talk and silence are very different from the ways of speaking outside those communities.

The unit of spoken interaction that Hymes identified he called a speech event, and after identifying the speech event, he proceeded to analyze a small number of what he called factors in the event. Hymes's way of identifying speech events was similar to Wittgenstein's way of exemplifying language games; that is,

> through words which name them. Some classes of speech events in our culture are well known: Sunday morning sermon, inaugural address,

pledge of allegiance. Other classes are suggested by colloquial expressions such as: heart-to-heart-talk, salestalk, talk man-to-man, woman's talk, bull session, chat, polite conversation, chatter (of a team), chew him out, give him the lowdown, get it off his chest, griping, etc. (Hymes, 1962/1974, p. 198)

Hymes's examples reveal a problem of scope in his conception of speech event because they include both Levinson's activity types as well as Austin's and Searle's speech acts. Nevertheless, the procedure of looking for names of speech events or language games has the advantage that if an event has a name, it must be recognized as a type within a culture, and members of that culture can distinguish between speech events that are of a given type and those that are not. The procedure is also "emic" in Pike's sense (Pike, 1967), in that this analysis of social interaction is a description treated by the people being studied as relevant to their system of behavior. It also implies that a translation of the name for a speech event into another language does not mean that the factors of the event are the same in the two language communities. Hymes gave the example of "cussing out," an English translation for a class of speech events of the Wishram Chinook who live along the Columbia River in Washington State (p. 199). The description of this speech event in Wishram Chinook involves asking who cusses out whom, when, and where, in what style, and about what? How are speakers rated for their ability at cussing out? What effect follows or is expected to follow? What is the role of this speech event in maintaining social values and personalities? Answers to all of these questions are specific to the culture in which the speech event occurs, and although we may have knowledge of a speech event that we call "cussing out" in our own culture, the answers to those questions are likely to be very different from Wishram Chinook. A consequence of the emic approach is that names of speech events should be translated with caution.

The analysis of the factors in speech events that Hymes conducted was, however, etic. The factors that Hymes identified in his early writing owed much to the communication framework presented by Jakobson (1960) and included the following: "1. a Sender (Addresser); 2. a Receiver (Addressee); 3. a Message Form; 4. a Channel; 5. a Code; 6. a Topic; and 7. Setting (Scene, Situation)" (Hymes, 1962/1974, p. 198). In a way that is analogous to the features of context of situation proposed by Firth, Hymes's terms are theories or categories that the outside analyst uses, which are not necessarily accepted or understood as relevant by the people participating in the speech event being analyzed.

Hymes's SPEAKING Model

In 1974, Hymes published a revision of his seven components of speech events. He called the revised terms Setting and Scene, Participants, Ends (purposes or outcomes), Act Sequence, Key (the tone or manner of the event), Instrumentalities (channel and form), Norms (social rules governing the event), and Genre (the kind of event). Listed in this order, the seven factors or components of speech events form the acronym SPEAKING and, thanks in part to this felicitous mnemonic, Hymes's "SPEAKING model" became well known. The components are briefly summarized below.

The *setting* and *scene* of a speech event are distinct. The setting is an etic description of the time and place of the event, whereas the scene is the cultural definition of an occasion of a particular type. In Hanks's (1996b) description of the exchange between Jack and Natalia, for example, he mentioned the setting as 7:28 a.m. on September 19, 1993, in a kitchen in Chicago—factors that make primary sense to the reader and analyst but may not be relevant for the participants. For Jack and Natalia, however, the scene may be first thing on a Sunday morning and the kitchen in the house shared by Jack and Natalia may be a different scene for them than a kitchen in a friend's house, where maybe they are staying as weekend guests.

Participants are not only the people who speak in the event, but, as described by Mitchell (1957/1975), participants are both personalities (the central participants) and persons—people who are "there" but whose contributions are not central to the event. Hymes goes beyond Mitchell's conception, however, in recognizing that certain participants may not be physically present but their participation is nonetheless central to the event. Hymes's example is again from the Wishram Chinook, where

> formal scenes are defined by the relationship between a source (e.g., a chief, or sponsor of a ceremony), a spokesman who repeats the source's words, and others who constitute an audience or public. The source whose words are repeated sometimes is not present; the addressees sometimes are spirits of the surrounding environment. (Hymes, 1974, p. 56)

This expansion of the concept of participation to admit persons as well as personalities and to include personalities who are not necessarily present was developed by Goffman (1979, 1981), and it may seem to open the door to the consideration of just about anybody as a participant. The question of which identities can and cannot function in participant roles in a speech event has, however, been described in general terms by Hanks (1996a) and is discussed further in chapter 4.

Ends in Hymes's taxonomy include the goals of a speech event (the ends toward which participants' efforts and activities are directed) and outcomes (the consequence or result of a speech event). In our earlier discussion of the different functions of questions in different activity types, I noted that the goal in Jack's question about whether the paper had arrived was interpreted by Natalia not as a request to obtain information about the paper's arrival but rather about its location. In Clarence Darrow's questioning of W. J. Bryan in the Scopes Monkey Trial, Darrow's goal was not simply to obtain information from the witness but rather to portray him in an unfavorable light to the jury. Finally, in the teacher's questions to the class of Norwegian schoolchildren reported by Seedhouse (2004), the teacher's goal was to get them to produce the linguistic forms that his lesson plan intended.

Different from participants' goals in a speech event, the outcome of a speech event is the effect that follows from it, which may be a change in the behavior, beliefs, attitudes, or knowledge of participants or indeed some change in the social or physical environment. The difference between ends-as-participants'-goals and ends-as-outcomes is apparent when participants' goals do not result in the outcomes intended. In discussing the organization of task-based foreign language learning, for example, Breen (1987) distinguished between the teacher's intended goal for a pedagogical task, which he identified as *task-as-workplan*, and the actual outcome of the task or *task-in-process*. A teacher may have designed a language learning task for students with the goal of students using and learning certain target language forms, but as soon as they begin to perform the task, the goals of the students may differ from the teacher's goal. As Breen described it:

> Task outcomes can be seen as the function of the actual contributions of the individual learner, the particular task type, and the situational conditions within which the task was completed. [. . .] Any learning outcome will be significantly shaped by the learners' own perceptions of all three. (p. 24)

The next component in Hymes's taxonomy is speech acts or *act sequences*. The minimum form of a speech event for Hymes is a speech act; for example, a cry of "Fire!" is both an act and an event, but most speech events consist of more than one speech act and, in many cases, participants have certain expectations about the sequence of acts. Sequences of speech acts have been investigated most rigorously by conversation analysts, who have observed that certain speech acts occur in ordered pairs and that the production of the first speech act in the pair gives rise to participants' expectations of the production of the corresponding second part by a different speaker. We have seen how this expectation works with question and answer (Schegloff & Sacks, 1973), but it applies equally to other sequences of two adjacent utterances produced by different speakers, including greeting-greeting, offer-acceptance/refusal, and call-response. Act sequences longer than adjacency pairs are not generally recognized by conversation analysts because the absence of one or more acts in a longer sequence does not generally result in an immediately noticeable perturbation in the interaction, but study of speech events of the same type does in fact show that more than two speech acts occur quite regularly together and that they usually occur in a sequence. This was Mitchell's (1957/1975) conclusion from observing commercial transactions in Cyrenaica, in which he observed that certain speech acts ("linguistic actions" for Mitchell) were only produced in certain participant roles and a complete transaction could be broken down into a number of stages, which, as Mitchell remarked, created a mutual expectancy between stages. The degree to which a sequence of acts creates participants' expectancy for certain acts to follow in a similar manner to an adjacency pair is evidence of how ritualized a speech event has become, and such a sequence has been referred to as a "script" by some (Schank & Abelson, 1977). An example of how a sequence of speech acts is expected in one speech event is Keenan's (1989) description of the *kabary* among a community of Malagasy speakers in Madagascar. This ceremonial speech event is associated with marriage proposals, burials, ancestral bone-turnings, and circumcisions. Many *kabary* involve two speechmakers, who engage in a ritual dialogue, but if the first speechmaker has made some error in the sequence of speech acts, the second will usually point this out. In communication across cultures, too, expectations of sequences may create misunderstanding because acts and sequences that are found in a speech event in one culture may be absent from a similar event in another culture. Such differences have led to claims of cross-cultural misunderstandings in areas such as medical consultations (Ranney, 1992).

The significance of *key*, the next component in Hymes's taxonomy, is the tone, manner, or spirit in which an event is done. The trope is of a musical key because music written in a particular key is often said to invoke certain emotions; for example, the key of B flat minor is often associated with sadness and loneliness, whereas the key of C major is associated by some with seriousness. In talk-in-interaction, the key of a speech event can be a clue to how it is to be interpreted, such that the same words in different keys can be interpreted in very different ways. Wittgenstein's challenge to "*Say* 'It's cold in here' and *mean* 'It's warm in here'" (2001, vol. 1, p. 510) can be met by altering the key of the utterance for, as Hymes (1974) wrote, when the key "is in conflict with the overt content of an act, it overrides the latter [as in sarcasm]" (p. 58). English provides a range of adverbs that describe the key of an event, including "sarcastically," "reluctantly," "politely," "ironically," and so on. The concept of key as being an indication of how talk is to be understood was later developed by Goffman (1974) as *frame*, and the verbal and nonverbal resources that conversationalists use in order to guide each other's interpretations of what is being said were investigated at length by Gumperz (1992) as *conversational inference*.

Channels and forms of speech are linked together in the next letter of Hymes's mnemonic: "I" for *instrumentality*. By "channel," Hymes referred to what earlier in this chapter I have called semiotic systems, but he limited his focus to those used for the transmission of speech. Today, this would include oral, written, and computer-mediated channels, and although most ethnographies of speaking have been limited to the oral channel, literacy practices have also been studied by ethnographers in a way similar to how Hymes advocated studying the ethnography of speaking. Because in ethnography social phenomena cannot be understood independently of one another, one thrust of this research has been to consider literacy activities in the context of other social activities that take place "around" them. As an example of this ethnographic approach to literacy, Brandt (1998) described literacy learning as an individual development in the context of economic development. By retelling the narratives of two women working in the clerical field between 1940 and 1970, Brandt illustrated how literacy learning opportunities exist in fragile and contingent contexts dependent on specific economic moments and are sponsored, or withheld, by agents who stand to gain some economic advantage by supporting or suppressing such opportunities. Researchers have also recently begun ethnographic studies of computer-mediated communication to investigate the construction of online communities, interaction, and identities, of which the recent collections by Androutsopoulos (2006) and by Magnan (2008) contain many interesting examples. In some of this research, the ethnographer's task has been to investigate relations among a range of social practices, software and hardware technologies, modes of representation, and interaction, which together construct an individual's Internet.

For Hymes, studying the "forms of speech" used in speech events meant including a very wide range of language varieties, including languages, codes, dialects, speech styles, and registers. Much recent work on speech events in multilingual communities has focused on participants' use of one or more language varieties or codes in different speech events and on the use of different speech styles in order to "cross" into an identity of a conspicuous out-group. In writing, also, there are codes that are associated with specific literacy practices. One example is the women's writing once adopted by generations of women in Jiangyong County (江永县) in the south of Hunan Province (湖南省), China (Endo, 1999). Before 1949, hardly any young women in this rural area attended formal schooling and so they never learned to write in standard Chinese; instead, the women learned a unique women's script (女书) from older women and used it among their "sworn sisters" (结拜姐妹)—closely trusted female friends. When one of the women married and left her own family to join the household of her husband, she was presented with a *sanzhaoshu* (三朝书), a cloth-bound booklet written entirely in women's script, bound and embroidered by the women. In the *sanzhaoshu*, the bride's sworn sisters and her mother expressed their hopes for the young woman's happiness and their sorrow at her departure from her childhood home. Women's script was unintelligible to men in the community, and in addition to the *sanzhaoshu*, the women used the code to write short autobiographies, folktales, poems, and songs.

The next component of Hymes's SPEAKING acronym is "N" for *norms*, which he interpreted in two ways: *norms of interaction* and *norms of interpretation*. A norm is a principle or statement asserting or denying that something ought to be done or has value, and a norm is therefore a basis for comparison. In talk-in-interaction, one of the pervasive features identified by Sacks, Schegloff, and Jefferson (1974, p. 700) is that, overwhelmingly, one party talks at a time and occurrences of more than one speaker at a time are common, but brief. Indeed, in certain cases where this does not occur (when somebody interrupts another speaker or when somebody refuses to cede the floor to another speaker), such actions may be considered sanctionable by the parties, who may respond with "don't interrupt me" or may describe a long turn-at-talk as a "speech-river" or "discorso fiume" in Italian.[6] The fact that such talk can be sanctioned shows the existence of norms in speech events, but such norms are by no means universal. Reisman (1989), for example, reported that in conversations among natives of Antigua in the Eastern Caribbean, "there is no regular requirement for two or more voices not to be going at the same time. The start of a new voice is not in itself a signal for the voice speaking either to stop or to institute a process which will decide who is to have the floor" (p. 113).

The interpretation of speech is also subject to certain norms, as Hymes indicated with "norms of interpretation." As with norms of interaction, when speech differs from the belief system of a community, such violations may be considered sanctionable. In contemporary American society, some people believe that the English language is going to hell in a handbasket because young people's style of speech differs from the norms that were taught to older generations. Norms of interpretation of talk are found in all societies that have been studied. Keenan (1989) in her description of styles of speaking in a Madagascan village distinguished between direct and indirect styles. Directness in speaking is not valued in the community and is associated with children and things that are contrary to tradition. In the speech event of *kabary*, which I used to illustrate act sequences, villagers do not consider it good to speak directly nor is it good to directly criticize someone who does so. Speaking indirectly is a skill that is prized and is associated with the men in the community. The women are expected to speak more directly than the men, and when directness is called for in village interactions, the job falls to a woman, as is recounted by Keenan in the following story. Some boys in the village were playing ball against the side of a newly whitewashed house and chipped off some patches of color:

> The landlord returned, observed this situation but after an entire day in the village, said only, "If you don't patch that, things might not go well between us." The next day he returned with his wife. As she approached the village, she accosted the first person she saw (which happened to be the eldest man in the village) with accusations. She told everyone within hearing range of their anger and just what must be done to repair the wall. This outburst caused a great deal of grumbling and unpleasant feelings among the villagers. But the outburst was almost expected. It was not a shocking encounter as it came from the wife and not the landlord himself. Such a display of anger is permissible, perhaps even appropriate, because it is initiated by a woman. (p. 138)

The norm of directness in the speech of men is interpreted as undesirable, whereas in the speech of women, the community interpretation is different and no sanctions need be applied.

The final component in Hymes's taxonomy is *genre*. In ordinary language, the term "genre" refers to a kind, sort, or category of compositions in literature or art, but for Hymes, genre involves the possibility of recognizing formal characteristics of a speech event. R. Bauman's definition is revealing (2000, p. 84). A genre is "a constellation of systematically related, co-occurrent formal features and structures" of a speech event, and examples of events that share formal characteristics are four-character idioms in Chinese. The title of the well-known kung-fu movie *Crouching Tiger, Hidden Dragon* is an example of this genre. The English title is a word-for-word translation of the four characters in the Chinese idiom 卧虎藏龙, which advises concealing strength from an enemy in order to preserve the element of surprise. Most Chinese idioms take the form of four characters, and one common dictionary of idioms includes more than 2,000.[7] Another example of a more structural genre is Propp's (1968) analysis of Russian folktales, in which he identified a finite number of characters (the hero, the villain, the princess, her father, the false hero, etc.) and a finite number of functions (the false hero presents unfounded claims, the hero and villain join in direct combat, the false hero or villain is exposed, the hero marries and ascends the throne, etc.). These "morphological" elements were combined in all the Russian folktales that Propp analyzed.

Genre serves as a conventionalized orienting framework for the production and interpretation of discourse because when an utterance is assimilated to a given genre, the process by which it is produced and interpreted is mediated through its intertextual relationship with prior texts. Genre is a component of speech events, and many genres are associated with primary speech events. So the genre of folktale, for example, may be closely associated with a group sitting around a campfire, but although both concepts bear a type-token relationship to specific utterances, genre and a speech event are not identical because a genre is still recognizable outside its primary context.

The intertextuality of genre links generic speech to historically prior events, and the social value of generic speech may be enhanced by its links to tradition.[8] Thus, a move in a Chinese conversation in which one participant invokes an appropriate four-character idiom is unlikely to be challenged unless another participant can come up with another idiom. The degree to which the formal features of genres are fixed or variable is related to the degree to which they serve an established an accepted authority. As R. Bauman (2000) comments:

> Prescriptive insistence on strict generic regimentation works conservatively in the service of established authority and order, while the impulse toward the widening of intertextual gaps and generic innovation is more conducive to the exercise of creativity, resistance to hegemonic order, and openness and change. (p. 87)

The components of Hymes's description of speech events provide a far more complete description of speech events than was given by Malinowski, J. R. Firth, or Mitchell. The components also provide a means to explain how speech events differ and to compare one speech event with another. Although the names of the categories themselves are not necessarily immediately recognizable by speakers (e.g., the terms "genre," "norm," and "key" may not be familiar to many), they do correspond to concepts that speakers recognize, as I have illustrated with the genre of Chinese four-character idioms, the norms of indirectness in Malagasy *kabary*, and the means that English adverbs provide for description of "key." Hymes's components thus provide a way into the description of speech events from the point of view of the participants in the events, and they are an ethnographic heuristic that can be used to begin a description of the social context of speech.

The unit of activity to be described by Hymes in an ethnography of speaking is the speech event, and this is a unit that Hymes admitted is culturally recognized and may even have a name used by a particular community of speakers. A similar definition of "activity type" was given by Levinson, but the necessity of the unit being culturally recognized was never explicit in Wittgenstein's description of "language games" nor was it in Austin or Searle's treatment of "speech acts." Malinowski's descriptions of a Trobriand Islander boasting about the superiority of his canoe or of the exchanges among a party of fishermen on a coral lagoon trying to imprison a shoal of fish in their nets are certainly culturally recognizable activities, just as is Mitchell's description of buying and selling in Cyrenaica, but neither author chose to theorize the unit he was describing. For Firth, the linguist, the unit was simply a text within a context of situation. Whether the unit of description is an event, an activity, or (as will be discussed shortly) practice, action, or praxis, such a unit must be goal-defined, bounded, with a configuration of components that constitute a type that is distinguishable from other types, and recognized as socially constituted by participants.

A focus on speaking (on language, that is) is central to Hymes's theory, but his approach should perhaps be broadened to recognize, as Levinson did, that culturally relevant activity may include more than speaking and need not include speaking at all. Recalling the discussion of semiotics with which this chapter began, if a practice is situated somewhere, at some time, and constructed by somebody, then the practice needs to be described in ways that go beyond a description of language. As Malinowski recognized and as Linell (2005) has recently emphasized, because of the ease with which language can be extracted from the context of situation by means of recording and transcription, there is always the danger that language is abstracted as well as extracted; that is, the semiotics of language are considered independently of the contexts in which the language was produced. Resituating language in context means that the linguistic system must be considered together with nonverbal semiotic systems that do not lend themselves so easily to recording and transcription. The positioning of participants with respect to each other and to the built environment, their bodily gestures, facial expression, and clothing must all be considered in an understanding of the social organization of participants. Indeed, the interaction among these systems may turn out to be the most appropriate way of explicating the practice.[9] Broadening the scope of analysis to include these nonverbal systems but keeping within Hymes's heuristic means that the focus of the study of talk-in-interaction will indeed be an ethnography— but of communication, not just of speaking.

Practice Theory and Discursive Practice

The role of language as one of several semiotic systems in communicative interaction and the importance of context in constructing and reflecting the meaning of social interaction imply that an exclusive focus on language is to ignore crucial dimensions of interaction. A broader concept is needed, one that includes both event and context of situation and both verbal and nonverbal semiotic systems. In social theory and anthropology, scholars have struggled with the problem of explaining the mutual interactions between human activity and social systems—between human agency and social structure. What they have been concerned with understanding is how social systems such as gender, class, and culture influence everyday human activity and also how humans are able to affect social structures through their actions. Research and theory development in sociology led by Bourdieu (1977, 1990), in anthropology led by Sahlins (1981, 1985), and the related work cited in Ortner's (1984) review of theory in anthropology since the 1960s have given rise to the development of *Practice Theory*. Practice Theory is an exploration of wider issues than the relationship between language and context of situation, but because of the power of the theory in explaining how individuals act in social situations and because of the role of language in social interaction, Practice Theory is relevant to any treatment of talk-in-interaction.

Practice Theory is an attempt to find a middle road that transcends the duality of materialism and idealism. The question is whether individual actions result from social forces that transcend the individual or whether individual agency is powerful enough to change those forces. Marx, as is well known, took the materialist position when he wrote in *Theses on Feuerbach*, "The human essence is no abstraction inherent in each single individual. In its reality it is the ensemble of the social relations" (Marx-Engels-Lenin Institute, 1949, vol. 2, p. 366). In contrast to Marx, Weber took the position that the ultimate unit of analysis in social life is the motivation for the actions of a single individual, and such motivation and actions may be influenced, but not determined, by social relations. Understanding the individual's motivations, according to Weber

(1957), involves taking the place of the individual and classifying motivation according to one of four "ideal types": *zweckrational* (rational means to rational ends), *wertrational* (rational means to irrational ends), *affektual* (guided by emotion), and *traditional* (guided by custom or habit).

In Practice Theory, there appeared a way of reconciling what had appeared to be a dichotomy between human agency and social structure. Practice is the construction and reflection of social realities through actions that invoke identity, ideology, belief, and power. A practice approach to talk-in-interaction thus seeks to examine both how the language, gesture, and positioning of specific interactions are determined by the social context of interaction and how that context—conceived broadly enough to include the implications of the practice in the society at large and the identities of the participants—is constructed by participants' verbal and nonverbal actions.

How does a practice approach parallel or diverge from the theoretical stances taken by the authors whose work I have so far discussed in this chapter? The way to approach this question is to ask three questions: What is a practice? What does a practice approach seek to explain? What does a consideration of talk-in-interaction as practice reveal about the relationship between talk and context? Responses to those three questions are perhaps best attempted by examining a particular practice, and the following transcript reproduces the linguistic part of a practice described by Block (2007). The conversation took place among three workers and was recorded in 2004 in the reception area of a public building in central London. The focal participant is Carlos, a Colombian migrant who had been living in London for 2.5 years at the time of the recording. The other participants are Carlos's workmate Bob, and Dan, a recently retired ex-workmate.

```
 1  Dan:     I feel a bit rough like I've got a bad cold and ( ) and
 2           erh (1) I can't shake it off I've had it for over a week so
 3           I thought I'd come up to town a bit ((Phones ringing in
 4           background)) oh, gosh thought I'd come down
 5  Carlos:  yeah?=
 6  Dan:     = and we had a poor performance/cause see he can't get down
 7           very often so he booked the tickets about four weeks ago=
 8  Carlos:  =and it was easy game for Chelsea
 9  Dan:     I know ( ) (1) and really I felt so rough I didn't feel
10           like going but I thought don't want to let im down
11  Carlos:  yeah=
12  Dan:     =cause what I've been taking and carrying this cold and
13           then they played like that awful! =
14  Bob:     =poor=
```

```
15  Dan:     =yeah, very poor=
16  Bob:     [no
17  Carlos:  he] was very poor performance for Chelsea=
18  Dan:     =but a lot of the play=
19  Bob:     =[yeah
20  Carlos:  yeah]
21  Dan:     °°we're not scoring the goals we're not scoring the goals I
22           can't make it out not scoring many goal°°
23  Bob:     ( )
24  Dan:     yeah but last Wednesday I mean ( ) I got the fucking
25           shivers and I that day all of a sudden I couldn't stop
26           shivering even though it wasn't that cold really=
27  Carlos:  =yeah
28  Dan:     I just had the fucking shivers later then I went to see the
29           doctor and me own doctor's been ill funnily enough so I see
30           another doctor (2) and he examined me and said ''no, don't
31           seem too bad'' so he says ''no use in giving you any
32           antibiotics'' HE WASN'T EVEN GONNA GIVE ME ANY MEDICINE
33  Carlos:  ((laughing))
34  Dan:     I said well what about you know cause I've been taking
35           Lemsips and all [that
36  Carlos:  that's] that's the worse really=
37  Dan:     and like last night I took a fucking Lemsip before
38           ((In the background, Bob asks if he can help someone who
39           has come to the reception counter)) about ten o'clock in
40           bed (2) and uh about two in the morning I've got this
41           fucking cough. Oh I couldn't shake it off (2) Oh, I just
42           feel terrible
```

I will try to ground answers to the three questions about Practice Theory in this data extract. First, what is practice and how is practice different from a speech act, a speech event, or an activity? In her review of Practice Theory, Ortner (1984) replied that practice is "anything people do" (p. 149), and linguistic analysis has not been a major part of Practice Theory, whose proponents have been more interested in rituals, *tabu*,[10] and *mana*[11] in Polynesia or in matrimonial choices, gift exchange, and the mundane economic conduct of everyday life of the Kabyle people of Algeria. When scholars such as Tracy (2002) focus on practices in which language plays a central role, *discursive practices* are defined as "talk activities that people do" (p. 21). Although practice is literally anything people do (including talk), most practice theorists are interested in the relationship between social forces and individual agency or how, in practices, participants reproduce preexisting social values and how those values are resisted and transformed. So, Ortner continued, "the most significant forms of practice are those with intentional or unintentional political implications"

(p. 149). An activity with political implications is clearly an activity that is defined culturally and in this it is easy to see that discursive practice parallels Hymes's conception of speech event, just as practice, in general, corresponds to Levinson's activity type. The conversation among Carlos, Dan, and Bob is a discursive practice because the transcript represents the talk that the three participants do, but analysis of the talk as practice involves understanding broader implications for society at large.

What, then, are the societal implications of the conversation among Carlos, Dan, and Bob? Answering that question involves expanding the focus of practice beyond the language used, beyond the type of speech event, and beyond the components of the event. If analysis is limited to the language and its immediate context as many applied linguists and SLA researchers might do, then applied linguists may be interested in this exchange as a token of the genre of small talk at work and SLA researchers may be more interested in it as evidence of native speakers of English conversing with a learner in which negotiation of meaning and, by implication, SLA takes place. From this perspective, the conversation appears uninteresting because, as Block (2007) admitted, "there do not appear to be any overt adjustments to linguistic form, conversational structure, or message content" (p. 93), and so from an examination that is limited to the talk and the immediate context of this conversation, there appears to very little of relevance to SLA. Yet, as Block pointed out, this level of analysis ignores features of context that *are* relevant to Carlos's acquisition of English but that can only be approached by extending the context to include Carlos's personal biography and his identity as an English speaker. A practice approach seeks to explain how Carlos's participation in this conversation is a way in which he and the other participants construct identities for themselves and how, through construction of their identities, participants reproduce or resist social categories such as class, gender, and ethnicity.

Carlos's participation in this conversation is minimal. He provides response tokens such as "yeah" at appropriate times, and his only topical contribution to the conversation is an assessment of the recent performance of the Chelsea Football Club. Carlos's lack of engagement in the conversation mediates an identity for himself different from that of his workmates. Block recounted Carlos's story as follows:

> Carlos grew up in a working-class family in a small city located in the southwestern part of Colombia. He studied philosophy and eventually became a philosophy lecturer at a university in Colombia. By the late 1980s, he was married and he had two children from this marriage, which

ended in 1991. In the late 1980s and early 1990s, Carlos was very active in leftist political movements working in opposition to the Colombian political establishment. On more than one occasion he was imprisoned and on two occasions he visited friends in London to get away from "hot" situations. During his second visit, in 1991, he met Kelly, whom he married soon after. Their son, Eduardo, was born in 1992. Carlos, Kelly and Eduardo lived in Colombia together from 1992 to 2001. Their life was middle class: Carlos was a philosophy lecturer at a university and Kelly worked as a Spanish/English translator. After more than eight years in Colombia, Kelly wanted to be close to her family in London again and there was some concern that Eduardo would never learn English, given that the couple spoke only Spanish at home. So they moved to London in autumn 2001. [. . .]

. . .throughout his formal education, [Carlos] had studied French, almost as a manner of protest against what he perceived as the imposition of English as the international language by the US. As a result, upon his arrival in London, Carlos spoke hardly any English and this meant that he could not find any employment beyond that of a manual labourer. In this sense, he was effectively declassed when he arrived in London, falling from professional middle class to unskilled low-level service provider in one fall [sic] swoop. (Block, 2006, pp. 153–154)

Because of his background as an intellectual in Colombia, Carlos had acquired what Bourdieu (1986) recognized as considerable cultural and social capital, and although his linguistic resources in English were limited, Carlos was able to use this cultural capital in his dealings with officials in Britain, such as immigration authorities, or professionals, such as doctors or lawyers. Having been declassed in his identity as an immigrant in London, his exposure to English was limited to short service encounters at work and longer interactions with his workmates, such as the one reproduced above. In such interactions, however, the working-class, White, male identity that his workmate Dan offers linguistically with his choice of topics about the local football team, his health problems, and his frequent expletive is not something that Carlos wishes to accept. As he later told Block:

Estoy escuchando y ya hay una parte de la conversación, que yo te digo, la pierdo porque la otra persona con quien habla. . . tiene el problema, es tartamudo, y luego su dicción, la forma de pronunciar, es muy cortante, y pierdo ya el ánimo, el interés, en la conversación. Entonces los dejo ya

entre ellos allí. Yo estoy allí pero. . . ((encogiéndose de hombros.))[12]
(p. 97)

In being there but not being there in the conversation—in resisting participation in the practice of informal conversation with his English workmates—Carlos's action is an act of resistance against an identity imposed upon him by his transmigrant status. For Dan and Bob, however, the conversational format and its familiar topics construct a practice that reproduces their identity as White, working class, and male. A practice approach to analyzing this conversation is thus a way in which both the materialist and idealist interpretations can coexist. A conversation like this is both a way in which social realities of social class, gender, and race are reproduced and thus reinforced, but it is also an opportunity for a participant (in this case, Carlos) to resist such positioning. His shoulder-shrugging attitude to participation in the conversation is a rational means to the end of positioning himself as an intellectual and resisting solidarity with his workmates.

As Ortner (1984, p. 149) concludes, a practice approach seeks to explain "the genesis, reproduction, and change" of social and cultural realities such as class, gender, and ethnicity. Such social movements as cultural reproduction are not an unthinking reaction of human automata to powerful social forces over which we have no control, nor is social change the result of the individual's struggle against such forces. Bourdieu and Wacquant (1992) argued for a middle ground that analyzes practice "by escaping both the objectivism of action understood as a mechanical reaction 'without an agent' and the subjectivism which portrays action as the deliberate pursuit of conscious intention, the free process of a conscience positing its own ends and maximizing its utility through rational computation" (p. 121). In this light, Carlos's participation in the conversation with Dan and Bob can be considered as neither an automatic expression of his own identity as a transmigrant nor a strategy that he uses to consciously resist identifying with his workmates. Instead, it is the practice itself—conversation among workmates—that creates the opportunity for Carlos, Dan, and Bob to construct their identities—identities that both reproduce and resist the social forces that formed them.

The third part of the question about what distinguishes a practice approach from language games, context of situation, and the ethnography of speaking is this: What does a consideration of talk-in-interaction as practice reveal about the relationship between talk and context? By providing a little of Carlos's personal history that question has already been answered. A practice approach differs from an ethnography of speaking in the recognition that ethnography *is* history. The tradition of considering present actions and language in the present as fundamentally different phenomena from past actions and language history is another dichotomy than can be traced to Saussure's distinction between synchronic linguistics and diachronic linguistics, but it is a distinction that obscures connections from the present to the past that explain much about the present. A practice approach to talk-in-interaction thus involves expanding, again, the notion of context to include the personal histories of participants and the generic history of the practice.

Participants' personal histories are relevant to practice because participants are predisposed to act and to talk in certain ways in particular situations, a predisposition that Bourdieu (1977) called *habitus*. Habitus refers to participants' socially acquired predispositions, tendencies, propensities, or inclinations, which are shown in mental phenomena such as opinions and outlooks, linguistic phenomena such as ways of talking, and physical phenomena such as deportment and posture, as well as ways of walking, sitting, and dressing. The linguistic features of habitus are national, regional, and social accent: Where individuals grew up and the people from the social class and race that they hang out with all influence how participants speak in a particular conversation. These features of personal history allow other people to categorize you as belonging to a larger group of people who share your geographical, class, and ethnic background. In Bourdieu's terms, accent and language choice are habitus, and habitus is something that does not generally reach conscious awareness, and unless it does, it limits the ways in which we can act and talk. In other words, habitus is temporal context; it is an index of personal history that every speaker brings to spoken interaction and that every writer brings to literacy practices.

Practices have histories also, and, as Sahlins (1985) pointed out, cultural schemata govern actions so that participants perceive experience through cultural categories that are already established in myth and legend. For Sahlins, practices provide "indigenous [interpretive] schemes of cosmological proportions" to members of a community (p. 76). As I remarked in the discussion of Hymes's components of speech events, ethnographers of speaking have also recognized the historical dimension of practice in the notion of *genre*, but when the focus is limited to formal linguistic features, the powerful influence of practice as genre may have been underestimated. One way in which the concept of genre has been extended beyond the purely formal analysis of language is exemplified by R. Bauman's work on the construction of tradition in folklore (e.g.,

R. Bauman, 1992), and the method may be loosely applied to the interaction between Carlos and his workmates that was presented earlier. Although I have focused on Carlos's participation in this practice, if we move our analytical focus to Dan, the interaction can be seen as several interrelated narratives in which Dan complains about his health and the performance of the football team he supports.

Most of the actions that Dan relates in his narrative are performed by others. In line 5, Dan invokes an unnamed participant as "he" and it is this person who booked the tickets for the football game and, although Dan is not feeling well, Dan doesn't want to let "him" down and accompanies this person to London. At the football game they watched, Chelsea's performance was "awful" and Dan uses a dramatic whisper in line 20 to state the trouble three times: "we're not scoring the goals." He then continues in lines 23–30 to relate his visit to the doctor, who refuses to prescribe medication, an action that Dan again dramatizes, this time by raising his voice in line 30: "HE WASN'T EVEN GONNA GIVE ME ANY MEDICINE." Dan relates that he told the doctor that he had been treating his cold with the well-known over-the-counter cold and flu remedy, Lemsip, but nonetheless he could not shake off his cold. His narrative is bounded with an opening in which Dan sets the scene: "I feel a bit rough" and concludes it by repeating: "I just feel terrible."

In all of the actions that Dan relates, he constructs himself as powerless. It was his friend, not Dan, who wanted to come down to London. Watching Chelsea play might have been worth the discomfort, but his football team did not score any goals, a situation that is incomprehensible to a supporter—"I can't make it out," he says. Additionally, although Dan expected his doctor to give him some medicine, the doctor refused. The only action that Dan took of his own accord—taking Lemsip—had no effect on his cold. In each of these four events, the structure of Dan's narration is the same: Other people (his friend, his football team, his doctor) act and, in each case, the effect of their actions on Dan is unpleasant until, finally, he tries to act himself by treating his cold with Lemsip, but this action fails and he is left, at the end, in the same state in which he began. It is indeed a series of unfortunate events and can be classified in the same genre as the series of children's books by Lemony Snicket. *A Series of Unfortunate Events* is a narrative of disasters that happen to the three Baudelaire children and over which they have no control. In the first book in the series, *The Bad Beginning*, the children's parents die and their house is burned to the ground (Snicket, 1999). They move in with a neighbor for just one day and then have to move to stay with a greedy man who wants to claim the Baudelaire fortune for himself. When he finds that he will not receive it, he treats the children like slaves and makes them do difficult chores for himself and his acting troupe. The story continues and worse happens.

Dan's narrative bears comparison with Snicket's books because they bear a generic resemblance. Genre, as R. Bauman (1992) described it, "is a classificatory concept, a way of sorting out conventionalized discourse forms on the basis of form, function, content or other factor or set of factors" (p. 138). The Baudelaire children are described by Snicket (1999, p. 1) as intelligent, charming, resourceful, and with pleasant facial features. Readers are encouraged to sympathize with the Baudelaire children because of these qualities and because they bear no responsibility for the dreadful things that happen to them, all of which are the consequence of actions performed by evil others. Recalling that cultural schemata govern actions so that participants perceive experience through established cultural categories, then, for Carlos and Bob, who listen to Dan's series of unfortunate events, do they not experience feelings of sympathy for Dan? Is Dan's choice of this genre not a strategy to elicit sympathy? Block (2006) does not tell us and we do not know, but a practice approach leads us to consider those implications of the genre.

Practice Theory goes beyond the primary focus on language of Hymes, J. R. Firth, Mitchell, Malinowski, and Wittgenstein, but the implications of Practice Theory for an approach to talk-in-interaction are clear. An approach to talk-in-interaction as practice expands the field beyond a consideration of what we can observe in an interaction. The idea put forward by Levinson in considering an instance of talk as an activity type is both a way to analyze the talk and to relate it to *other* talk, an approach that Hymes extended by specifying the components of speech events. In their attempts to explain speech events in exotic places, Malinowski and Mitchell inevitably had recourse to the cultures in which those events were embedded and without which they could not be understood. Even in our daily lives, Wittgenstein recognized that the uniform appearance of words confuses us into believing that an utterance always means the same although we do not know the language game in which the utterance is a move. Practice Theory goes even further in recognizing that every instance of talk is a *discursive* practice and that what participants bring to that practice is a habitus that has accumulated over a lifetime. The practice itself is an interpretive schema—a way of organizing experience in the mind, a way that participants make sense of themselves, a way in which they construct and reconstruct identities and cultural categories that are already established by the myths and legends of the cultures in which they live.

Chapter Summary and a Look Ahead

In this chapter, I have tried to provide a rationale and a methodology for considering talk-in-interaction as discursive practice. In this, I have been guided by a relationship between talk and the contexts in which talk happens. I recognize that we know much more about language in isolation than about language in context, and I have reviewed how scholars have tried to correct the imbalance. The chapter began with a description of a theory of semiotics in which members of a community were believed to share a common understanding of signs, a common knowledge of the relationship between linguistic form and meaning. A challenge to that view was Peirce's proposal that a sign that a speaker creates simply creates another sign for a hearer, and the relationship between form and meaning for the hearer does not necessarily correspond to the relationship created by the speaker. Philosophers of language came to a very similar fork in the road, reflected by the difference between the theory of semantics developed by Wittgenstein (1933) in the *Tractatus*, in which every utterance is a picture of reality and is seen as a logical proposition with a truth value, and his later view of utterances as moves in a language game, the meaning of which depends on the game being played. Semioticians and philosophers described their own language within a taken-for-granted cultural context, but linguistic anthropologists came to a very similar understanding of the role of context when they had to make sense of utterances in cultural contexts that were radically different from the ones they knew. First Malinowski and then J. R. Firth and Mitchell incorporated the "Where?" "When?" "Who?" and "Why?" of context of situation into a developed theory of language, which was later greatly expanded into the fully developed set of components of speech events in Hymes's ethnography of speaking.

The work of linguistic anthropologists and sociologists has also been foundational in the latest development of the theory of language in context: discursive practice, which is a language-centered view of Practice Theory. In discursive practice, the context of talk-in-interaction extends beyond the speech event to include the social-historical trajectories of participants and the role of the practice itself as a cultural schema governing participants' actions such that they perceive experience through established cultural categories.

A good condensation of one argument that I have tried to make in this chapter is Erickson's (2004) assertion that "the conduct of talk in local social interaction is profoundly influenced by processes that occur beyond the temporal and spatial horizon of the immediate occasion of the interaction" (p. viii). However, such a statement omits the agency of individuals, which, as we have seen in comparing the talk of Carlos and Dan, can be both a consequence of the social processes beyond the horizon of the speech event and an attempt to influence them. I have recited arguments that demonstrate that the traditional linguistic approach to language structure and meaning as context-free, as occurring nowhere, nowhen, and produced by nobody is untenable. Instead, as Erickson again asserted, "the conduct of talk in local social interaction as it occurs in real time is unique, crafted by local social actors for the specific situation of its use in the moment of its uttering" (p. viii). In other words, all talk happens somewhere and somewhen and is produced by somebody for some purpose. Ignoring the context of talk cannot lead to an understanding of its function. The discursive practice approach to talk-in-interaction, which will be the topic of the remaining chapters, is grounded in these insights.

Notes

1 Pierce often uses the terms "sign" and "representamen" to mean the same thing, although at one point he distinguished between them as follows: "The concrete subject that represents I call a sign or a representamen. I use the two words *sign* and *representamen* differently. By a *sign* I mean anything which conveys any definite notion of an object in any way, as such conveyors of thought are familiarly known to us. Now I start with this familiar idea and make the best analysis I can of what is essential to a sign, and I define *representamen* as being whatever that analysis applies to" (Peirce et al., 1933, vol. 1, p. 540).

2 Peirce has a view of the infinite regression of representamen and interpretant: A sign is "anything which determines something else (its *interpretant*) to refer to an object to which itself refers (its *object*) in the same way, the interpretant becoming in turn a sign, and so on *ad infinitum*" (Peirce et al., 1933, vol. 2, p. 303).

3 Two contexts in which I can say "It's cold in here" and mean "It's warm in here" are (a) in my incredulous response to somebody's comment that "It's cold in here" and (b) if I am a sarcastic person who often makes what I believe to be witty comments about states of affairs that are manifestly false.

4 Conventions used by Seedhouse (2004) to transcribe talk-in-interaction are explained in the Appendix.

5 Malinowski (1923) had recourse to the same procedure in explaining the meaning of the language activities of the Trobriand Islanders to an English readership.

6 A campaign speech by Italian Prime Minister Silvio Berlusconi was criticized in the Italian media as a "discorso fiume": *Il premier tiene un discorso fiume. Parla a braccio per circa due ore davanti a una platea di settemila sostenitori (anche se il padiglione non è completamente pieno) che sottolineano con cori di ≪Silvio, Silvio≫ i passaggi chiave del suo intervento (Corriere della Sera*, April 6, 2006). Translation: "The Prime Minister's speech was very very long. He spoke without

notes for about two hours before an audience of seven thousand supporters (although the hall was not completely full), who responded with cries of 'Silvio, Silvio' whenever he made an important point."

7 Wei (1978) listed the following well-known Chinese four-character idioms among over 2,000 in his dictionary: 立竿见影 (raise pole see shadow) "have an immediate effect," 半斤八两 (half catty eight ounces) "six of one and half-a-dozen of the other," 老生常谈 (old scholar often says) "platitude," 有血有肉 (has blood has flesh) "true to life," and 破釜沉舟 (break cauldrons burn boats) "burn your boats."

8 The term "intertextuality" originally coined by Kristeva (1974) and developed in Kristeva (1980) has been used in many senses by different scholars and has migrated away from the sense that it had in the work of Kristeva. It was defined in Kristeva (1974) as the transposition of one or more systems of signs into another, accompanied by a new articulation of the enunciative and denotative position. In the sense in which I use term here, I adopt the meaning of "constitutive intertextuality" (Fairclough, 1992), in which genre serves as a conventionalized orienting framework for interpreting speech.

9 McDermott (1980) recalled an apt image that Ray Birdwhistell used to understand context: "I like to think of it as a rope. The fibers that make up the rope are discontinuous; when you twist them together, you don't make them continuous, you make the thread continuous. [. . .] The thread has no fibers in it, but, if you break up the thread you can find the fibers again. So that, even though it may look in a thread as though each of these particles is going all through it, that isn't the case. That's essentially the descriptive model" (p. 2).

10 Things or places that are *tabu* must be left alone and may not be approached or interfered with. In some cases, they should not even be spoken about. The English word "taboo" derives from this usage.

11 *Mana* is a traditional term that refers to a concept among the speakers of Oceanic languages, including Melanesians, Polynesians, and Micronesians. It is an impersonal force or quality that resides in people, animals, and inanimate objects, which instills in the appreciative observer a sense of respect or wonder.

12 Translation: "I'm listening and there is a part of the conversation, that I tell you, I lose it because the other person he is talking to . . . he has this problem, he stutters, and then his diction, how he pronounces, it's very sharp, and I lose spirit, interest, in the conversation. So, I just leave them there, to talk among themselves. I'm there but . . ." ((He shrugs.))

Language Learning ISSN 0023-8333

CHAPTER THREE

Investigating Context

All talk happens somewhere, at some time, and is produced somehow by somebody for some purpose, and the approach that practice theorists have taken is that talk and its context are inseparable. It has to be admitted, however, that the melding of talk and context in Practice Theory is of quite recent origin and many scholars have taken the contrasting position that in order to understand the relationships between talk and context, it is necessary to focus attention and resources on one to the near exclusion of the other. Disciplinary boundaries determine which of the two a particular researcher chooses to focus on, with linguists focusing their attention on language and sociologists or anthropologists focusing on context. It is perhaps not surprising that scholars should differ in their interpretations of the relationship between language and context because the concepts—and the relationship between them—are difficult to define. An indication of the variety of approaches to that relationship was provided by Goodwin and Duranti (1992), who, in their introduction to a collection of essays on context written by anthropologists and sociolinguists, reviewed eight different traditions in the analysis of social context. In all eight traditions, however, Goodwin and Duranti noted that "the notion of context . . . involves a fundamental juxtaposition of two entities: (1) a focal event; and (2) a field of action within which that event is embedded" (p. 3). The focal event, for our purposes, is talk and the field of action is the context of talk.

Once the distinction between talk and context is accepted, the question becomes whether to begin the investigation of talk-in-interaction with talk, the focal event, or to start with the context of talk, the field of action within which talk is embedded. These are in fact two very different approaches and are presented in two separate chapters. In the present chapter, I review the approaches that have been taken to investigate context and the methods that have been adopted by second language (L2) researchers to describe and analyze context. In chapter 4, I take a complementary approach to talk-in-interaction and present the linguistic and interactional resources that are employed by participants in talk-in-interaction and describe the methods that have been developed to relate language to context.

Locating Context

Ethnomethodology

In contrasting a view of language as an abstract system with discursive practice, in chapter 2 I argued that the "Where?" "How?" "When?" "Who?" and "Why?" questions about language in practice have not received as much attention as the question of "What?" Theories of language in practice have differed in their interpretations of the scope of these contextual questions: To oversimplify, theories have differed in considering how far outside the focal event one should look in order to locate the context. One of the principal fault lines in the treatment of context can be found in the Conversation Analysis (CA) literature. In the tradition of ethnomethodology, from which CA draws its theoretical stance and many of its practical procedures, the "Who?" question asks about characteristics of social participants, such as age, gender, and social class, whereas the "How?" question requires us to specify the activity that the participants engage in, such as an interview, a seminar, or a service transaction. In the CA tradition, these questions are not considered in advance of analysis of social interaction. As Pomerantz and Fehr (1997) remarked, in CA, context is used in two senses. In the first sense:

> Conduct is produced and understood as responsive to the immediate, local contingencies of interaction. What an interactant contributes is shaped by what was just said or done and is understood in relation to the prior. (p. 69)

In another sense, context is brought into being by the actions of interactants. Pomerantz and Fehr continued:

> Rather than treating the identities of the participants, the place, the occasion, etc., as givens, conversation analysts and ethnomethodologists recognize that there are multiple ways to identify parties, the occasion, etc. and that the identifications must be shown to be relevant to the participants. (p. 69)

In the ethnomethodological tradition, then, the distinction made is not between language and a context lying beyond the immediate interaction; rather, it is between people's conduct in a moment of interaction and the immediate sequential context (what was just said). To the extent that participants invoke other aspects of context, those aspects influence the interpretation of their conduct, but if other context is not invoked, then the analyst must ignore it.

The ethnomethodological approach to context has been criticized by some scholars who have been working within the CA tradition because it appears that so much of an analyst's interpretation of what happens in interaction depends on the analyst and the participants sharing a common cultural (i.e., contextual) background. Cicourel (1992), for example, pointed out that such an extreme empiricist approach can be problematic because it obscures information that was available to the researcher during collection and analysis of data, and he distinguished between "narrow" and "broad" senses of context—the broad sense incorporating extrasituational information. Cicourel (1992) supported his argument with examples from his own work on interactions among physicians, patients, and technicians in a teaching hospital (Cicourel, 1983, 1992) and especially from his work on the construction of expertise in the same community (Cicourel, 1995, 2000). In his work on the construction of expertise in medical settings, Cicourel found that in order to understand interaction, it was necessary to go far beyond the sequential context and to explore fully the background of participants.

The extended context that Cicourel (1995) described goes far beyond the situational context of a particular interaction, but it is essential in order to understand how participants make inferences about expertise from their talk. It also goes far beyond the methods of CA. Cicourel criticized CA approaches, saying that because they deal with interactions and participants with which the researchers and their readers are familiar, they make use of analysts' implicit sociocultural knowledge without acknowledging it and that as soon as researchers move outside a cultural context with which they are familiar, it is necessary to do the kind of ethnographic work that Cicourel advocated in order to understand participants' conduct in interaction.

Sentences and Utterances

Others have expanded the view of context beyond the sequential context of talk and one of the first to provide a much broader analysis of context was the Russian philosopher and literary critic Mikhail Bakhtin, who developed profound insights into the use of language in context that were based on his studies of European literature, especially the development of the novel from classical times to the 19th century. Bakhtin's approach to language in context is founded on his distinction between a sentence and an utterance. For Bakhtin, utterances are different than sentences—although sentences are the stuff that makes up language, rather like paper and ink make up this book. An utterance can be as short as a sentence or as long as this book, or it can be a single turn-at-talk in a conversation. Morson and Emerson (1990), in an extensive review and evaluation of Bakhtin's work, crafted the distinction skillfully when they wrote "Sentences are repeatable. Sentences are repeatable. . . . But each utterance is by its very nature unrepeatable. Its context and reason for being differ from those of every other utterance" (p. 126). From this differentiation, it is now a short step to answering the "Who?" question: Each utterance is spoken or written by a particular someone and is addressed to a particular someone else. This has the important consequence that the meaning of a word in an utterance is neither the meaning that a speaker originally intended nor the meaning that a listener interprets; it is somewhere in between. Neither is the meaning of a word in an utterance its dictionary meaning. As Bakhtin's colleague Voloshinov (1973) wrote, the "*word is a two-sided act*. It is determined equally by *whose* word it is and *for whom* it is meant. As word, it is precisely *the product of the reciprocal relationship between speaker and listener, addresser and addressee* . . . I give myself verbal shape from another's point of view" (p. 86, emphasis in the original). This relationship is what later scholars have called co-construction. A very similar position on the distinction between sentences in isolation and utterances in context was taken by Schegloff (1978), who wrote:

> Taking sentences in isolation is not just a matter of taking such sentences that might appear *in* a context *out* of a context; but that the very composition, construction, assemblage of the sentences is predicated by their speakers on the place in which it is being produced, and it is through *that* that a sentence is context-bound, rather than possibly independent sentences being different intact objects in or out of context. (p. 101, emphasis in original)

The "How?" and "Why?" questions are discussed by Bakhtin (1986) in his theory of speech genres. A genre is a pattern of communication that is created in a recurring communicative situation. Genres aid communication by creating shared expectations about the form and content of the interaction, thus easing the burden of production and interpretation. In other words, life is not full of surprises, and people create meaning in routine ways. We see the importance of genres when we move out of our daily communicative routine and try to learn a foreign language. Although we may know the grammar, vocabulary, and pronunciation of a foreign language well, we may nonetheless "feel quite helpless in certain spheres of communication precisely because we do not have a practical command of the generic forms in the given spheres" (Bakhtin, 1986, p. 80). Genres are crystallizations of earlier interactions, and whenever we communicate, we do so in one or another genre. Unlike R. Bauman's (2000, p. 84) linguistic definition of genre as "formal features and structures" cited in chapter 2, for Bakhtin, genres are not simply fixed grammatical structures or combinations of words (although certain words and ways of speaking may be associated with a particular genre), but each implies a set of values: a way of thinking about the world and the appropriateness of a given genre in a particular social context. Genres are also not simply ways of producing talk; they are just as important in interpreting what is said because they help listeners and readers understand social relations between the speaker/writer and others, the speaker/writer's values, their tone, and the purposes of the communication.

Bakhtin's (1986) concept of genre is revisited in Gee's (1999, 2007) distinction between "Discourse" with a "big D" and "discourse" with a "little d." Discourse with a little d is the way that applied linguists, such as those whose work I review later in this chapter, consider how stretches of language like conversations or stories are used in situ to enact activities and identities. With a big D, Discourse (or more often Discourses in the plural) involves far more than language. As Gee (1999) explained:

> If you put language, action, interaction, values, beliefs, symbols, objects, tools, and places together in such a way that others *recognize* you as particular type of who (identity) engaged in a particular type of what (activity) here and now, then you have pulled off a Discourse (and thereby continued it through history, if only for a while longer). (p. 18, emphasis in original)

Like Bakhtin's genres, Discourses with a big D are therefore ensembles of semiotic systems that must be considered not only to have a history but whose history is part of the way in which participants construct meaning. The role of Discourses in constructing language learners' identities is considered later in this chapter.

The time and place of an utterance are, in one sense, the physical circumstances of utterance, but what counts in the interpretation of an utterance is not a physical description of time and place; rather, it is the meanings that a specific time and a particular place take on for the participants. Bakhtin (1981) goes much further in his discussion of "Where?" and "When?" and makes a connection between the actions and interpretations of communication and the time-space context of the interaction.[1] The time-space context, in a similar way to genre, provides possibilities for action and a calculus of likely interpretations of any action. Bakhtin's discussion of time-space context is carried out entirely by reference to the history of the novel in European literature from classical times to the 19th century, but it can easily be extended to spoken interaction. Take, as an example of the temporal dimension of context, the utterance

"Though the sex to which I belong is considered weak . . . you will nevertheless find me a rock that bends to no wind." In this utterance, a female speaker expresses a view of her gender that was prevalent in certain historical periods but is much less common today. It is unlikely that a woman in 21st-century Europe or North America would claim that women are considered weak. The speaker then goes on to claim for herself an unshakeable determination and strength, in effect claiming a powerful identity in contrast to what her addressee might believe about her gender. Knowing that the temporal context of the utterance is 16th-century England helps us understand the reasons why the speaker formulated it in this way. In fact, the remark is attributed to Queen Elizabeth I of England when speaking to the French ambassador.

Another example, provided by Gumperz (2000, p. 132), shows the influence of the spatial dimension of context on the interpretability of language.

```
1 A: But she's a FLAKE.
2 B: (fast tempo) Ya know we should probably watch it.
3    They're probably sitt'n there.
4 A: (overlapping B's last three words) I know
5 B: It's just nice going to cafes now and I feel like
6    I don't have to avoid anybody
7 A: (overlapping B's last three words) THIS is the LIFE.
```

In this conversation, Gumperz pointed out that the speakers share a common normative principle to avoid gossiping about other people when there is a chance that they may overhear you. The shared knowledge is indexed by A's overlapping of B's statement of the principle with "I know" in line 4. The motivation for B's overt statement is that "they're probably sitt'n there"; in other words, the public location of the conversation is the reason for B's warning in line 2. Then, in line 5, the spatial context of the conversation is explicitly indexed by B: "It's just nice going to cafes."

In addition to Bakhtin's (1981) insights into the context of utterance, he also provided some observations about the "What?" of language use that go beyond a description of a single linguistic system. Bakhtin recognized that a single language like English, Russian, or Japanese has an official form (the standard language) but, in addition, has many unofficial forms that are used by different speakers to create identities and establish membership in communities. The term that Bakhtin used for the coexistence of many different varieties within a single language is *heteroglossia*. Dialects of a language are examples of the different varieties of language that make up heteroglossia. Dialects are expressions of a regional identity—of New York or of Edinburgh, of Shanghai or of Hong Kong—but language also indexes social class within particular communities, so that a working-class New Yorker speaks a different variety of English from an upper middle-class New Yorker. Other identities that are indexed by different language varieties are gender (women's talk, men's talk, and the talk of other gendered identities), age (teenagers speak very differently from senior citizens), and ethnicity (African American varieties of English differ from Hispanic varieties, and both differ from White varieties). Then, of course, there are many varieties of language that index the profession of the speaker as a vendor at a farmers market, as a lawyer, as an information technology consultant, and so on. Speakers of one language command a number of different varieties of that language, and the creation of an identity involves use of certain varieties that index that identity. As Bakhtin put it,

> Consciousness finds itself inevitably facing the necessity of having to choose a language. With each literary-verbal performance, consciousness must actively orient itself amidst heteroglossia. It must move in and occupy a position for itself within it. It chooses, in other words, a "language." (p. 295)

In discussing the narrow approach to context adopted by ethnomethod-ologists and the much broader approach of Bakhtin and his circle, I have sketched some of the challenges that face analysts of discursive practice. Those challenges are threefold: how to describe and analyze the context of talk-in-interaction, how to describe and analyze the talk itself, and how to unite the two aspects of practice into a coherent theory of discursive practice. For the remainder of this chapter, I discuss methods for identifying, describing, and analyzing context and follow this discussion with a presentation of methods for analyzing talk-in-interaction in chapter 4. The studies reviewed here are chosen because they provide rich descriptions of context and because the researchers have focused on talk in those contexts and related what participants say to the context. This approach to grounding a discussion of context in utterances means that many interesting discussions of context, such as Norton (2000), that provide no transcripts of conversations are not reviewed here. In the remaining chapters of the book, I argue for ways in which a holistic approach to context and talk provides insight into the development of language and identity, the creation of community, and language learning through social interaction.

Four Perspectives on Interaction and Context

The investigation of the context of language learning and language use is a very different enterprise from the explication of the development and use of language, one which demands methods quite different from linguistic analysis. In this section, I review four ways in which scholars understand the connection between context and language and I report the methods that they have used to make the connection. In all four approaches, researchers have focused on L2 learning and use and have related learners' language to the contexts in which it develops over weeks, months, and years. To begin at one end, there are those scholars who have started with an analysis of learner language and correlated language development with the context in which it occurs. Because researchers in this tradition start from linguistic form and work outward to context, I have called this tradition "an applied linguistic perspective" and have chosen Liu (2000) as a paradigm. Working within a different paradigm, other researchers have taken what I have called "an ethnographic perspective" to describe the physical, social, and institutional context in which language development occurs and have made specific connections between features of context and talk-in-interaction. The majority of these studies have focused on young children in school, and Toohey's (2000) work is the paradigm here. These ethnographic studies of the context of talk-in-interaction have extended the notion of context in two contrasting but complementary directions, asking, first, how far institutional cultures are internalized by individuals and then, critically, how the everyday discursive practices of learners reflect, maintain, and challenge forms of personal and institutional power. I address the first of the two questions by discussing the role of self-stories as data sources to investigate what I have called "emotional perspectives" on language learning. Finally, in addressing the second question I return to the critical ethnography of schooling to show in political relief the relationship between the social world outside the classroom and the Discourses within it.

An Applied Linguistic Perspective on Language in Context
The distinction between emic and etic approaches to linguistic and cultural analysis has been adopted by many linguists, psychologists, and anthropologists and, because of the widespread use of these two terms, the distinction has been interpreted in slightly different ways (Headland, 1990). In what follows, I use an etic approach to context to label investigations in which a theory of a specific instance of language in context is developed in order to provide an understanding of other instances; that is, an observer's etic description of context is made in terms that can be applied to other cultures and other contexts and is not specific to the context in which it is identified. An etic description is not necessarily either an insider's or an outsider's perspective on a specific context, but it is a perspective that is, in principle, applicable to other talk in

other contexts. Ways of arriving at such an etic perspective are by conducting an analysis of talk-in-interaction from a specific theoretical perspective or by using a common metric that is applied to many different contexts of talk-in-interaction.

Several examples of contexts that have been described from particular theoretical perspectives are provided by longitudinal studies of learners. Some of the classics are the four-volume diary study by Leopold (1939, 1947, 1949) of the acquisition of English and German by his daughters growing up in Milwaukee in the 1930s and unpublished theses by Fillmore (1976) and Nicholas (1987). Several researchers have published more recent studies of the context of second language acquisition (SLA) by children. Cathcart (1986) recorded children using English as a second language in a kindergarten class in which she identified contexts that she described as "recess," "seatwork," "free play," "ESL," "playhouse," and "interview and story-telling." Nemoianu (1980) studied two 3-year-old German children playing with their age-mates and speaking English in a context that she called "conversation play." The most significant of these longitudinal studies, however, is Liu's study of a Chinese child's acquisition of English as a second language in Australia (Liu, 2000; Tarone & Liu, 1995).

Liu (2000) studied the development of spoken English by a child of Chinese immigrants to Australia. The child, named "Bob" by Liu, was studied for 26 months from when he was almost 5 years old. Bob was born in Beijing and his family moved to Australia when Bob was 4 years old so that his father could pursue an advanced degree in statistics. His family spoke Mandarin Chinese at home and had only limited knowledge of English. Liu studied Bob's spoken interaction in English in several different physical settings. In the first 5 months of the study, Bob was in a preschool program organized by the university at which his father was enrolled. After he finished the preschool program, Bob then moved into the first grade of a primary school. In both contexts, Liu gathered data about Bob's interaction with his teachers and his classmates in the classroom by means of a radio microphone attached to Bob's clothing. The third physical setting was at Bob's home, where, throughout the 26-month period of the study, Liu recorded 22 conversations mostly in English between Bob and himself.

Liu's (2000) study documented two developing dimensions of Bob's use of English in conversations: his functional use of English and his developing interlanguage grammar. Bob's functional use of English was described using the interlanguage functions established by Nicholas (1987), which include a mixture of grammatical categories such as "statements" and "questions," speech act categories such as "greetings" and "commands," and sequential interactional categories, including "responses to questions" and "responses to commands." His developing use of grammar was measured against the six developmental stages for the acquisition of English question formation proposed by Pienemann, Johnston, and Brindley (1988). According to this model of question formation, Stage 1 is single units including words and lexical chunks. Stage 2 is questions formed with SVO word order and rising intonation as in "You like number one?" Stage 3 involves fronting of some element (e.g., a *wh*-word or unanalyzed *do*) without inversion, as in "Why you do that?" In Stage 4, learners produce inversion in *yes/no-* and *wh*-questions with copula *be*, as in "Where's my book?" In Stage 5, learners invert auxiliaries after *wh*-words, as in "What're you doing?" In the final stage, learners produce inversion across the full range of contexts in which it is required in the target, and they produce negative and tag questions, including "You didn't work this the whole story, do you?" and "You just want to copy, do you?"[2]

Liu's (2000) analysis of the context of Bob's conversations is not limited to their physical setting; he identifies, in addition, the roles of the other participants in the conversations. At the preschool, Liu recorded conversations between Bob and his peers and between Bob and the adult preschool supervisors. In the primary school classroom, Liu distinguished between Bob's conversations with his peers and with his teachers. In the physical setting of the home, Liu recorded his own conversations with Bob. The information that Liu provided about each of Bob's interlocutors goes beyond a simple description of their institutional roles. In the preschool, for example, Bob "had the opportunity to mix with a group of native English-speaking children and one Chinese-speaking girl" (p. 113), but little information is given about his adult preschool supervisors. In the early weeks of his preschool experience, Bob spoke mostly in Chinese, but his use of English increased so that toward the end of his preschool attendance, his utterances were mostly in English. During this period, however, Bob produced vocalizations such as his "woo—woo—" to initiate interactions with the adult supervisors and in the early recording sessions produced private speech in Chinese. When Bob moved to the first-grade classroom in the primary school, Liu provided considerable background information about his teachers: "One was the regular teacher, a female of about thirty years of age (T1), who was responsible for the class most of the time. The other was a relieving [substitute] teacher, a male in his mid-thirties (T2), replacing the regular teacher when she was absent" (p. 163). Liu described the participation structure of Bob's interactions with the adults in the preschool and in first grade as follows:

In the beginning, Bob perceived the supervisors in the pre-school center as his teachers. In line with his previous experience and cultural understanding, he expected that the supervisors would come to teach him English . . . However, it turned out that he was not able to learn very much from the supervisors.

According to Liu, Bob's lack of opportunity to learn English from the adults in preschool influenced how he structured his participation with his first-grade teachers:

He tended to avoid using English with his teachers . . . his main concern seemed to be his image as a good pupil. (pp. 164–165)

According to Liu (2000), Bob's interactions with his teachers both in preschool and first grade seem to have had very little influence on the development of his English. Most of Bob's production of English was in response to elicitations from the teachers, and Bob was concerned with presenting himself as a competent pupil and competent user of English. These concerns led Bob to produce utterances with relatively simple syntax. Markers of syntactic development did not occur in Bob's interaction with teachers but emerged instead in his interactions with peers and with Liu himself.

Bob's interactions in English with his classmates and with the neighborhood children were very different from his interactions with teachers. His conversations with peers ranged over a number of topics, including sports, personal interests, games, family, and food, whereas the social actions performed included arguing, quarreling, and even verbal abuse. Liu (2000) surmised that the rich verbal environment and varied functions of language in Bob's interactions with his peers were the grounds for his syntactic development in English. Because Bob took a very competitive stance with his peers, much of his syntactic development emerged in ritual oppositions with his male friends. One example comes from his interaction with rivals Mark and Ben during an in-class drawing assignment.

```
1 Mark:  You can't draw the same sorts as in everything
         you know. Like the original. (Pointing to Ben's work
         of wave lines.)
2 Bob:   Yeah. Yeah. You can draw. Look at that. (To Ben.)
3 Mark:  You can't, can you? So I can't either.
4 Bob:   Look he doesn't know how to draw. (To Ben about Mark.)
```

```
 5  Mark:   I can draw better than both of you.
 6  Ben:    Can you draw peak? (Meaning mountain peak.)
 7  Mark:   Yes, I can.
 8  Bob:    OK, you draw.
 9  Ben:    Can you draw school?
10  Mark:   Yes, I can.
11  Ben:    Can you draw the whole world?
12  Mark:   Yes, I can.
13  Ben:    Ah ha, no one can draw the whole world.
            (Paul comes to the table.)
14  Ben:    Can you draw the whole world? (To Paul.)
15  Mark:   He would.
16  Ben:    You don't know because you don't know how to draw.
17  Mark:   I don't know how to draw the whole world.
18  Bob:    You don't know.
19  Ben:    Do you know how to draw stars?
20  Bob:    No, he don't know.
21  Mark:   I don't know how to draw stars. There's no one
            in the world knows how to draw stars.
22  Bob:    I know how to draw stars. It's it's very easy.
            You doesn't know.
```

The boys in this interaction engaged in ritual verbal oppositions that are often found in interactions among boys (Ong, 1981). In turn 1, Mark tells Bob that he cannot draw in one way, to which Bob immediately responds that he can and points to Ben's drawing in support. Bob increases his opposition to Mark in turn 4 by telling Ben that Mark does not know how to draw. After Ben challenges Mark to draw a mountain peak, Bob repeats the challenge in turn 8: "OK, you draw." The ritual opposition between Ben and Mark continues until Mark admits that he does not know how to draw stars and, in fact, "no one in the world knows how to draw stars" (turn 21). This gives Bob an opportunity to challenge Mark's denial by repeating with reverse polarity the complex structure that Mark had used: "I know how to draw stars" (turn 22).

The social context of interaction with peers and the ritual verbal opposition between Bob and his classmates provide a context in which, simply by reversing the polarity of clauses produced by the other boys, Bob is able to produce previously unspoken structures. According to Liu (2000), in interactions with his peers, Bob produced almost 10 times the number of utterances than he produced with his teachers. It is not just the number of utterances and their occasions of use that facilitate emergence of new grammatical structures, however; rather, it is the participation structure that Bob and his peers create that allows his English syntax to develop. This contrasts with the participation structure of Bob's interaction with his teachers, in which Bob's role is a respondent to the teachers' initiations and disciplinary directions.

In addition to Bob's interactions with his teachers and peers, the final context in which Liu recorded Bob's syntactic development was in the physical setting of Bob's home, in which Liu recorded his own conversations with Bob. These conversations occurred over a period of just over a year. Liu was originally asked by Bob's parents to help with his English, and the role that Liu played in these early conversations was that of a teacher. Bob addressed Liu as 老师 (teacher) in these early sessions and appeared to take what Liu said as instructions from a teacher. His relationship with Liu, however, was dynamic and, after Bob entered school, he came to see Liu as a family friend and began to address him as 叔叔 (uncle). As time went on, the social distance between Liu and Bob continued to change, and Bob began to address Liu by his personal name in the same way that Bob's parents did. Liu remarked that this is unusual in Chinese culture and was evidence of Bob's acculturation to the different relationship between adults and children in Australia.

Liu's conversations with Bob were dyadic and, not surprisingly, the total number of utterances produced by Bob in this context was twice the number produced in interaction with his peers and 22 times as many as in his interactions with his teachers. In the first few conversations with Liu, Bob responded to Liu's questions and requests, but after seven meetings, Bob's initiations far outnumbered his responses to initiations by Liu. In this period also, Bob was often asked to tell stories, a particular style that was not found in Bob's interactions with other interlocutors. Bob's many opportunities for talk with Liu and the variety of participation structures that Liu and Bob created led to faster development in Bob's English syntax. Liu reported that his interactions with Bob played an important role in the development of Bob's interrogative forms:

> The emergence of all stages [of interrogatives], with the exception of Stage 3, which emerged in Bob's interactions with his peers, occurred in this interactional setting. It demonstrates that the particular type of interaction between Bob and [Liu] made it possible for the development of interrogative forms to proceed more rapidly than in his interaction with the teachers and his peers. (2000, p. 308)

Given the importance of context in the development of this learner's interlanguage, the question of what features of context can be implicated in his development arises. In the primary school classroom, Liu again distinguished two contexts: Bob's conversations with his teachers and with his peers; in the physical setting of Bob's home, Liu recorded his own conversations with Bob. The role of Bob's interlocutors in these contexts differed, creating different participation structures involving Bob's greater initiation in some contexts (those with his peers and in his later conversations with Liu) and less in others (with his preschool supervisors, first-grade teachers, and his earlier conversations with Liu). The physical settings of those conversations were related to the roles that participants took, showing the reciprocal roles of adults and pupils in conversations in the preschool and first-grade settings, but the change over time in the conversational roles taken by Bob and Liu shows that Bob could interpret the physical setting of his home as either institutional with Liu as teacher or as more intimate when Bob considered Liu an "uncle." The genre of Bob's speech in different contexts is only occasionally described by Liu as, for instance, when Bob told narratives in his later sessions at home with Liu and when, in his first-grade conversations, Bob created ritual verbal opposition with his male peers.

The contexts of interaction cannot thus be taken as simply a constellation of independent features of setting, participants, and genre as might be inferred from Hymes's SPEAKING model discussed in chapter 2. Instead, the features of context are interrelated and must be described in full in order to accurately depict the development of Bob's interlanguage. This approach contrasts with the context-independent approach to interlanguage development proposed by Pienemann and Johnston (1987). These authors claim that there exists a universal (i.e., context-independent) sequence of acquisition of interrogative forms in English as a second language. Stage 5 follows Stage 4; Stage 4 follows Stage 3; and so on. When the context of acquisition is considered, however, the sequence does not hold. As Tarone and Liu (1995, p. 122) reported:

> In Bob's case, Stage 4 and 5 interrogative forms did emerge in interactions with the researcher long before Stage 3 forms emerged. [...] It would appear, then, that Bob's participation in the interactional context with the researcher altered a so-called universal sequence of acquisition of interrogatives in Bob's IL.

An Ethnographic Perspective on the Context of Second Language Learning

In his study of Bob's acquisition of English, Liu (2000) took a specific linguistic perspective on talk-in-interaction and he applied a common metric to the many different contexts in which he recorded Bob's talk-in-interaction. In this respect, therefore, Liu's approach to analyzing talk-in-interaction was etic. A different approach to the relationship between language and context is one in which the contexts of specific instances of talk-in-interaction are described in terms that are locally situated and specific to those contexts, and the language used is described in relation to the specific, local, historically constructed, and changing contexts of use. Examples of this approach are found in longitudinal studies of learners by researchers who take an ethnographic approach to describing the richness of situational contexts or by individual learners who, in their self-reflections and memoirs, describe their own experiences as learners. Toohey's (2000) book *Learning English at School: Identity, Social Relations, and Classroom Practice* is an example of the former approach. A sample of learners' memoirs and self-stories is surveyed later in this chapter.

In her book, Toohey (2000) reported a longitudinal study of six minority-language children in English-medium classrooms in Canada. She followed the children from kindergarten through Grade 2, observing classroom behavior, recording classroom talk, and conducting interviews with the children, their teachers, and parents to trace the development of the children's identities. Unlike Liu's (2000) study of Bob, Toohey did not focus on the development of any specific linguistic patterns in the children she observed; instead, her analysis focused on how the children's identities were constructed through the activities that they and their teachers engaged in at school. The aspects of school identity that Toohey discussed were the children's academic competence, their physical presentation, their behavioral competence, their social competence, as well as their language proficiency.

By the end of kindergarten, the children's teachers had evaluated the *academic competence* of their pupils and had established that five of the focal children were academically "average" and adequately prepared for Grade 1; the teachers recommended that one child be assessed for learning difficulties that went beyond the child's lack of knowledge of English. Toohey (2000) described the teachers' judgment of the academic competence of Amy, who had arrived from Hong Kong the week before kindergarten started and whose family used Cantonese exclusively at home. Her academic competence was established as described by Toohey:

> Amy [. . .] came into kindergarten already familiar with the use of many
> kindergarten materials and keenly interested in completing the crafts
> projects the teacher set up every day. [. . .] Mrs. Clark's judgement that
> Amy was of average intelligence, and would be only temporarily
> handicapped by her lack of experience with English, no doubt rested on
> Amy's increasing participation in classroom conversations, as well as her
> adept participation in the classroom craft activities. (pp. 64–65)

The children's *physical presentation* was also important in creating an identity:

> Amy, for example, was smaller than any of the other children in her class [...]. Children clearly noticed this; indeed Agatha commented, "She's a little girl" and told me the school was providing a kind of daycare for Amy. Sometimes children tied Amy's shoes for her or lifted her up as they might a much younger child. (p. 65)

The children's *behavioral competence* was constructed by their teachers primarily on the basis of the children's compliance with the teacher's directives, including whether they paid attention to what was going on in the class. The *social competence* of the children was an aspect of the children's identity determined by how they interacted with their peers. An example of one child's lack of social competence is the case of Harvey, a boy who spoke English at home but who had difficulty being understood by his classmates. Toohey (2000) reported that he also had many disputes with classmates over resources and other children frequently refused to play with him:

> Once, for example, Harvey carried around a Bingo game and wanted playmates; he approached two other boys in the class (one Anglophone, one Chinese-speaking):
>
> (38)
>
> Harvey: Bingo, guys! (*enthusiastic*)
> Earl: Ah, stupid Bingo.
>
> He asked another boy who did not respond [...]. A few minutes later, Harvey said to me: "Mrs Toohey, nobody's playing with me Bingo. Nobody ever plays with me." Indeed he spent a great deal of time playing alone. (p. 51)

Finally, the aspect of the children's identity that relates most directly to their development in English as a second language was their *language proficiency*, but even that, Toohey (2000) argued, is constructed by the children's display of language in social contexts. In order to understand the role that social context plays in allowing children to display their language proficiency, it is useful to compare the two cases of Julie and Surjeet. Julie was the daughter of Polish-speaking immigrants to Canada. Her mother had cared for her since birth, speaking only Polish, and Julie's exposure to English was through her contacts with English-speaking children in her neighborhood and during her 1-year attendance at an English-medium preschool program. According to her mother, Julie knew only a few words of English before she entered kindergarten. Surjeet was the oldest of three children in her Punjabi-speaking family. Before entering school, she had been cared for by her family members, who could speak both Punjabi and English. Her mother reported that Surjeet understood Punjabi reasonably well but could not really speak it and she was primarily an English speaker. This observation was confirmed by Toohey, who reported that she "never observed Surjeet speaking Punjabi or playing with children who were speaking Punjabi at school" (p. 31).

Although Surjeet and Julie had very different exposures to English before they entered school, both were, nonetheless, identified as "ESL" (English as a second language) on the basis of interviews that their teacher had with them and their parents before school began. Part of the reason for this ascription of ESL identity was institutional. As Toohey explained, "The children [. . .] enrolled in the Language Development class were defined as 'ESL' for purposes of identification in the school and also for funding arrangements involving the school district and the provincial Ministry of Education" (2000, p. 69).

Although it would appear that Surjeet's exposure to English before entering kindergarten was greater than Julie's, by the end of the kindergarten year their teacher and the school's ESL specialist determined that Julie had enough English to no longer need specialist support in Grade 1. Surjeet, however, was considered to require further ESL support. This apparent reversal of ESL proficiency in the two children is considered by Toohey to be a consequence of the different ways that the two children constructed contexts for interaction with adults and peers in the kindergarten classroom. Toohey described their interactions with their peers as follows:

> Julie had relatively easy access to many classroom interactions and resources. She successfully established friendly relations with the adults in her classroom. She seemed able to play with or beside the children whom she sought as playmates. (2000, p. 70)

> Surjeet, on the other hand, by the end of the year appeared to have no particular allies in her classroom; on several occasions others usurped her place in conversations. Her access to classroom resources (including conversations with peers) never appeared secure, and her verbal contributions at such times seemed somewhat incoherent. (2000, p. 71)

The association between context and the development of ESL proficiency that Toohey (2000) made is not without precedent in the literature on social interaction, and she reviewed theoretical and empirical studies that provide a background. In gender studies, for example, Goffman (1979) noted how, in commercial advertising, the social identity of gender is displayed by an individual and interpreted by those who witness the display, such that gender identity is constructed both by the subject and others on the basis of physical appearance. Other physical features, including the use of one's body and language, combine in the construction of identity in the work of Bourdieu (1984). As I argued in chapter 2, Bourdieu used the term *habitus* to index socially acquired predispositions, tendencies, propensities, or inclinations that are realized in the bodies of human agents by eye gaze, posture, mobility, bodily movements, and speech in discursive practice. In Bourdieu's writing, *hexis* describes the embodiment of habitus by means of which power and social divisions are constructed, maintained, and reproduced. The ways that, through their bodies, agents exert power over others is expressed by Bourdieu in a passage quoted by Toohey:

> Bodily *hexis*, a basic dimension of the sense of social orientation, is a practical way of experiencing and expressing one's own sense of social value. One's relationship to the social world and to one's proper place in it is never more clearly expressed than in the space and time one feels entitled to take from others; more precisely, in the space one claims with one's body in physical space, through a bearing and gestures that are self-assured or reserved, expansive or constricted ("presence" or "insignificance") and with one's speech in time, through the interaction time one appropriates and the self-assured or aggressive, careless or unconscious way one appropriates it. (Bourdieu, 1984, p. 474)

An extension of Bourdieu's (1984) ideas on the role of physicality to physical interaction in learning is found in the sociocultural theory of Vygotsky and in research by Hall and by McDermott. For Vygotsky, children's cognitive development occurs through social (i.e., physical) interaction with other children, and talk-in-interaction involves the physical presence and movement of the children's bodies. Extending Vygotsky's assertion to adult interaction, this physical and social interaction occurs in repeated engagement in discursive practices—what Hall (1993) called "oral practices," which she defined as "socioculturally conventionalized configurations of face-to-face interaction by which and within which group members communicate" (p. 146). For Hall, "language acquisition is bound to this notion of oral practice and [. . .] the ability to participate as a competent member in the practices of a group is learned through repeated engagement in and experience with these activities with more competent members of a group" (p. 148).

An individual's competent participation in group activities, however, does not necessarily mean that the individual is measured on some external standard of "English proficiency" or "good behavior." As McDermott (1993) parsed it, an individual's competence means being "good at what they do," even if that means being learning disabled. The practices (or activities) that Toohey (2000) observed in the Grade 1 classroom were opportunities for the children to display their competence. As was noted in chapter 2, in Practice Theory the organization of talk and bodily positioning have political implications; they are, in other words, ways in which some individuals exert power over others. Three practices that Toohey described in the Grade 1 classroom clearly have norms of interaction and demonstrate the politics of interaction. The Grade 1 teacher, Ms. Reynolds, taught the children three ways in which each child should be differentiated from other children and thus create an individual identity for themselves. Each child should sit in their own desk, each child should use their own things and not those of others, and each child should use their own words and ideas and not borrow from others. The norms of these practices are physical instantiations of interpellation,[3] a process by which concrete individuals are constructed as subjects by ideology, as theorized by Althusser (1972).

The norms of these classroom practices were enforced by the teacher, internalized by the children, and brought about what Toohey (2000) called a "breaking up" of the children. The degree to which a child observed the norms influenced their competence as perceived by the teacher and other children. Surjeet was observed violating several of the norms. When she went over to another child's desk, she was censured by a classmate and told: "Surjeet, get in your desk!" During a whole-class activity, she also violated the rule of using her own words. As Toohey (pp. 88–89) recorded it, under Ms. Reynold's guidance, the children were estimating the number of seeds in a pumpkin. The teacher was writing the numbers on a chart next to the children's names:

```
1              Martin:  One zillion.
2  Ms. Reynolds:  I don't know how to write that.
3              Martin:  One and a lot of zeros.
4  Ms. Reynolds:  Pick a smaller number.
5              Martin:  One million.
6                 May:  One thousand!
7            Surjeet:  One million.
8  Ms. Reynolds:  Somebody already guessed that. You
                       can choose a number above or below.
9  (Surjeet turns away.)
```

In this activity, Martin's contributions in turns 1 and 5 met the requirement that the children use their own words, as did May's contribution in turn 6. Surjeet, however, by her repetition of Martin's words in turn 7, violated the rule and drew censure from Ms. Reynolds in turn 8, resulting in Surjeet's withdrawal from the practice in turn 9.

By the end of Grade 1, despite her initial exposure to English at home, Surjeet was considered to still need special attention from the ESL specialist, whereas Julie had "graduated" from ESL. In kindergarten, Surjeet had relied on help from her peers and was not differentiated from them. In Grade 1, however, the classroom practices and norms imposed by Ms. Reynolds and internalized by the children "broke up" the children and interpellated them as individual subjects. Toohey commented:

> If the practices of their community had been different, if the girls' access to its tools had been different, their identities as language learners might have been different. However, how they were seen in terms of their academic, physical, behavioural, and social competence overlapped considerably with how they were seen as language learners. These aspects of their identities interacted in complex ways to construct them as differentially able. (2000, p. 71)

The practices of the Grade 1 classroom are contexts with political implications for the children. Their performance in classroom practices resulted in their separation into classes, one which must take further ESL and one which need not. The results of being interpellated as a subject in a certain way through participation in discursive practices has two implications: one for the beliefs of the person himself or herself and another for global processes in society. These are discussed in the following two subsections.

Emotional Perspectives on the Contexts of Learning

What effect on Surjeet's and Julie's beliefs about themselves did their interpellation as "ESL" or "graduated from ESL" have? In the cases of these children and the other focal children in Toohey's (200) study, the methodological challenges of getting children to talk about their own identities result in no information in this area. In studies of the internalization of culture by older children and adults, however, there are a number of studies that have shown that a community's interpellation of an individual as subject does not necessarily reproduce a similar identity in the individual. As Strauss (1992) put it, cultural interpellation of a subject identity is not simply copied ("faxed") into an individual's internal values and beliefs. Being called "limited English proficient" (LEP) does not automatically imply that a subject takes on an LEP identity. A difference between institutional identity and personal identity may come about through individuals actively resisting interpellation by powerful others, as in the rebellion of poor and working-class kids against school authority documented by Willis (1977). The extent to which culturally interpellated identities are internalized, resisted, or transformed by individuals can be investigated by examining the stories that individuals tell about themselves. Telling stories about the self as a member of new community or as a learner of a new language is, as Eisenhart (1995) has argued:

> not only a way to demonstrate membership in a group or claim an identity within it. Telling stories about self is also a means of becoming; a means by which an individual helps to shape and project identities in social and cultural spaces. (p. 19)

In L2 learning, these self-stories—called "diary studies," "language learning memoirs," or "learner autobiographies"—have recently received much attention by, among others, Schumann (1998), Pavlenko (2001b), and Young (1999). These stories of identity construction and transformation through language learning are in fact a subgenre of reports of self-stories by anthropologists interested in learning. These include Holland and Eisenhart's (1990) study of the attitudes of young college women to romantic relationships, Cain's (1991) study of learning to be a member of Alcoholics Anonymous, Traweek's (1988) report of how scientists developed as experts in high-energy physics, and Harkness, Super, and Keefer's (1992) study of how first-time American parents work to fashion an identity.

The self-stories of language learners provide ways of understanding the relationship between social context and language learning and use in ways very different from the longitudinal studies that have been described thus far. Although some learners have expertise in linguistics, language learning, or language teaching, most do not; for this reason, only some parts of self-stories by a minority of learners reflect on their linguistic progress in the way that Liu (2000) reflected on the acquisition of English by Bob. In their self-stories, L2 learners reflect on linguistic features that they find particularly salient because of the role that a particular feature plays in the development of a new identity. In Kaplan's (1993) book-length memoir of her experiences learning French, for example, she writes at length about her struggles to pronounce the French "r." She first hears the new "r" from her first French teacher in Minnesota, Madame Holmgren, and remembers,

I knew what it was supposed to sound like. I heard Holmgren's "r." And I
knew that by comparison our resistant "r" was a flat, closed-off smashed
version of the truer sound. So let's say I did decide to risk it, make it ok,
this foreign "r," I still had a dilemma: the American "r" sounded stupid,
Midwestern, but to get the French one right I knew there would be an
awkward apprenticeship where it would come out all slobbery and wrong.
Like kissing a boy with braces on. (p. 128)

Later, during a study-abroad experience in France, Kaplan recalled recognizing
that pronouncing the French "r" correctly was one her greatest difficulties:

So that feeling of coming onto the "r" like a wall was part of feeling the
essence of my American speech patterns in French, feeling them as
foreign and awkward. I didn't know at the time how important it was to
feel that American "r" like a big lump in my throat and to be dissatisfied
about it. Feeling the lump was the first step, the prerequisite to getting rid
of it. (p. 54)

Kaplan's experience of noticing the gap between her own pronunciation and
the pronunciation she desired changed to a feeling of great satisfaction when
eventually she pronounced the "r" correctly:

I looked up at my teacher, M. Herve Frichot, former colonial school
teacher from Madagascar. He had a goatee and glasses with thick black
frames. He was a skeptic but he was looking at me now with deep respect.
He hadn't thought I could do it. He said, "You've done it." He added:
"Vowels next." But that was minor. I wasn't worried about the vowels
because I knew that since I had gotten the "r," I had already started
opening up my vowels. I could perfect them with the same method I had
used for the "r": First feeling them wrong, like an impediment, feeling
them again and again in their wrongness and then, one day, opening up
and letting the right sound come. Relaxing. The "r" was the biggest
hurdle; my system was now in place. (p. 55)

With her newly acquired confidence, Kaplan went outside the school to practice
her new found skill in the community:

I went into the village in search of French. I went to the train station. I
bought tickets to Geneva, "aller et retour à Genève"—that is what you had
to say to get a round trip ticket. I loved to let it roll off of my tongue,
"alleretretour" in one drum roll, "to go and return." I bought tickets just to

say it. Most of what I did, in town, I did in order to speak. Complicated conversations at the Tabac, the newsstand, the grocery. (p. 53)

Toward the end of her book, Kaplan, now a professor of French at a prestigious American university, reflects on what learning French has meant for her, and again she turns to the importance of that one phonological achievement:

> Learning French and learning to think, learning to desire, is all mixed up in my head, until I can't tell the difference. French is what released me from the cool complacency of the R Resisters, made me want, and like wanting, unbuttoned me and sent me packing. French demands my obedience, gives me permission to try too hard, to squinch up my face to make the words sound right. French houses words like "existentialism" that connote abstract thinking, difficulties to which I can get the key. And body parts which I can claim. French got me away from my family and taught me how to talk. Made me an adult. And the whole drama of it is in that "r," how deep in my throat, how different it feels. (pp. 140–141)

Kaplan's self-story revealed not only her struggles with a particular linguistic feature but also the emotional resonances that it had for her. She wrote about the "foreign" and the "American r's" and how the process of learning the French "r" would be an awkward apprenticeship. Her description of what Schmidt has called "noticing the gap" in SLA (Schmidt, 1990; Schmidt & Frota, 1986) involves feeling dissatisfied with the feeling of a big lump in her throat. The noticing phenomenon, which has received considerable attention in the discussion of consciousness in cognitive development in SLA, has emotional resonance for this learner. However, it is only by means of data elicited from a self-story, in which a learner talks about their emotional and social development in addition to their cognitive development, that it is possible to gain insight into the role that emotions play. This important difference is stressed by Pavlenko (2001a):

> L2 learning stories [. . .] are unique and rich sources of information about the relationship between language and identity in second language learning and socialization. It is possible that only personal narratives provide a glimpse into areas so private, personal, and intimate that they are rarely—if ever—breached in the study of SLA, and that are at the same time at the heart and soul of the second language socialization process. (p. 167)

Self-stories of learners have become an established literary genre. Pavlenko (2001b) listed 16 full-length books and 7 shorter essays written in English in which, like Kaplan, learners have described their own development in an L2 and culture. Shorter and less literary but nonetheless relevant to understanding identity and context in L2 learning are the diary studies. In the 1970s, Schumann and a number of colleagues collected 30 or more of these, many of which were reported in publications by Bailey (1983, 1985, 1991; Bailey & Ochsner, 1983) and by Schumann (Schumann & Schumann, 1977). Underlining the importance of self-stories as data sources in social-psychological fields such as SLA, Pavlenko and Lantolf (2000) commented:

> In recent years narrative genre and personal narratives per se have gained increasing stature in psychology, sociology, sociolinguistics, and anthropology as legitimate and rich data sources for a variety of investigation including that of narrative construction of selves and realities. (p. 159)

The narrative method is not without its critics, however. Some have questioned the relation between a narrative and the events it depicts (Carr, 1986; White, 1980). White raised the question of the narrative's capacity to represent reality due to the story nature of narrative structure, particularly the configuration given to the sequence of events by a story's beginning, middle, and end, which do not necessarily take place in the event itself. Carr (1986) attacked "self-authorship" or "authenticity" as idols of modern individualism and self-centeredness. He believes that narration is constitutive not only of action and experience but also of the self that acts and experiences. Rosenwald and Ochberg (1992) also questioned the narrative "self," arguing that the sense of self is partly one's sense of who one is in relation to others. These authors have also questioned the presence of an interviewer in the creation of the oral narrative of an interviewee. Thus, many critics caution readers to question the contextual nature of narratives and the depiction of reality created by the narrator.

Partly in response to these criticisms of narrative and phenomenological research, sociologists have developed the procedures of grounded theory. Grounded theory emphasizes the meaning of experience for participants and at the same time allows a researcher to generate or discover a theory within which social processes can be described and explained (Charmaz, 2006; Glaser, 1978; Glaser & A.L. Strauss, 1967; A.L. Strauss, 1987; A.L. Strauss & Corbin, 1990, 1998). By adopting these procedures, a theory of a social and psychological process such as language learning can be "grounded" in data from the field, especially in the actions, interactions, and social processes of learners. Within grounded theory, the response to criticisms of the role of the narrator in narrating events is the systematic method of data collection and analysis described by Creswell (2007). The researcher first asks participants to focus on how they experience a process and to identify the steps in the process. Such issues are described in interviews and then participants' responses are openly coded. In open coding, the researcher segments the talk in the interview into salient categories of information and then finds, within each category, several properties or subcategories that construct a larger level of explanation. The next stage is axial coding, in which the researcher first identifies a *central phenomenon* and then (a) explores conditions that influence the phenomenon, (b) identifies actions or interactions that result from the central phenomenon, (c) identifies the conditions that influence the actions, and (d) delineates the outcomes for this phenomenon. The researcher may then select a storyline that connects the categories. The processes of open, axial, and selective coding result in a theory written by the researcher, which emerges with the help of written notes on the evolving theory made throughout the process of open, axial, and selective coding.

One of the very few reports of the emotions of an L2 learner that has used grounded theory is the research that Garrett and I conducted of Garrett's affective responses to an intensive Portuguese language course (Garrett & Young, 2009). In the summer of 2005, Garrett, an experienced teacher of French, attended an intensive 8-week Brazilian Portuguese course at a university in the American Midwest. The course met for two hours in the morning and reconvened for two hours in the afternoon for five days a week. The morning session was taught by an experienced male native speaker of Brazilian Portuguese, who had taught the program for over 15 years and coauthored the textbook used in the program. In the morning session, the instructor introduced new grammatical structures and contextualized them in authentic language materials such as Brazilian songs, advertisements, and articles from magazines. The afternoon session was taught by a female nonnative-speaking teaching assistant. The afternoon session focused on language use and cultural awareness. Students watched movies, listened to guest speakers, and engaged in communicative activities that required them to use Portuguese.

Twice each week throughout the course, Garrett met with Young, when she talked at length about her language learning experiences. The meetings were very casual and were recorded on audio tape, resulting in a total of six hours of data. Young did not have a predetermined set of questions or an agenda during these meetings. Most recording sessions started with Young asking, "How is your Portuguese class going?" Garrett did most of the talking and Young's contributions to the sessions were minimal, consisting of active listening, empathic reflection, and minimal encouragers. Garrett transcribed the tapes three weeks after the end of the program.

The process of analysis consisted in immersion in the data and the repeated sorting, coding, and recoding that characterize the grounded theory approach. Analysis began with open coding, which consists of examining the data for individual words and utterances. Open coding was done by Garrett, who, after transcribing and reading through the transcripts several times, coded the data for emerging topics and continually refined the categories being coded.

Open coding was followed by axial coding, whereby the researcher makes connections between a coding category and subcategories. Glaser and Strauss (1967) propose an inductive strategy in grounded theory, whereby the researcher discovers concepts and hypotheses through constant comparative analysis. In Garrett and Young's (2009) study, the main category that was found was that the transcripts were rich in Garrett's affective responses to the learning experience. Using Schumann's (1998) definitions of affect in learning, affective appraisal of stimuli that appeared to be driving the learner's decisions were coded. The transcripts were coded for words and expressions that appeared to be related to emotional reactions and patterns of appraisal. Next, a list of affective responses was made and linked to the event that elicited the response.

Subcategories of topics that appeared to elicit the learner's affective reactions were identified and coded. After several refinements of the subcategories that emerged from the transcripts, they were reassessed. The four main topics that eventually emerged from the transcripts as eliciting the most affective responses were (a) language awareness—the learner's awareness of her own knowledge of Portuguese and her comparisons of the language with other languages she knew; (b) teacher voice—the learner's own professional teacher's voice that appeared in the way that she evaluated her instructors' teaching styles, the course materials, and her own learning strategies; (c) social relations—with other students in the class and with her instructors; and (d) culture learning—her responses to the Brazilian culture to which she was exposed.

Codes and categories were sorted, compared, and contrasted until saturated—that is, until further analysis produced no new codes or categories and when all of the data were accounted for in the core categories. In order to estimate which topics were most frequently mentioned as eliciting an affective response, the individual comments in each of the four topic areas were totaled. In each comment, the learner expressed either positive or negative affect,

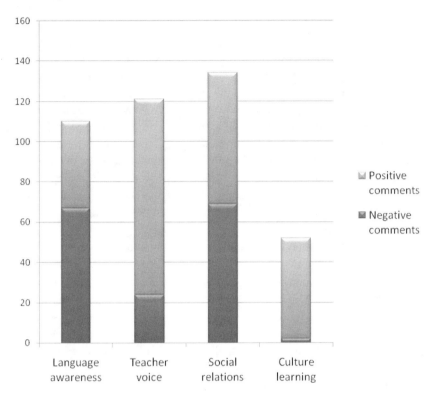

Figure 3.1 Numbers of affective comments on four topics (from Garrett & Young, 2009). Reproduced with permission from Wiley-Blackwell.

and the totals of positive and negative affective comments in each of the four categories are displayed in Figure 3.1.

These quantitative results are aggregates of the learner's affective comments over the whole of the 8-week course. They show that positive emotions were elicited most often by the learner's reflections on her instructors' teaching styles, the course materials, her own learning strategies, and the Brazilian culture to which she was exposed. Negative emotional responses were elicited by her developing knowledge of Portuguese and her comparisons of the language with other languages. Her social relations with other students in the class and with her instructors elicited negative emotions as often as positive. These aggregate figures, however, do not provide a representation of how the learner's appraisal of different stimuli changed over the 8 weeks, which was done by analyzing her responses week by week in order to describe an affective trajectory of her learning experience.

Given the increasing attention paid to emotion by cognitive scientists and the neurobiological demonstrations by Leventhal and Scherer (1987) and others that cognition derives from emotionally colored perception, the emotion of language learners is an issue that needs to be addressed in SLA. What Garrett and Young's (2009) study showed in weekly detail is how one learner's emotional responses influenced her desire to approach or avoid particular situations and how some of those responses are modified by new experiences and change the learner's affective appraisal over time. In Garrett and Young's study, emotion thus became the explanatory premise for the learner's focus of attention in her acquisition of Portuguese. The learner testified to her emotional assessment of her experiences as pleasant or unpleasant, and this was the basis for categorizing her comments into those that expressed positive or negative effect. This binary distinction, however, masks the different ways in which the learner experienced emotion. Her responses should not be interpreted as simply ☺ or ☹. To distinguish among the learner's emotional responses to events, Garrett and Young used the system of stimulus evaluation checks devised by Scherer (1984a, 1984b). This system guides the researcher to identify the events that the learner evaluated as (a) novel, (b) intrinsically pleasant or unpleasant, and (c) enhancing or inhibiting progress to achieving her goals or needs. The learner may also evaluate an event in terms of (d) the degree of control that she believes that she has over the event or its consequences and (e) whether the event is consistent or inconsistent with her ideal self-concept and whether it conforms to the norms of her social group. The learner's evaluation of events as novel or not, their goal significance, her ability to cope with them, and their compatibility with her self-image and social norms are evident in the data, as the following examples show.

The learner mentioned on occasion the novelty of an event; for example, she expressed her delight after watching a film about wildlife in Brazil: "This is just the funnest little summer I'm having! This little sofa travel experience I'm having, traveling the world via my sofa. I feel like I'm going to Brazil without the effort." On other occasions, she expressed frustration over repeating an activity that she had done already: "Student C proposed practicing dictations and my initial thought was, 'that's a waste of time.' "

On several occasions, she reported events that enhanced her progress toward her goal of learning Portuguese; for example, she described refocusing her attention on spoken input from her teacher: "Rather than focusing on the sounds he was making, I was focusing on what was written and focusing on the pronunciation of the individual words whereas today was the first day I realized

I needed to focus on the prosody, so I felt like that was a success—that I've switched from the need to focus on the individual words to focusing on the flow." At other times, however, she experienced an event that did not further her goals as stressful: "I feel I can hear things being done [spoken] differently than I'm saying them, but I can't quite identify where the problem is."

The learner often remarked on her ability to cope with an event. Sometimes she felt overwhelmed, as when she complained: "We were supposed to memorize a page of Portuguese dialogue and I thought, 'How can I memorize this when I don't even know how to pronounce it?'" On other occasions, she expressed pleasure at some events in which she found herself managing well. At the end of her 8-week language program, for instance, she reflected that "I really feel like I'm becoming more knowledgeable about this culture and language."

The learner's self-image was enhanced by some experiences; for instance, when she managed to talk more in class, she reported: "I'm starting to talk in class. It's fun." On other occasions, however, her ideal self-image was challenged: "I've just kind of been getting by. I haven't been the stellar Portuguese student." She was also aware of the image that she was projecting to other students in the class, especially after students received their grades on an exam: "Everyone's success is private. Or it could just be that people don't talk to me about it because I'm such a bad speaker that they don't want to embarrass me. I don't know. In general I don't talk to people about grades." On other occasions, she felt that she was projecting an image of a stellar student: "I can write this language like a star, and I can read it and understand it within the upper tier of my class." On a few occasions, she experienced an event that went against accepted social norms and beliefs; for example, "Student S would do irritating things like how he said that he thought Barcelona was an awful city to a bunch of Spanish speakers."

Garret and Young (2009) described the emotional responses of one beginning learner to her experiences in one foreign language classroom and the means by which her responses were recorded and analyzed. This learner and her experiences were unique, and they made no claim that other learners respond in similar ways to similar experiences. What is of more general interest in their study, however, is that the affective responses of foreign language learners and, in particular, their responses to events in the classroom are an underresearched area of SLA. Greater attention to affect in language learning is needed because of the emotional grounding of higher order cognitive and metacognitive processes such as attention, memory, planning, and hypothesis construction. Affective appraisal of language learning events by individual learners results in approach or avoidance when similar events occur in the future and influences these cognitive processes and other lower order processes. What Garrett and Young's research shows is the use of grounded theory to discover an individual learner's affective states and the trajectory of change in those states throughout the language learning process.

The affective responses of L2 learners to their learning experiences may be understood from the study of learner memoirs, diary studies, and self-stories. I have argued that learners' emotions are an important part of the context of L2 learning, and in stimulus appraisal theory, emotional responses play a central role in cognitive development. These data provide a nexus between societal judgments and their interpellation by individuals, but is there an influence in the opposite direction? That is, how does Practice Theory frame the relationship between the L2 learning and using activity of individuals and organized social situations and political institutions? This relationship is considered in the next and final subsection of this chapter.

The Local and the Global: Political Perspectives on Language in Context

Practice Theory, as presented in chapter 2, is concerned with the intended or unintended political implications of discursive practices. Block's (2007) analysis of the conversation among Carlos, Dan, and Bob that was reproduced in that chapter showed how knowledge of participants' social class, gender, and ethnicity are essential to understanding the nonnative speaker Carlos's participation in the conversation in English with his two native-speaking workmates. Earlier in the present chapter when discussing Toohey's (2000) study, the interpellation of ESL was applied to some children as required by the Canadian provincial Ministry of Education and by the school district, and its effects were clear on the children's identity formation and language learning. In these examples, global social forces are seen to influence the local ecology of talk-in-interaction and thus of L2 learning.

A clear example of the way that societal values are communicated through instruction is the comparison that Baquedano-López (1997/2001) made between the ways that different identities are created for children through religious instruction in Spanish and English. Baquedano-López observed religious instruction of children at a Catholic parish church in Southern California. Over 20 months, she observed two classes: one in Spanish and one in English. The *doctrina* class of 24 students was taught by a Spanish-speaking teacher and the catechism class of 15 students was taught by an English-speaking teacher. Both teachers told their students stories of appearances of the Virgin Mary. In the *doctrina* class, the teacher and her students constructed a shared Mexican identity, a shared history of oppression, and a collective dark brown skin color through stories of the apparition of *Nuestra Señora de Guadalupe* to an Aztec craftsman named Juan Diego in the year 1531. An example of how the teacher constructs ethnic identity based on skin color is when the teacher explains to her class that the physical features of *Nuestra Señora de Guadalupe* are similar to their own:

> La Santísima Virgen quiso ser parecerse morenita como nosotros. Porque la Virgen de Guadalupe no es blanca como la Virgen del Carmen que se apareció y es la patrona de España. La Virgen del Carmen es blanca y la Virgen de Guadalupe es morenita como nosotros.[4] (p. 353)

In the catechism class taught in the same church to a multiracial class including Latino, Asian, and White children, the monolingual English-speaking teacher describes the Virgin Mary as multiethnic and positions Mexican ethnicity as only one of many ethnicities in the society that the teacher images:

> Now remember that Mary has appeared in many countries to many many people differently. Our Lady of Guadalupe she appeared to the Indian, she looked like an Indian. When she appeared over here ((walking towards a cast statue on the desk)) Our Lady of Grace ((touching the statue)) she's crushing the snake with her feet because the snake represents the Devil and she's standing on top of the world. This is our Lady of Grace. We have our Lady of Mount Carmel. We saw the Pilgrim Virgin, Our Lady of Fatima. She has appeared to many many many many places. She's appeared in Lourdes and when she was in Lourdes, she wore the costume of the French ladies, she looked like a French lady. When she appears in Japan, she appears Japanese. When she appears in Hawaii, if she does, she'd appears Hawaiian. So Our Lady can change her features to look like the country she's appearing in. (pp. 354–355)

The ideological differences between the two teachers' presentations of the Virgin Mary are quite clear. In the catechism class taught in English, the emphasis is on a generic, multiethnic Mary, whereas in the *doctrina* class taught in Spanish, the teacher creates a Mexican racial identity based on skin color and Spanish oppression of the indigenous peoples in Mexico.

In studies of L2 learning and teaching, the effects of societal ideologies on classroom discourses are described by Gebhard (2002/2004, 2005) and their influence on teachers' instructional practices are described by Conteh (2007) and Shameem (2007). In Gebhard's two studies, she explored the ways in which the phenomenon of classroom SLA is shaped by the institutional context in which it is embedded. Her data sources and her methods of analysis are summarized in Table 3.1.

Several differences emerge when comparing Gebhard's (2002/2004) methodology with ways of analyzing interaction employed by authors of other studies reviewed in this chapter. The most salient difference is that transcription and analysis of actual classroom interaction is only one part of Gebhard's studies, and a small part at that. Many of Gebhard's data sources are interviews with stakeholders in the educational context, including administrators, teachers, aides, students, and parents. A second difference is that, in order to investigate the institutional context in which classroom interaction happens, Gebhard draws upon written records, both pedagogical such as textbooks and student work as well as institutional student records, including school reports and correspondence between the school and parents. Gebhard's analysis of the oral and written data is conducted according to critical discourse analysis, a procedure defined by Fairclough (2001) that aims "to show up connections which may be hidden from people—such as the connections between language, power and ideology" (p. 4).

This is the way that not only Gebhard but also Toohey and Baquedano-López have analyzed talk-in-interaction. It is a methodology that, according to Gebhard (2002/2004), "asks educational researchers to become linguists and SLA researchers to become educational anthropologists" (p. 260).

Gebhard's (2002/2004) critical analyses of the discourses of reading and writing instruction and of a text produced by an L2 learner named Alma show the ways in which classroom literacy practices constrained Alma's efforts to acquire academic literacy. This legitimated the school's decision to interpellate Alma as a remedial student and advise her to transfer to another school where, as her teacher advised her mother, she would not be the lowest. In her 2005 study, Gebhard used a similar combination of ethnography and critical discourse analysis to show how a temporary state policy encouraged a teacher to create a classroom discursive space that "allowed Hmong and English-only students room to negotiate linguistic and cultural differences in ways that fostered and legitimated the display of multicultural identities and supported the acquisition of academic literacy practices, particularly for less proficient English language learners" (p. 206).

The studies by Gebhard and Baquedano-Lopéz have demonstrated how global societal policies influence the ways students learn to produce and interpret language at school and the consequences of those policies for

Table 3.1 Data sources and analysis for a study of how classroom SLA is shaped by institutional context

Unit of analysis	Observations	Transcripts from audio tapes and/or video tapes	Document collection	Method of analysis
School (n = 1)	General staff meetings	Interviews with district personnel	Student records	"Thick" descriptive field notes (Geertz, 1973)
	Committee meetings	Interviews with administrators	State records	Content analysis (Bogdan & Biklen, 1992)
	In-service workshops	Interviews with restructuring coordinators and committee chairs	School reports	Critical discourse analysis of transcriptions (Fairclough, 1989)
	Special events (e.g., open house)	Interviews with teachers	Correspondence with parents	
		Interviews with ESL and bilingual teachers	School maps	
		Interviews with bilingual aides		
Focal student (n = 3)		Recordings of classroom social and linguistics interactions	Student work	"Thick" descriptive field notes (Geertz, 1973)
		Interviews with students	Teacher-created materials	Content analysis (Bogdan & Biklen, 1992)
		Interviews with parents	Textbooks	Critical discourse analysis of transcriptions (Fairclough, 1989)
			Correspondence with parents	

Source. Gebhard (2002/2004, Table 1). Reproduced with permission.

development of their identities. Crucially, the interpretation of these policies is in the hands of classroom teachers, and two recent studies focus on how two different teachers have interpreted them. In her study of bilingualism in mainstream primary classrooms in England, Conteh (2007) told the story of British government policy on bilingualism in schools by recounting the developing position expressed in position papers and policy directives published over 30 years, all of which recognized that children whose home language is not English are an asset to the school and the community, and at the same time, it recognized the need to provide special services such as bilingual teaching assistants to help children transition to monolingual English schooling.

One of the systemic obstacles to achieving the status of a child's home language as an "asset" in education that Conteh mentioned is that the majority of teachers in English primary schools are not bilingual, and although the number of bilingual teachers is increasing, they may not know the languages of all their pupils in a multilingual community. Language alternation by a bilingual may influence and be influenced by the social context in at least three ways: Choice of language may reflect social expectations, it may index resistance to those expectations, or it may be a playful exploration of self-identity (Young, 2007). If the overt government policy is to view bilingualism as an asset, a teacher who does not share the language of her pupils is, in effect, expressing resistance to that policy. As Apple (2000) has argued, the school curriculum is never a neutral assemblage of knowledge but is selected by someone or some group's vision of "legitimate knowledge." The teacher is able to construct legitimate knowledge as expressed in the majority language and implicitly sanction knowledge expressed in another language. Conteh showed a rather different situation of a bilingual teacher who regularly alternates between the majority language (English) and the community language (Punjabi). She noted that such alternation altercasts an identity of her Punjabi pupils as sharing access to legitimate knowledge, but it also demonstrates to her monolingual English-speaking students that knowledge expressed in the community language is legitimate.

Whereas the implications of the classroom conversations that Conteh described can be seen as supporting official bilingual policy in England, Shameem's (2007) research shows the disconnect between the official language education policy in Fiji and the language used in multilingual primary school classrooms. In multilingual Fiji, the community language of Fijians of Indian origin is Fiji Hindi, a common language that evolved over the years from the dialects of Hindi spoken by indentured laborers brought to the Fiji islands by the British in the 19th century. Fiji Hindi has diverged significantly from the varieties of Hindi and Urdu spoken on the Indian subcontinent. The colonial government of Fiji established a different variety of Hindi, known as Shudh (or "pure") Hindi as the standard because this variety enjoyed the status of the official language in India. It was a variety that was already codified and was incorporated as a language of education in Fiji. The diglossic situation of Fiji Hindi and Shudh Hindi is complicated by the colonial language, English, which is the official language. Shameem reported that the official language policy is to use Shudh Hindi for teaching Indo-Fijian children in the first 3 years of primary school before transitioning to English in the later years of schooling, although the community language is Fiji Hindi, which differs from the standard. Shameem's research shows that, in their responses to questionnaires, primary school teachers reported much greater use of Shudh Hindi than was the case when she observed actual language use. She reported that "while three [first grade] teachers had reported using English and three a combination of F[iji] H[indi] as language of instruction in their English lessons, observation showed that in fact six of the eight teachers were using only English while the other two used both" (p. 209). The divergence between reported and actual language use has two important implications when viewed from the perspective of Practice Theory. First, although official policy may constrain language choice by these teachers to some degree, the constraint is much more effective on their consciousness (i.e., the way that they mediate their own language choice): Official policy provides a ready-made internalization for these teachers of their own practice, a practice that actually diverges from their mediation of it. Second, the systematic encouragement of the use of the High variety of Hindi over the Low variety in education appears to do little to maintain either variety as a community asset and, in fact, encourages maintenance of the colonial language—English.

From the perspective of Practice Theory, the two studies by Conteh (2007) and by Shameem (2007) demonstrate certain interesting relationships between local talk-in-interaction and societal policies. It is evident that societal values shape, guide, and, to some extent, dictate behavior, but the effect is more evident and more insidious in the ways that individual actors make sense of their practice—in fact, by mystifying them about the nature of their own behavior. The Fijian primary school teachers believe that they are practicing a language policy that is more in line with the official ideology than in fact they are doing. As Bourdieu (1990) has argued, the social conditions and official ideology of which actors are aware do not result in automatic reproduction of systemic values by people through discursive practice. In fact, actors' resistance to the expectations of the system may lead to change within the system itself.

In the case of the mainstream English primary schools that Conteh describes, the use of the community language by a bilingual teacher does not simply recognize bilingualism in minority communities as an asset that the official policy encourages, but it demonstrates to the children who speak the dominant language that they can at times be excluded from interactions and denied access to teacher-legitimated knowledge as a consequence of their normally privileged position as monolingual speakers of the dominant language.

However, are learners' knowledge and beliefs determined by global societal forces? Are individual learners' interactions political in the sense that they exert an influence on social institutions? Bourdieu and Thompson (1991) have argued for a negative answer to the first question, and I have also argued earlier in this chapter that self-stories demonstrate that societal interpellation of a language learner's identity is not simply reproduced in the individual's internal values and beliefs. Erickson, in his 2004 book, *Talk and Social Theory*, has addressed the second question by arguing that the coin of social influence has two sides and it is incorrect to construct solely a top-down view of large-scale societal structures that determine local ecologies of talk-in-interaction. For, in Erickson's view:

> There is a local-global connection, and the connections of influence between the two run in both directions—inward to the local encounter from the social world outside it, and outward from the local encounter to actions that take place beyond the temporal and spatial horizon of the encounter itself. (p. 191)

However, with the exception of Erickson's own speculations about the relationship between a family dinner conversation and the election of Ronald Reagan to the White House in 1980, researchers have not been able to show the obverse of Erickson's coin; namely the societal consequences of particular sites of social interaction.

Chapter Summary and a Look Ahead

This chapter began with a discussion of the distinction between talk and context and with Bakhtin's insights into sentences and utterances. Taking Bakhtin's utterances as a starting point, my discussion of context ran through the famous five ("Where?" "How?" "When?" "Who?" and "Why?") questions that must be asked about every utterance to make it into a discursive practice. The discussion then moved on to examine why conversation analysts reject four of the five questions (all except the "Why?"). I argued that the radical empiricism of CA has rejected those questions as irrelevant unless they are apparently and overtly raised by speakers. Although the ethnomethodological assumptions of CA have resulted in a very powerful methodology for understanding talk-in-interaction, the context beyond the transcript is necessary in order to proceed further and, in fact, conversation analysts tacitly use social and cultural context in interpreting talk within its cultural context.

Taking the five questions seriously was the goal of the second half of this chapter, in which I reviewed four very different ways in which scholars have investigated the connection between context and L2 development, and I reported the methods that they have used to make the connection. All four approaches involve studying language learners over extended periods of time, but they differ in their focus. An applied linguistic approach is one in which a close linguistic analysis of sentences (in Bakhtin's sense) is correlated with the situational contexts in which those sentences were realized as utterances, although the analysis of context in this approach is quite superficial. Researchers who have taken an ethnographic approach are much more serious about describing context, but their analysis of learners' language is understandably less detailed than applied linguists. In the other two approaches, the focus is not so much on learners' language as it is on what learners, their teachers, their parents, and their friends *say* about their language learning experiences. In their self-reports, language learners report on what they noticed and paid attention to, much of which is mediated by their emotional responses to actions and practices in the classroom and beyond. Finally, researchers who have taken a political perspective on language in context are closest in approach to those practice theorists in anthropology that were discussed in chapter 2. From the political perspective, social and economic inequities are reproduced in the Discourses of schooling, and they make apparent what is normally hidden as one way of challenging those inequities.

With the exception of the applied linguistic approach, the analysis of the stuff of talk taken by researchers in the other three approaches has been quite cursory. As I argued in the introduction to this chapter, the decision whether to begin the investigation of talk-in-interaction with talk (the focal event) or to start with the context of talk (the field of action within which talk is embedded) produces two very different narratives. In this book, I present them in two separate chapters. In the present chapter, I have reviewed the approaches that have been taken to investigate context and the methods that have been adopted by researchers to describe and analyze context. In chapter 4, I take a complementary approach to discursive practice. I present the participation framework in which discursive practices are created and then detail the verbal, interactional, and nonverbal resources that are employed by participants to create them. I go on to describe the methods that have been developed to understand how participants employ resources to create context and how contexts are brought into being by talk.

Notes

1 Bakhtin's term for the time-space context of utterance is *the chronotope*.
2 Examples of interrogative forms in the six stages are taken from Liu's recordings of Bob.
3 Interpellation represents "how an individual's identity is absorbed into, and produced by, the dominant ideologies within a society. Interpellation is when a person recognizes and acquiesces to their position within structures of ideology" (Gauntlett, 2004).
4 Translation: "The Blessed Virgin wanted to be to look a little dark like us because the Virgin of Guadalupe is not white like the Virgin of Carmen who appeared and is the patroness of Spain the Virgin of Carmen is white and the Virgin of Guadalupe is a little dark like us" (Baquedano-López, 2001, p. 353).

CHAPTER FOUR

Discursive Resources

In the approaches to context that were reviewed in chapter 3, the focus rested on expanding context beyond the words of a transcript or the pages of a text. Taking a broader perspective on context and systematically investigating participants, their history, their emotions, and power relations has two advantages. The first is that it removes language from its position at center stage, challenging the autonomy of linguistics in which language is considered a self-contained system that can be documented and filed in grammars and dictionaries. A second advantage that Practice Theory brings to the study of context is to question what is to be compared: linguistic forms or contexts in which linguistic forms are used. Practice Theory begins with practice, and when language is part of a practice, it begins with discursive practice. As defined in chapter 2, a discursive practice is any talk activity that people do. What do participants do? They construct and reflect social realities through actions that invoke identity, ideology, belief, and power. How do participants do that?—by verbal and nonverbal actions, actions involving talk and other semiotic systems.

The questions addressed in this chapter have to do with the resources that participants employ in order to perform those actions. The issues that arise include how discursive resources are combined into a participation framework and how, with the help of this framework, an instance of discursive practice is identified and compared with a class of discursive practices. The presentation is in four parts. In the first section, the idea of participation framework is introduced, in which the focus is on how gaze, posture, and gesture reinforce verbal and interactional discursive resources to create a discursive practice. In the sections that follow, discursive resources are considered to be of three types: verbal, interactional, and nonverbal resources. The discussion of these three types of resources is aided by locating each of them within different analytical procedures: Verbal resources are considered as ways of making meaning in context and are analyzed according to the principles of Systemic Functional Grammar; interactional resources are presented as ways that participants create order in interaction that reflects and constructs their social roles and positions, and these are analyzed using the methods of Conversation Analysis. Finally, the nonverbal resources presented in the first section are revisited, this time as part of situated practices analyzed as embodied participation frameworks.

By framing what participants do in discursive practices as "resources," the emphasis is on a kind of repertoire that participants employ to achieve their goals in interaction, goals that may include a conscious desire to persuade or resist another participant, or to accept or reject a proposed action. In this case, participants appear as actors with strategies developed to achieve their goals, but many actions in interaction happen without participants' awareness and include the choice of a particular register in a particular context or the sequence of actions in a conversation. Repertoires of resources of which very few participants are consciously aware are the semiotic systems of gesture, gaze, and bodily positioning, which, nonetheless, create actions and achievements. The terminology of "resources," "repertoire," and "actors" will be used whether or not participants are aware of using resources strategically. Categorizing and analyzing these resources brings them to a level of awareness at which actors may evaluate discursive practices in many different ways.

Participation Framework

Language is the human semiotic system par excellence. Because of the centrality of language in social life and the permanence of written language, it has received a great amount of attention to the detriment of other "nonverbal" semiotic systems, including bodily gesture, facial expression, clothing, spatial positioning, ritual practices, and expressive systems such as the visual arts. However, as was elaborated by Goffman (1979) in his essay on "footing," a communicative social event is much more than the production and reception of language: The relative positioning of participants with respect to each other and to the built environment, their gaze, and their facial expressions must all be considered in an understanding of the social organization of participants, which Goffman referred to as "participation framework." The importance of these dimensions of interaction has been demonstrated by M. H. Goodwin (1990) in her study of interaction among adolescent African American children and by C. Goodwin (1981) in his study of family interaction; it has also been illustrated by Hanks (1996b) in his analysis of communicative practice. In addition to the evidence that these scholars and others have demonstrated of the importance of nonverbal semiotic systems in the analysis of interaction, much recent work by Kendon (1980, 1990), McNeill (1992, 2005), and C. Goodwin (1979, 2007) has described in great detail the function of gesture in communicative interaction.

Hymes (1974) believed that of all the factors in speech events, the participants were central and, in his elaboration on Hymes's theory, Goffman (1981) began not with language but with the participants and he defined "participation status" and "participation framework" in the following oft-quoted passage:

> If one starts with a particular individual in the act of speaking [. . .] one can describe the role or function of all the several members of the encompassing social gathering from this point of reference (whether they are ratified by the participants of the talk or not) [. . .]. The relation of any one such member to this utterance can be called the "participation status" relative to it, and that of all the persons in the gathering the "participation framework" for that moment of speech. (p. 137)

Goffman's (1981) identification of different participation statuses is well known. He criticized the simple idea that we can identify speaker and hearer simply by looking at the names that are indicated on the left-hand side of a transcript, and he distinguished among several different participation statuses of production and reception of speech. The production roles he identified are animator, author, and principal. The participant out of whose mouth words flow is the "animator," an individual engaged in the activity of speech production. However, the words spoken may not originate in the mind of the animator, who may simply give voice to the expressed thoughts and actual words of another. An "author" is someone who has selected the sentiments being expressed and the words in which they are encoded. Then, in any interaction, there may be a participant whose "position is established by the words being spoken, someone whose beliefs have been told, someone who is committed to what the words say" (Goffman, p. 144), a participant Goffman called the "principal." These production statuses may be taken by different participants in the same conversation, but the same participant may change footing in the conversation to move from one status to another.

Examples of how a single participant may change footing during a conversation are often found when journalists explain their personal opinions about an issue. Journalists, of course, are trained to report the actions and views of others without interpretation, but when they are asked to express their personal views, journalists can animate the voices of others to express their own opinions. This is illustrated in an extract from an interview with foreign correspondent Charles Sennott just after he returned from Iraq, where he was an embedded reporter with the U.S. Army's 28th Infantry Regiment.[1] He replied to a question from Terry Gross, the host of the radio program *Fresh Air*, about whether the United States should withdraw its troops from Iraq:

Terry Gross: A lot of people are saying we could stay there forever with these grudges and long time wars will still exist so why not just kinda get out?

Charles Sennott: Exactly. And I think that, that is an understandable impatience with the complexity of where we are and the timeless sense of what it is. I think I can also, just as a reporter, as a person who's got to know a lot of the soldiers and a lot of the veterans who are coming home and really listen to them. What I hear that really resonates with me is when they say, "Look. We broke it. We need to fix it." And I hear that on every level from people who are against the war, who have served in it, people who are very smart who know the region. But I do think that there is a very strong sense that I relate to and I feel resonates with me an obligation to fix something that we broke.

In Sennott's reply, his status is always as animator, as he and Terry Gross are the only participants who speak the words that are broadcast on the program, but when he explains his personal opinion, he invokes the status of other participants who are not present in the studio at the time of the interview: U.S. soldiers in Iraq and veterans. Their actual words that he reports, "Look. We broke it. We need to fix it," construct their status as authors. In his concluding remarks, he reports that he agrees with many people, whom he invokes as principals to support his own view that there is an obligation to fix something that the United States broke in Iraq. This example shows how invoking the participant status of author in a conversation can construct the participant status of animator with greater authority.

A similar way in which participants rapidly change footing in a conversation and how invoking statuses of author and principal alters the status of animators can be found in the foreign language classroom. Mori (2004) reports a conversation between two students in a Japanese as a foreign language (JFL) class. Using handouts and information written on the board, their class teacher first introduced key Japanese expressions for delivering opposing views while acknowledging others' stance, as well as vocabulary for discussing the issue of gun control, which was selected as a suitable topic for practicing the key expressions. After the teacher-fronted instruction, students discussed their opinions in pairs, using the key expressions. Two students, Alan and David, begin their pair work by gazing at the board, where the teacher had written the structure to be used and some vocabulary. Alan says:

ano seekatsu wa abunai node, watashi wa juu o motsu koto o kinshisuru
bekida to omoimasu.
*"Well, life is dangerous, so, I think owning a gun. I think we should
prohibit."*

David replies:

tashikani,
"Certainly,"

Throughout this exchange, both speakers are gazing at the board and much of
their speech is authored by the teacher, who wrote the grammatical structure
and vocabulary on the board. That is to say, the participation framework of
this fragment of conversation includes a participation status for the teacher as
author. As Goffman (1981) proposed, participation does not require physical
presence, and although the teacher is present in the JFL classroom while Alan
and David are talking, many student pairs are conducting similar conversations
and she is not physically co-present in the dyadic interaction between Alan and
David. Thus, a participant need not be physically present in an interaction but
must be oriented to by those who are physically present, and the orientation of
Alan and David to the teacher is evident by their mutual gaze at the board on
which the teacher has written the words that they animate. Orientation of the
body to nonpresent participants is a criterion for participation in rituals that has
been described by Hanks (1996a).

Change of footing (change of participation status) is often indexed nonverbally, and this is precisely what occurs as the conversation between Alan and
David continues. Immediately after the exchange quoted above, mutual gaze
between Alan and David gets established for the first time when Alan initiates
a self-repair in English:

Not *senpai* I got a wrong word. *sei- seika*? Is that world? Which one's life?
Which is it?

Mori (2004) explained Alan's problem with word choice as follows. "In
Japanese, the length of a vowel constitutes a minimal pair, that is, whereas
sekai means 'world,' *seekai* means 'correct answer.' Furthermore, the long
vowel *ee* and the absence of the last vowel *i*, as pronounced in the word *seeka*
means 'outcome'" (p. 542). David provides an accurate model of the word
sekai in the next turn, which Alan had pronounced incorrectly in their earlier
exchange, and the correct pronunciation is immediately echoed by Alan. In
this exchange, the teacher's words on the board are no longer used. The change

of footing of both participants in this exchange is indexed both nonverbally by Alan and David moving their gaze from the teacher's words on the board to each other and verbally by switching from Japanese to English, their first language (L1).

Extending his critique of the simple message exchange format, Goffman (1979, 1981) identified several participant statuses of hearers. The main hearer status is the addressee, who is the person known, ratified, and directly addressed by the speaker, but other persons in the audience may also influence the speech style of the speaker. These include those who are known and ratified but not directly addressed, called "auditors" by Bell (1984), as well as those overhearers who the speaker knows to be there but has not ratified, and eavesdroppers—persons whose presence is unknown. Unofficial participants may be engaged in the encounter in one of two socially different ways, as Goffman (1981) described:

> Either [the hearers] have purposely engineered this, resulting in "eavesdropping," or the opportunity has unintentionally and inadvertently come about, as in "overhearing." In brief, a ratified participant may not be listening, and someone listening may not be a ratified participant. (pp. 131–132)

Some of the differences among theses statuses are illustrated in the following conversation reported by Tannen (2004):

> A couple who live together are having an argument. The man suddenly turns to their pet dog and says in a high-pitched baby-talk register, "Mommy's so mean tonight. You better sit over here and protect me." This makes the woman laugh—especially because she is a petite 5 ft, 2 in.; her boyfriend is 6 ft, 4 in. and weighs 285 lb.; and the dog is a 10-lb. Chihuahua mix. (p. 399)

In this conversation, the man chooses his addressee as the dog but, clearly, his girlfriend is a ratified auditor, and he is using the dog strategically as a resource for him to communicate with her. In other cases, however, speakers may not use auditors and overhearers as resources, but, nonetheless, their receptive participation status influences the interaction. Such is the case when bilinguals do not wish to be understood by a person in their vicinity. Back (2009) gave an example of this from an interview with a member of a group of male Ecuadorean folk musicians touring the United States. The musicians are bilingual in Spanish and Quichua and one of them explains occasions on which they use Quichua strategically because of the participation status of an overhearer:

> Algo que deberías haber preguntado es en qué casos hablamos quichua aquí en los Estados Unidos. Claro porque una conversación normal se tiene, pero hay otras situaciones que utilizamos, por decir vemos una linda chica y decimos ooo, *aligu nachu*? O sea, estamos viendo de frente pero como no saben ese idioma, entonces [. . .] es como lo dices, a veces lo usamos [el quichua] como código, la de ventas, de admiración por una chica, o para vacilar un chico, o para decir alguien está viniendo, todo eso usamos el quichua más como código cuando estamos en el trabajo.[2]

In this example, the participation status of a pretty girl or a customer for the group's music CDs influences which of their languages the bilingual musicians use. In the case of the pretty girl, the musicians wish to express their admiration secretly, and in the case of the customers for their CDs, they wish to create an exotic identity that may make their music more attractive to their customer. Both of those changes in footing are indexed by a switch from Spanish or English to Quichua. In the foreign language classroom, too, norms of using the target language as much as possible may result in students' alternating between their L1 and the second language (L2) when the teacher is in earshot (i.e., when the teacher's participation status as overhearer or auditor becomes known to the students).

If nonpresent participants are taken to be a relevant part of the context of interaction and if participants' footing is constantly changing throughout interaction, this leads to an increasingly complex description of talk-in-interaction and interpretation of utterances. Increasing complexity does, however, bring with it the need to choose a description that is no more elaborate than is needed. The question is thus: How do you limit the description of a participation framework such that only socially relevant participant statuses are included? A procedure for doing just that was described by Hanks (1996a) in his description of participant roles in the course of a ritual performance by a Mayan shaman. His assumptions are summarized in the following constraints on interpretation:

1. Barring [. . .] indications to the contrary, the speaker bodily given is the source of words, propositions and sentiments expressed. Hence, animator, author, and principal coincide until further notice.
2. Gaze, posture, gesture, and speech [. . .] are deployed in a mutually reinforcing fashion.

3. [...] the actor(s) bodily present to whom an utterance is addressed is (are) the target. ·

4. [...] participants must be able to identify the same referential objects (more or less) in order for canonical acts of verbal reference to be successful. (p. 168)

These four constraints can be seen in my interpretation of the examples given earlier. In Charles Sennott's interview, he indexes participants first with indefinite reference "a lot of the soldiers and a lot of the veterans" and then continues by assuming that they are known to his hearer when he says that he listens "to them" and "they say 'Look. We broke it. We need to fix it.'" The two students in the JFL class use gaze and speech consistently in indexing the words that their teacher wrote on the board. The tone of voice that the man uses to address the dog in the third example is "a high-pitched baby-talk register" indexing a change of footing. By referring to his girlfriend in the third person and the co-present dog in the second person he has changed her participant status from addressee to auditor. Finally, the pretty girl in the audience is visually co-present to all members of the Ecuadorean folk music group and the use of Quichua as a "secret" language that all the musicians understand but which (presumably) the girl does not ensures that the addressees are able to identify the same referential object.

Verbal Resources

Within a framework, participants create meanings—meanings that are intimately connected to the context in which they are created—and in this section I consider the ways in which language functions in the creation of meaning. Given the importance of context in discursive practice, any analysis of language must take the function of language in context into account. Unfortunately, this is not the starting point of most contemporary theories of grammar. One aim of generative grammar, for example, is the discovery of a finite number of rules from which all grammatical sentences of a language can be generated. This aim bears no relation to the situational contexts in which the sentences can be generated; that is, a sentence is determined to be grammatical or ungrammatical independently of context, and generative grammar does not say anything about whether a particular sentence may be judged to be appropriate in one context and inappropriate in another. In addition, the domain of most grammars is the sentence, and very few formal theories have anything to say about linguistic organization above the level of the sentence. Sentences are essentially constructs of the written language, however, and units of talk-in-interaction differ from sentences—they may be as small as a single participant's turn-at-talk or as large as a complete discourse. Finally, according to Chomsky's well-known account, linguistics as properly conceived is a branch of cognitive psychology, and linguists are to study a state of mind, which is our knowledge of the language that we speak. Such decontextualized knowledge is expressly distinguished from how that knowledge is applied in actual use.[3] In Chomsky's (1986) later formulation, internalized language or "I-Language" is to be distinguished from externalized language or "E-Language." E-language (corresponding to what was once called "performance") is the external observable behavior and is, by Chomsky and others, considered to be a poor candidate for systematic study. Out of the disordered and nonsystematic E-language to which a human child is exposed and using an innate language faculty, the child constructs an internal representation—a set of rules mapping meanings onto forms. This set of rules is the child's I-Language. It is the I-Language that is the state of mind deemed to be the proper object of linguistic inquiry. E-Language is considered to be unsystematic because the relationship between utterances and the social and cultural contexts in which they are produced is poorly understood. From the perspective on discursive practice that has been adopted in this book, however, ignoring E-language means conceding defeat before the starting whistle has blown. If we are to search for systematic connections between language and context, we must start with E-language.

This is the approach taken in Systemic Functional Grammar (SFG). This is an approach to instances of language use that takes meaning as its organizing principle. It is appropriate for the analysis of language in context because (a) it relates language structure systematically to situational and cultural contexts; (b) its unit of analysis is *text*—any instance of language produced in speech or in writing and is not limited to the sentence; and (c) it views the language system (the I-language) as sets of options for making meaning that are instantiated in any given text (the E-language). Because of the close relation between language and context in SFG, it has been a particularly attractive model for applied linguists. Butler (1993) made the connection clear when he wrote that the focus in SFG is:

> language in relation to the social system, and therefore in the texts which language users create, and the relationship of these texts to their contexts of creation. The text is viewed as a semantic unit, which is realized by, rather than consisting of, sentences. The production of a text is seen in terms of successive choices by the speaker(s) or writer from the "meaning potential" offered by the language in use, these choices being sensitive to

a range of contextual parameters concerned principally with the nature of the social process in which the language users are engaged, the social relationships between addressor and addressee(s), the medium of interaction, and the purpose for which interaction is taking place. (p. 4500)

Systemic Functional Grammar

Founded by Michael Halliday in the 1960s, SFG has its origins in the tradition of European linguistics that developed following the work of Saussure. It is functional and semantic rather than formal and syntactic in orientation, it takes the text rather than the sentence as its object, and it defines its scope by reference to usage rather than grammaticality. As Halliday (1994) wrote, its primary source was the work of J. R. Firth and his colleagues in London. While SFG accounts for linguistic structure, it places the function of language as central (what people do with language and how language mediates meaning). An SFG analysis starts with context of situation, and explains how language both acts upon and is constrained by that context. The name "systemic" derives from the term *system*, in its technical sense as defined by J. R. Firth (1957). System is the theoretical representation of paradigmatic relations, contrasted with *structure* for syntagmatic relations.

The analysis of context in SFG is inherited from Malinowski, who differentiated among verbal context, nonverbal context, context of situation, and context of culture. Steiner (1983) represented the differences in Figure 4.1.

The initial branch of Malinowski's context tree is the distinction between verbal (or linguistic) context and nonverbal (or nonlinguistic) context. Similar distinctions were made in the discussion of context in chapter 2. Malinowski's verbal context is similar to Goffman's frame and Gumperz's conversational inference, by means of which an utterance is interpreted in terms of utterances

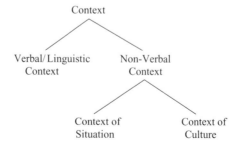

Figure 4.1 Malinowski's analysis of context (Steiner, 1983, p. 56). From Steiner, Erich. (1983). *Die Entwicklung des britischen Kontextualismus.* Heidelberg: Julius Groos Verlag. Reproduced with permission.

that precede it. In addition, in Conversation Analysis (CA), the verbal context is the sequential positioning of an utterance in the stream of talk. The nonverbal context does not necessarily imply for Malinowski the use of nonverbal semiotic channels such as gesture, gaze, and bodily positioning; it does, however, comprehend those elements of context introduced in Practice Theory, including social relations among participants, emotion, habitus, and genre. Nonverbal context is further divided into context of situation and context of culture. Malinowski (1923) argued that the cultural context of any interaction is indispensable if the interaction is to be understood:

> The study of any language, spoken by a people who live under conditions different from our own and possess a different culture, must be carried out in conjunction with the study of their culture and their environment. (p. 306)

The other category of nonverbal context is context of situation, which, as was discussed in chapter 2, was theorized first by Malinowski and later developed systematically by Firth and in detail by Mitchell. A specification of the context of situation of a given communicative act would include the seven components included in Hymes's SPEAKING model. In SFG, context of culture is the totality of all possible meanings within a given culture, whereas context of situation includes only those meanings that are invocable by participants in a specific communicative act. The major contribution of SFG is to explicate systematic correlations between the organization of language itself and specific contextual features.

What is the nature of that correlation between language and context? On the language side, the basic unit of analysis in SFG is the text. A text can be as short as a single-word utterance such as "Vote!" or longer than Clarence Darrow's examination of W. J. Bryan in the Scope Monkey Trial that was discussed in chapter 2. In SFG, a text is considered both a specimen of the linguistic system and an artifact—a tool designed to achieve some purpose. On the context side, Halliday (1978, 1985/1989) argued that there are just three aspects of context that have linguistic consequences: field, tenor, and mode. These are defined by Butt, Fahey, Feez, Spinks, and Yallop (2000) as follows:

> Field: what is to be talked or written about; the long and short term goals of the text;
>
> Tenor: the relationship between the speaker and hearer (or, of course, between writer and reader);
>
> Mode: the kind of text that is being made. (p. 5)

These three aspects of context correspond closely to the main functions of language in relation to participants' ecological and social environment, which Halliday (1994) called ideational, interpersonal, and textual metafunctions.[4] The three metafunctions are then realized by various aspects of linguistic substance. The *ideational metafunction* is how language mediates participants' construction of their experiences of the external physical and biological world, their own internal thoughts and feelings, and the logical relations among them. The ideational metafunction correlates the context of *field* with the phonic or graphic substance of language. The *interpersonal metafunction*, as its name implies, is how language mediates speakers' and writers' personal and social relationships with other participants such as their interlocutors and readers. The interpersonal metafunction correlates the context of *tenor* with the phonic or graphic substance of language. The *textual metafunction* is how participants build sequences of discourse, organize the discursive flow, and create cohesion and continuity within a linear and time-dependent flow. The textual metafunction correlates the context of *mode* with the phonic or graphic substance of language. Every text instantiates[5] all three metafunctions within the same text, just as all three contextual features are present in all communicative exchanges. Describing exactly how the linguistic resources of the lexicon and grammar (lexicogrammar in SFG terminology) mediate the correlations between context of situation and linguistic substance is, unfortunately, beyond the scope of this book and, in what follows, I will assume some familiarity on the part of the reader with the analytical procedures of SFG. Comprehensive explications of the relations between metafunction and context are provided by Halliday and Matthiessen (2004) and Eggins (2004), whereas Butt et al. (2000) provide a very accessible introduction to the theory with implications for language teaching.

Systemic Analysis of a Spoken Text

In the following pages, I work through a stylistic comparison of two discursive practices. The systemic functional analyses of these two texts demonstrate the symbiotic relationship between text and context in SFG. Both texts—one spoken and one written—are derived from Young and Nguyen (2002).[6] Because text both instantiates and creates context, each text is first presented with minimal contextual information in order to demonstrate how contextual information can be derived from the text. The spoken text is reproduced in Extract 4.1, in which turns at talk are numbered and speakers are identified simply by letters or by "?" if the speaker cannot be identified. The analysis of this spoken text makes only occasional reference to the interactional nature of the discourse. An interactional analysis is presented in the third section of this chapter, in which interactional resources are the focus.

Extract 4.1: Spoken text

```
1   C:  If he moves, how far he is away?
2   T:  Well as he moves away,
3   C:  If he's three feet away, would he be smaller?
4   T:  Nuh. Well, think about it. If I'm standing here,
        and looking at my face. Okay here- here let's say.
        This is maybe easier to see. I'm looking at my eyeballs
        and I'm gonna see the top of my head, so I have to look
        up at an angle about that much. Right? Cuz I'm this
        height. As I move away, does my height get different?
        No.
5   ?:  No.
6   T:  I look smaller, because I'm farther away. Right?
7   ?:  Yeah.
8   T:  But really my- the height- my eye-. Now look at the
        rays from my eyes, eeeehh ((imitating high pitch
        sound of a ray gun)). They're still going
        at the same angle, aren't they?
9   ?:  Yeah
10  T:  Eeeehh ((imitating high pitch sound of a ray gun)).
        So I must be the same height. I look smaller cuz
        I'm farther away.
11  D:  So then it would be one quarter, wouldn't it?
12  T:  I don't know. But I don't wanna spend any more time on
        this.
```

Field and Ideational Metafunction

In Extract 4.1, speakers' experiences of the world are related in their talk, and each experience may be seen as having three constituents: participants, processes, and circumstances. Participants are those objects or persons who experience; processes are their experiences; and circumstances are the time, place, and manner of their experience. Processes are central to the ideational metafunction and they are realized by verbal groups and verbs of action. They are of two kinds: experiential and logical. Experiential processes may be material, behavioral, mental, or verbal, whereas logical processes are those that establish existence of a participant or relations among participants.

Examples of verbal processes instantiating material processes are underlined in these three clauses from the text:

If I'm standing here (turn 4)
As I move away (turn 4)
They're still going at the same angle (turn 8)

Participants in the processes are realized as nominal groups (and sometimes
as prepositional phrases and embedded clauses): "I" (the person speaking)
in turn 4 and "they" (the rays from the person's eyes) in turn 8, and these are
ACTORS—the doers of the processes. Information about how, why, where, and
when the process happened is considered as the circumstance of the process,
which is realized by adverbial groups, prepositional phrases, and even nominal
groups. In the first example, from turn 4 the circumstance is LOCATION
(Where is the process occurring?); in the second example, it is EXTENT (How
far is the process occurring?); in turn 8, it is MANNER (How is the process
occurring?).

Material processes construct "a world of action in which physical and
biological entities interact, by themselves, or on other things" (Halliday &
Martin, 1993, p. 27), but material processes are not, of course, the only type of
process that participants experience; others include mental, verbal, and logical
processes. Mental and verbal processes construct "a world of semiotic activity in
which typically conscious entities negotiate meaning" (p. 27). Mental processes
encode cognition, perception, and affect, and the participant role in mental
processes is SENSER. Examples include:

Think about it (turn 4)
I'm gonna see the top of my head (turn 4)
I don't know (turn 12)

There are also quite a few logical processes instantiated in Extract 4.1. In
these processes, the verbal group is instantiated by copula verbs as in these
examples, in which copula verbs instantiate a relational attributive process
between subject nominal groups and subject complements:

how far he is away? (turn 1)
if he's three feet away would he be smaller? (turn 3)
I'm this height (turn 4)
Does my height get different? (turn 4)
I look smaller because I'm farther away (turn 6)

What does this analysis of the ideational metafunctions of the oral text tell us about what is talked about? In other words, what does a systemic analysis tell us about the field of the text? This question may be approached by finding the frequencies with which the various process types are instantiated in the text, a process that is repeated with the other metafunctions in order to relate interpersonal metafunction to tenor, and textual metafunction to mode. In this way, we see the meaning-making resources that participants have selected in creating the text. There are 11 material processes, 14 relational processes, and the 5 remaining processes are mental. This shows that the text is about relations among material things. The participants in these processes, however, all refer to persons either as individuals (*he* or *I*), as parts of the individual T (*my face, my eyeballs, my height, my eyes*), or as emanating from the same individual T (*the rays from my eyes*). Although the participants are human, they do not participate in behavioral processes representing "the outer manifestations of inner workings and acting out of processes of consciousness (e.g., *people are laughing*) and physiological states (e.g., *they are sleeping*)" (Halliday & Matthiessen, 2004, p. 171). Instead, it is simply the physical movement of their bodies in space that are represented in the text.

Tenor and Interpersonal Metafunction

Moving from ideational metafunction, we can now investigate the relationship between interpersonal metafunction expressed in Extract 4.1 and the tenor of the context of situation (the relationship between speaker and hearer). Interpersonal metafunction is realized by the Mood element, consisting of two parts: the Subject, which is a nominal group, and the Finite operator, which is part of a verbal group. The Finite has two interpersonal roles in the verbal group: It may realize the time of an event in relation to the speaker by means of grammatical tense or it may realize the speaker's attitude toward or opinion about an event by means of modality. Subject and Finite form the Mood element, which realizes the selection of mood type. The absence of Finite characterizes imperative, whereas declarative and interrogative types are realized in English by the different sequential relations between Subject and Finite. Each clause also participates in a system of polarity, whose terms are "positive" and "negative" and the negative is often explicitly marked.

Table 4.1 shows how an analysis of Mood structure of the clauses produced by speaker T in turn 4 illustrates the interpersonal metafunction of Extract 4.1.

The clauses in Table 4.1 are typical of clauses throughout the text: Most tenses are present, polarity is generally unmarked (i.e., positive), and mood

Table 4.1 Mood structure in turn 4 of Extract 4.1

Clause	Subject	Finite	Polarity	Mood type
Nuh.			−	Declarative
Well, think about it.			+	Imperative
If I'm standing here,	I	Tense: present	+	Declarative
and looking at my face	(I)	Tense: present	+	Declarative
Okay here- here let's say.	Us		+	Imperative
This is	This	Tense: present	+	Declarative
maybe easier to see.			+	Declarative
I'm looking at my eyeballs	I	Tense: present	+	Declarative
and I'm gonna see the top of my head,	I	Tense: present	+	Declarative
so I have to look up at an angle about that much.	I	Tense: present	+	Declarative
Right?			+	Interrogative
Cuz I'm this height	I	Tense: present	+	Declarative
As I move away,	I	Tense: present	+	Declarative
does my height get different?	My height	Tense: present	+	Interrogative
No.			−	Declarative

type is frequently declarative. This analysis indicates that T generally makes positive statements about events occurring in present time. A detailed analysis of all 43 clauses in Extract 4.1 shows that all tenses are realized as present. An additional system in Mood structure (not shown in Table 4.1) allows speakers to express meanings that lie between "yes" and "no," between positive and negative polarity. This system enables speakers to express opinions about what they are saying, to take a stand on the probability of something occurring, on how (un)usual something is, on whether the speaker or an interlocutor is obliged or inclined to do something, and how typical or obvious a state of affairs is. The system that allows this is known in SFG as MODALITY (not to be confused with Mood, although MODALITY is often instantiated by modal verbs). In Extract 4.1, MODALITY instantiates in four modals verbs. They are all epistemic; that is, they express how much certainty or evidence the speaker has for the proposition expressed by his or her utterance. The only modality in T's utterances is in turn 10: "I must be the same height" expressing T's certainty about his height; the modality (indicated by underlines) in other speakers' utterances expresses less confidence in their propositions:

C: If he's three feet away, <u>would</u> he be smaller? (turn 3)

D: So then it <u>would</u> be one quarter, <u>wouldn't</u> it? (turn 11)

Another difference between how T and the other participants make meaning is in mood type. Both T and the other participants in the dialogue realize mood type by declaratives (23 clauses out of 31 produced by T and 6 clauses out of 10 produced by other participants are declarative), but T is the sole participant to make demands on others by means of imperatives in turns 4 and 8. All participants demand information of others by means of interrogatives, although other participants express interrogatives more frequently than T by means of a *wh*-interrogative in turn 1, a yes/no interrogative in turn 3, and a modal tag in turn 11. Out of 10 clauses produced by other participants, 3 are interrogatives, and out of 31 clauses produced by T, only 4 are interrogatives. T expresses interrogative mood type by means of the mood adjunct "right?" or a mood tag "aren't they?"—the function of which is to elicit agreement with the previous proposition. T only once appears to demand information by means of the yes/no question in turn 4, but he immediately provides that information himself.

To summarize: What are the meaning-making resources that participants have selected in creating Extract 4.1 and how do these resources express the relationship among participants? The clearest evidence presented by the semiotic analysis is that the social role played by T differs from the roles played by the other participants. T makes statements about the world as it is with certainty, whereas the other participants are less certain; T makes demands on the attention of other participants by means of imperatives, whereas the other participants demand information from T by means of interrogatives; T does not demand information of the other participants, only their agreement with his propositions by means of modal adjuncts and mood tags. He answers his only yes/no interrogative immediately: "As I move away, does my height get different? No."

One way of framing the relationship between T and the other participants in Extract 4.1 is in terms of discursive power, which Fairclough (2001) has defined as "controlling and constraining the contributions of non-powerful participants" (pp. 38–39). The relative status of T and the other participants is unequal and T takes the more powerful discursive role by his statements, the epistemic security with which he makes them, his demands for attention, and his demands that other participants agree with his description of the world. T's more powerful role is co-constructed by the other participants, who construct their less powerful roles by less certain modalization, by demanding information from T (information that they do not possess), and by confirming his interpretation of the world by their answers to his modal tags and adjuncts. The lexicogrammatical choices made by participants in Extract 4.1 construct the contextual variable of tenor: the relative statuses of participants and their social distance.

Mode and Textual Metafunction
The third aspect of context that is revealed by a semiotic analysis is mode: the kind of text created by the textual metafunction, which organizes a message into a sequential and coherent whole. The analysis of clause as message in SFG is based on the analysis of functional sentence perspective first proposed for Czech by linguists of the Prague School (Daneš, 1974b; Firbas, 1992; Vachek, 1964). Many languages, including Czech and Japanese, distinguish between the syntactic function of subject and the communicative function of topic by means of morphology. Topic is the element of a clause about which something is said, and comment is what is said about this element. Japanese marks topic by the particle は "wa" and subject by が "ga," although in many cases, the same constituent functions as both subject and topic. In English, there is no morphological distinction between the topic and subject, and the topic is generally the first sequential element of a clause. SFG borrows the terminology for the distinction between topic and comment from the Prague School by referring to the communicative starting point of clause-as-message as Theme and the remainder of the clause-as-message as Rheme. The analysis of a text as message thus consists in identifying Theme in each clause (its thematic structure) and describing the relationship between Theme and Rheme in different clauses (its texture).

Communicative Theme and syntactic subject may be instantiated by the same element in a clause, most often when that element is a nominal group. Thus, in "I look smaller," the element "I" is both Theme and subject of the verb "look," but often Theme and subject do not coincide; for instance, one clause in the previous paragraph is "In English, there is no morphological distinction between the two functions," in which the prepositional phrase "In English" functions as Theme and "there" is the grammatical subject. Theme in SFG is broader than topic because several elements may form part of clausal Theme, but only one (often the last in the sequence) is topic, known in SFG as topical Theme. Another element of Theme may relate the clause to preceding or following clauses and is known as textual Theme, or a clause may begin with an interpersonal meaning that indicates the kind of interaction between speakers and is known as interpersonal Theme. In Extract 4.1, for example, the Theme in the clause "If I'm standing here" consists of textual Theme "If" and

Table 4.2 Thematic structure in major clauses in turn 4 of Extract 4.1

	Theme			Rheme
	Textual	Interpersonal	Topical	
1	Well,	think		about it.
2	If		I	'm standing here,
3	and		(I)	(am) looking at my face, . . .
4	Okay		here- here	let's say.
5			This	is maybe [easier to see]
6			(this)	easier to see.
7			I	'm looking at my eyeballs
8	and		I	'm gonna see the top of my head,
9	so		I	have to look up at an angle about that much.
10	Cuz		I	'm this height.
11	As		I	move away,
12		Does	my height	get different?

topical Theme "I," with the rest of the clause "'m standing here" as Rheme. The clause "does my height get different" begins with interpersonal Theme "does," followed by topical Theme "my height." Most thematic elements have a topical Theme, but textual and interpersonal thematic elements may be absent and, if they do, they occur in the sequence *textual^interpersonal^topical*.[7] Table 4.2 is a thematic analysis of major clauses in turn 4 in Extract 4.1. The minor clauses "Nuh," "Right," and "No" are not shown because they have no thematic structure.

Table 4.2 shows that T's turn begins with the textual Theme "Well," which links to a preceding question. The topical Theme in most of the following clauses is "I" referencing the same individual, whereas the topical Theme of the last clause refers to a physical property of that individual: "my height." In the middle of this thematic sequence, T thematizes "here" and "this" in Clauses 4–6 to index a physical place in the environment. The nature of this text thus appears to be an interactive call to other participants, followed by a description by T of his own material processes, a description interspersed with talk about a physical location.

Apart from the thematic structure in each clause of this text taken in isolation, it is possible to see how Theme in one clause connects by means of

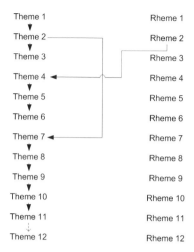

Figure 4.2 Repetitive thematic progression in turn 4 of Extract 4.1.

coreference to the thematic structure of nearby clauses, thus producing thematic progression or texture. The thematic progression of turn 4 in Extract 4.1 is shown in Figure 4.2, in which Theme N and Rheme N refer to the thematic structure in clause N of Table 4.2; Theme 2 and Rheme 2, for example, refer to the thematic structure of Clause 2: "If I + 'm standing here." Arrows indicate that Theme or Rheme in a previous clause reappears as Theme in a subsequent clause.

Figure 4.2 shows that "I" is the predominant topical Theme throughout T's turn-at-talk. His turn concludes with the topical Theme "my height" in Clause 12, which is semantically related to the Theme in the preceding clause. The topical Theme "here" in Clause 4 was introduced as Rheme in Clause 2 and the same referent is repeated in Clauses 5 and 6. Extract 4.1 illustrates a form of texture in which the same Theme is repeated from clause to clause. The repetitive texture found in turn 4 and illustrated in Figure 4.2 is characteristic of the whole of Extract 4.1. Theme in the early clauses is "he," which then becomes "I" or "my height" in most of T's turns 4 and 6. The new Theme "the rays from my eyes" is introduced by T in turn 8 and "I" returns as Theme in the remainder of T's talk. The attempt by D in turn 11 to introduce a new Theme is not taken up by T.

Texture is one verbal resource that speakers and writers use to create different discursive practices. Figure 4.2 illustrates the repetitive texture imposed

Figure 4.3 Thematic progression illustrating zigzag texture.

on the text by T. In other discursive practices, however, texture may be created by different patterns of thematic development, of which Daneš (1974a) provides three patterns. In Figure 4.3, a zigzag thematic progression is illustrated, in which Theme of Clause 2 derives from Rheme of Clause 1 and so on. Figure 4.4 illustrates an iterative thematic progression in which the same Theme enters into a relation with several successive Rhemes. Fries (1995) called the third type of thematic progression illustrated in Figure 4.5 "a progression with derived Themes," in which the text as a whole concerns a single idea and the Themes of the clauses constituting the text are all semantically derived from the single main idea but are not identical with it or with each other. The extent to which it is possible to characterize different discursive practices or genres by different thematic progressions has been debated by Daneš (1974a), Ghadessy (1995), and Fries (1995).

This analysis of the textual metafunction in the oral text parallels some of the analyses made of ideational and interpersonal metafunctions. The thematic structure of the text shows that the Theme "I" and related Themes ("my height," "the rays from my eyes") predominate and the repetition of this Theme characterizes texture. This Theme is only used in turns produced by a single speaker, T, and it is not repeated as "you" in the contributions of other speakers. Recall that in the analysis of the ideational metafunction of the verbal groups in this text, it was found that they instantiated material processes, so the absence of

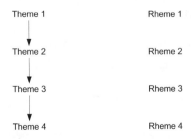

Figure 4.4 Thematic progression illustrating iterative thematic texture.

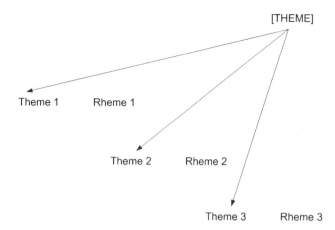

Figure 4.5 Thematic progression with derived themes.

first- or second-person Theme in the contributions by the other participants is coherent because T is not talking about his mental or verbal processes, but rather he is using real and imagined actions of his body to illustrate material processes.

Systemic Analysis of a Written Text

Systemic Functional Grammar has been used extensively in the comparative study of texts in order to distinguish ways of making meaning in different texts and the verbal resources that are available and normative in different styles. Stylistic studies in SFG, many of which have been collected in anthologies by Birch and O'Toole (1988), Carter and Stockwell (2008), and Chatman (1971), describe ways of making meaning in literary texts and in nonliterary texts such as oral narratives, jokes, and instructional discourse. A comparison of presentations of the same scientific topic orally by a physics teacher and in the students' physics textbook was carried out by Young and Nguyen (2002) in order to distinguish the modes of meaning employed by the authors of the two texts and to describe how the semiotic choices made by the textbook writer and the teacher socialize readers and students to the semiosis of physicists. The oral text that Young and Nguyen compared was Extract 4.1, which is a transcript of a 45-second segment of a 12th-grade physics class at a high school in the American Midwest. The written text was taken from the textbook *Conceptual Physics* (Hewitt, 1992), which was assigned to the same class. Extract 4.2 is a passage from the textbook that treats the same topic—reflection in a plane mirror—that the teacher was explaining in Extract 4.1.

Extract 4.2. Written text

Consider a candle flame placed in front of a plane (flat) mirror. Rays of light are reflected from its surface in all directions. The number of rays is infinite, and every one obeys the laws of reflection. Figure 29–4 shows only two rays that originate at the tip of the candle flame and reflect from the mirror to someone's eye. Note that the rays diverge (spread apart) from the tip of the flame, and continue diverging from the mirror upon reflection. These divergent rays *appear* to originate from a point located behind the mirror. The image of the candle the person sees in the mirror is called a **virtual image**, because light does not actually pass through the image position but behaves virtually as if it did.

Your eye cannot ordinarily tell the difference between an object and its reflected image. This is because the light that enters your eye is entering in exactly the same manner, physically, as it would if there really were an object there. Notice that the image is as far behind the mirror as the object is in front of the mirror. Notice also that the image and object have the same size. When you view yourself in a mirror, your image is the same size your identical twin would appear if located as far behind the mirror as you are in front—as the long as the mirror is flat.

The two texts bear comparison because both the teacher and textbook writer have a common aim: to explain the physical phenomenon of reflection in a plain mirror. Both texts are designed for the same audience of students in a 12th-grade American high school and they are of comparable length: 40 clauses in the oral text and 34 clauses in the written text. In order to compare the modes of meaning employed by the authors of the two texts, their ideational, interpersonal, and textual metafunctions may be analyzed and comparisons may be made of how each metafunction is realized by the lexicogrammar chosen by the authors of the two texts. The analysis of the written text is presented here in summary form, but the process of analysis is the same as that for the oral text.

Just as in the oral text, processes instantiated in the verbal group are central to the ideational metafunction. They are of two kinds: experiential and logical. Experiential processes may be material, behavioral, mental, or verbal, whereas logical processes are those that establish the existence of a participant or relations among participants. Examples of some of these processes in the textbook are as follows:

Material: Rays of light <u>are reflected</u> from its surface in all directions
Mental: When you <u>view</u> yourself in a mirror
Relational: Figure 29–4 <u>shows</u> only two rays

The textbook instantiated 11 material processes, 7 mental processes, 14 relational processes, and a few behavioral and existential processes, and their distribution in the teacher talk was 11, 5, and 14, respectively. Similarity of distribution of process types indicates that both the written and spoken texts are about relations among material things. The difference between the ideational metafunctions in the two texts, however, lies in the two authors' choice of agency. In the teacher talk, the agents in the material processes refer to the teacher in the first person or to parts of the individual teacher's body, whereas in the textbook, the agents of material processes are objects such as *a candle flame*, *rays of light*, and *light*, all of which are referenced by third-person pronouns. The contrast in agency in material processes appears from the beginning of both texts where the textbook author and the teacher employ a mental process to introduce contrasting material processes: The textbook author writes, "Consider a candle flame placed in front of a plane (flat) mirror," whereas the teacher tells his class, "Well, think about it. If I'm standing here and looking at my face." Third-person agents in the textbook cast the writer and the reader as observers and keep the reader at a distance from the process. In so doing, the textbook author presents scientific processes as observed objective entities independent of the reader and the writer. In contrast, the teacher is an agent in the material process of reflection in a plane mirror, bringing science into the lived relationship between speaker and hearer. Thus, whereas the textbook casts the reader as an observer, the teacher casts himself—and by implication, his students—as participants. Turning now to relational processes, in both the textbook and the teacher talk these are instantiated most often by copula "be." The textbook author, however, uses a far wider range of ways of expressing relational meaning than the teacher. The teacher uses only copula "be" and one other verb: "look" in "look smaller." The textbook author, on the other hand, not only uses copula "be" and verbs of near-being but also employs a wide range of less obviously relational verbs such as "every one obeys the law of reflection," "the image . . . is called a virtual image," and "[light] . . . behaves virtually as if it did."[8] The textbook author's greater range of vocabulary for expressing relational processes in the textbook has the advantage of precision but, at the same time, may make it harder for his readers to comprehend that a relation between entities is his intended meaning.

The communicative relationship between the teacher and his class can be compared with the communicative relationship between the textbook author and his readers. In doing so, a comparison between the tenors of the two texts is made by investigating the interpersonal metafunction. Recall that the interpersonal metafunction is realized in lexicogrammar by the Mood element.

Given that the oral text forms part of live interactive communication between teacher and students and that the interaction between the textbook writer and his readers is asynchronous, we would expect the structure of Mood in the two texts to show differences. Although similarities exist—the predominant mood type selected in both texts is declarative (23 declarative clauses produced by the teacher and 30 by the textbook author) and imperatives are used by both (3 by the teacher and 4 by the textbook author)—the obvious difference between the two is that the teacher (and his students) frequently select interrogatives but the textbook author never does. Most Finites in both texts are tensed, and tense is realized throughout both texts by the unmarked present. A more revealing stylistic difference, however, is how the two texts instantiate modality. As was mentioned earlier, the only modal Finite in the teacher talk is "I must be the same height," which expresses the teacher's certainty about his height, whereas the modal Finites in the students' utterances "would he be smaller?" and "It would be one quarter, wouldn't it?" express less confidence in their propositions. In the textbook, the author does not express any degrees of certainty or evidence for his propositions; that is, he does not employ epistemic modality. Other modalities are used, however. There is one instance of deontic modality that expresses or denies permission in "Your eye cannot ordinarily tell the difference between an object and its reflected image" and several irrealis modals in these clauses:

> the light that enters your eye is entering in exactly the same manner, physically, as it would if there really were an object there.
> your image is the same size your identical twin would appear

The irrealis modals do not, however, express the author's certainty or uncertainty about propositions in the way that the epistemic modals in the students' talk do. Instead, in the textbook, they help the author construct a counterfactual world to compare with his claims about the real world.

The different modalities in the classroom talk and in the textbook index different relationships among the participants. In the classroom talk, propositions about how light is reflected in a plane mirror are negotiated, with the teacher expressing certainty about his statement while the students express uncertainty. In the textbook, however, there is no epistemic modality and no negotiation. The writer tells his readers how it is by denying them permission to tell the difference between an object and its reflected image and by comparing the real world with an imaginary one. The only image used by the teacher has a different function: It is the way he casts himself as a cartoon character with rays coming out of his eyes, an image that may have emotional appeal to his teenage students.

Finally, we turn to comparisons of how the two texts are organized by comparing their thematic structure and texture. We noticed that the thematic structure of the teacher talk primarily involves the first person, in which the teacher refers to himself or to properties of his physical body. In the textbook, however, no first-person referent functions as topical Theme. The passage begins with third-person Themes: "a candle flame," "rays of light," "Figure 29–4," and "the image of the candle that the person sees." About halfway through, the textbook author transitions to Themes related to a second-person reader: "your eye," "you" and "your identical twin." Textual Themes in both texts are very similar. Both the teacher and textbook author use mostly explicit conjunctions such as "and," "but," "because," "so then," and "as long as" to index relations between adjacent clauses, and most conjunctive relations in both texts are external—that is, they relate events in the physical world of light rays, mirrors, and observers that together constitute the field of discourse. Most of the conjunctive relations expressed in both texts are consequential (cause and effect) and temporal (before, after, and simultaneously), reflecting the fact that both texts are descriptions of a process. These relations—as well as comparative (contrast and similarity) and additive conjunctions—connect most adjacent pairs of clauses in both texts. Interpersonal thematic elements are more common in the classroom interaction than in the textbook because of the question-answer interactive nature of the classroom. All four interpersonal elements in the textbook Themes are imperatives, whereas only three interpersonal elements in the classroom talk are imperatives and five are interrogatives.

The final element of message organization is texture—the relationship between Theme and Rheme in the clauses that make up a text. Extract 4.1, as we noted, is characterized by repetitive texture, in which a Theme is introduced in one clause and repeated in several following clauses. A similar structure can be found in the textbook. "Rays (of light)" is the Theme repeated in the first paragraph, which ends with new Themes, "the image of the candle" and "light" introduced in the final sentence of the paragraph. Themes in the second paragraph are more varied, and in several clauses, Rhemes in previous clauses are thematized, producing a multiple-Rheme texture:

18   Your eye + cannot ordinarily tell the difference between an object and its reflected image.

      . . .

24   Notice +
25   that the image + is as far behind the mirror
26   as the object + is in front of the mirror.

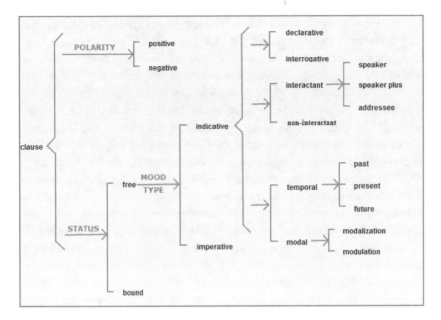

Figure 4.6 System of interpersonal metafunction (Wu & Matthiessen, 2007). Reproduced with permission.

27 Notice +

28 also that the image and the object + have the same size.

The Rheme in Clause 18 includes two elements "an object" and "its reflected image," which are thematized in Clauses 25, 26, and 28. The second paragraph concludes with repetitive texture in which second-person "you" and related elements ("your image" and "your identical twin") are repeated. The textuality of the textbook passage thus seems to be a combination of the repetitive textuality found in the teacher talk interspersed with the more formal multiple-Rheme pattern.

What does a stylistic comparison of these two texts reveal about discursive practice? In SFG, the I-language of both teacher and textbook author is not a set of rules that produce grammatical sentences; rather, it is a set of resources from which speaker and writer make meaning by selecting from among sets of alternatives at different levels. These selections are usually unconscious choices; at each level of analysis in SFG, a speaker or writer makes selections from a system of hierarchically ordered levels. An example of how these hierarchical levels are arranged in a system that realizes the interpersonal metafunction in a clause and the paradigm at each level is shown in Figure 4.6.

The speaker's or writer's selection among the paradigmatic choices at each level determines the interpersonal metafunction of a clause. As these systemic choices accumulate over many clauses in the production of a text, a relationship between the speaker and hearer or the writer and reader (the tenor of the discourse) is created. We have seen in the analysis of the interpersonal metafunctions in the teacher talk and textbook that experts in the academic discipline of physics are communicating with novices. The expertise of these participants is created by their choice of imperatives and by their choice of modality and, in the case of the teacher talk, by the reciprocal modality chosen by the students. The difference between the two styles is in the choice of interrogatives by teacher and students and their absence in their textbook. Another important difference between the two styles lies in the textual metafunction of the two texts. The topical themes in the teacher talk are instantiated as first-person nominal groups, in which the teacher refers to himself or to properties of his physical body. However, no first-person referent functions as topical Theme in the textbook, where the passage begins with third-person Themes and transitions to second-person Themes in the second paragraph.

Systemic Functional Grammar, as demonstrated in the analysis of these two texts, involves selection among classes of elements at different levels. The system of meaning potentials thus consists, at each level, of what Saussure called an associative organization of elements (Saussure et al., 1966), or a paradigm. Figure 4.6 illustrates the paradigms at different levels of the interpersonal metafunction; for instance, an obligatory choice of polarity in a clause involves selection of one of two alternatives—positive or negative. Selection of mood type means that either indicative or imperative is selected; selection of indicative mood involves selection of the three binary realizations of declarative/interrogative, interactant/noninteractant, or temporal/modal; and selection of temporal involves selection among past, present, or future.

Paradigmatic organization in the system of meaning potential that constitutes I-language in SFG is, as Saussure indicated, one of two kinds of linguistic organization. The other is the relation among items in a temporal sequence, which Saussure called a syntagmatic relation. In contemporary approaches to spoken language, the syntagmatic principle of ordering has been investigated most successfully by researchers who have asked the guiding question of CA, "Why this now?" in their attempts to describe the orderliness, structure, and sequential patterns of talk-in-interaction. In the next section I turn to the interactional resources that speakers employ in order to create social order in spoken interaction.

Interactional Resources

The account of discursive resources presented so far has considered text as the central feature of a discursive practice and, in SFG, text is seen as the instantiation in lexicogrammar of choices among semiotic alternatives at different systemic levels. Yet, there are other important features of a discursive practice that go beyond the properties that we have isolated as text. A spoken discursive practice is done in real time and in a constantly varying social context. Whereas a systemic functional analysis of practice as text has treated text as an object, and we have assumed that the meaning of texts is not in dispute, in this section I consider that in constructing spoken texts, speakers are doing social actions in real time and, throughout the constantly evolving interaction, meanings are not fixed but emerge from negotiation among speakers. The framework for understanding discursive practice as talk-in-interaction that is taken here is that of CA, and it is quite different from the systemic functional analysis that has been presented so far. The contrast between CA and SFG (or any linguistic approach to practice) is described by Hutchby and Wooffitt (1998):

> CA is only marginally interested in language as such; its actual object of study is the *interactional organization of social activities*. CA is a radical departure from other forms of linguistically oriented analysis in that the production of utterances, and more particularly the sense they obtain, is seen not in terms of the structure of language, but first and foremost as a practical social accomplishment (p. 14).

Conversation Analysis has its roots in a phenomenological tradition in sociology that Garfinkel (1967) developed and termed *ethnomethodology*. The innovative character of an ethnomethodological approach to talk-in-interaction parallels the view of social interaction in context that anthropologists developed in Practice Theory. As presented in chapter 2, Practice Theory seeks to explain "the genesis, reproduction, and change" of social and cultural realities such as class, gender, and ethnicity" (Ortner, 1984, p. 149). Practice theorists assume that the social order is not automatically reproduced by the actions of individuals but examine, instead, the ways that individual actors in social settings create, transform, reproduce, and resist the cultural forces of society. The development of ethnomethodology in Garfinkel's writing is very similar. According to Garfinkel, sociologists had interpreted the famous aphorism of Durkheim (1966) that "the objective reality of social facts is sociology's most fundamental principle" to mean that social phenomena such as social order, discrimination, justice, social class, and so on should be taken as formal realities to be described and measured. The question of how these facts are reproduced from one generation to the next was taken to be a process of first socializing children through positive and negative reinforcement enacted by the institutions of school and family. In their own interactions, individuals would then reproduce the same social phenomena unconsciously. Garfinkel's interpretation of Durkeim's aphorism was radically different and produced a radically different research agenda. For Garfinkel, the social fact to be investigated is how humans *achieve* or *construct* social phenomena through social practices; that is, macrosocial constructs of social order are not taken as a given; instead, what is to be investigated is how they are achieved. Ethnomethodology is, then, the study of the *methods* used by the *ethnie*[9] (the folk) to achieve intersubjectivity and create social phenomena. As Garfinkel wrote, the central recommendation of ethnomethodology is that "the activities whereby members produce and manage settings of organized everyday affairs are identical with members' procedures for making those settings 'account-able'" (p. 1). Just as in Practice Theory, I have stressed that habitus is an index of personal history that every participant brings to interaction, so Garfinkel emphasized the indexicality of language and the difficulties this creates for the production of objective accounts of social phenomena. Such a view places ethnomethodology firmly on the side of phenomenology and against the positivism of formal social science. This means that accounts are dependent on the settings in which they are produced for their meaning.

This approach is very different to the analytical approach of SFG because whereas SFG assumes that an analyst's understanding of the meaning of a text is the same meaning that is intended by the producer of the text, ethnomethodology takes it for granted that the individuals who participate in a conversation are constantly attempting to make sense of what they are doing. Garfinkel and Sacks (1970) highlighted the difference when they wrote:

> However extensive or explicit what a speaker says may be, it does not by its extensiveness or explicitness pose a task of deciding the correspondence between what he says and what he means that is resolved by citing his talk verbatim. (p. 344)

The ethnomethodological roots of CA are also a challenge for what Seedhouse (2004) has called "linguistic CA" (p. 50). Some linguists have adopted the methods of CA to study how a specific linguistic form such as "no" is used in different contexts or have taken certain patterns of turn-taking as norms for the analysis of power in teacher-student interaction. Linguistic CA, as exemplified by these two examples, fails to recognize the dependence of any segment of talk on its context and that an objective meaning of any action cannot be substituted for its indexical meaning in the context and moment of action.

For conversation analysts, language is a structured system for the production of meaning (a very similar formulation to that adopted by systemic functional grammarians) and is a vehicle for communicative interaction understood in the widest possible sense. Communication and interaction, however, are social processes that are fundamental to the production, reproduction, and maintenance or social order and social institutions of all kinds, including intersubjectivity in dyadic conversation, the family, up to and including the nation-state.[10]

The procedures of ethnomethodological CA involve the following: (a) an emic indifference to any social or sociolinguistic theory that appears relevant to an understanding of social action, (b) a perspective on social action that tries to take it as the very first experience of that particular action by an observer, (c) the study of the practices by which participants in actions achieve social order rather than the order itself, (d) the investigation of the consequences when participants deviate from a recognized and shared social order, (d) the recognition of the context dependence (the indexicality) of all social action and the impossibility of objective knowledge, and (e) the documentary method of interpretation (Mannheim, 1952/1971). The documentary method of interpretation is central to ethnomethodological CA and is defined by Garfinkel (1967) as follows:

> The method consists of treating an actual appearance as "the document of," as "pointing to," as "standing on behalf of" a presupposed underlying pattern. Not only is the underlying pattern derived from its individual documentary evidence, but the individual documentary evidences, in their turn, are interpreted on the basis of "what is known" about the underlying pattern. Each is used to elaborate the other. (p. 78)

The procedures of ethnomethodological CA may become apparent when they are used in a sample analysis of a conversational interaction—the same oral text that was subjected to a systemic functional analysis earlier. Extract 4.3 is a revised and expanded version of Extract 4.1. In this extract, a teacher (T) is standing at the front of a class of about twenty 12th-grade students in a high school in the American Midwest, who are sitting at their desks facing the teacher. An overhead projector (OHP) is projecting, on a screen behind the teacher, an image of a cartoon man looking at his reflection in a mirror. From where the students are sitting, the cartoon man is facing to their right. At the beginning of Extract 4.3, the teacher is standing in the light of the OHP pointing with his left hand at the image and gazing at the students.

Extract 4.3. I'm looking at my eyeballs

```
 1  C:  if he moves, how far he is away.
 2      (1.5)
 3  T:  ⌈well as he moves
 4      ⌊((T gazes at C.))
 5      ⌈away, =
 6      ⌊((T moves back out of the light of the OHP. ))
 7  C:  = if he's three feet away, would he be smaller?
 8      (2.0)
 9  T:  ⌈nuh-. well, ↑think about it.
10      ⌊((T raises his R arm with his index finger in the air. ))
11      ⌈(.) if I- if I'm standing here, and looking at my face,
12      ⌊((T walks across in front of the projected image toward
13      the students' R side of the room while gazing at the
14      wall. ))
15      okay here- (.) here, let's say this is maybe easier to
16      ⌈see.
17      ⌊((T reaches the wall on the right side of the room and
18      gazes at it. ))
19      I'm looking at my eyeballs and I'm gonna see  ⌈the top of
20      'my head, (.5)                                 |
21                                                    ⌊((T glances
22      briefly at the students. ))
23      so I have to look up at an angle about ⌈that much, (.5)
24                                             ⌊((With his R
25      hand, T indicates a place on the wall at the height of
26      his head and gazes at it. ))
27      right? (.2) cuz I'm ⌈this height, (0.8)
28                         ⌊((T moves his R hand from the wall
29      toward the top of his head and back to the wall. ))
30      ⌈as I move away, (.5)
31      ⌊((T steps backward away from the wall continuing to gaze
32      at the wall, keeping his R hand level with the top of
33      his head. ))
34      does my height get different? no.
35  ?:  °no.°
36  T:  ⌈I look smaller because I'm farther away, right?
37      ⌊((T drops his R hand and turn his head to gaze at the
38      students. ))
39  ?:  yeah.
```

```
40 T:  ⌐but really my- the height- my eye-
41     ⌊((T turns his gaze back at the wall and steps backward
42     away from the wall toward the center of the room. ))
43     now look at the rays from my eyes,  ⌐ee::: ((imitating
44     high pitch sound of a ray gun))     |(0.5)
45                                         ⌊((T moves his R hand
46     rapidly to and fro in front of his eyes in the direction
47     of the wall. ))
48     ⌐they're still going at the same- (0.5) angle, aren't
49     |they.
50     ⌊((T continues to step backward away from the wall toward
51     the center of the room moving his hand rapidly to and fro
52     in front of his eyes as he moves. ))
53 ?:  yeah. =
54 T:  = ee::: ((imitating high pitch sound of a ray gun)) so I
55     must be the same height.
56 ?:  ⌐you s-
57 T:  |I look smaller cuz I'm farther away.
58     ⌊((T turns his head to gaze at the class. ))
59     (0.8)
60 D:  so then it would be one quarter, would ⌐n't it?
61 T:                                          |I don't know.
62                                             ⌊((T drops his R
63     hand and turns to face the class. ))
64     ⌐but I don't wanna spend many more time on this.
65     ⌊((T raises his R hand in a gesture of refusal and looks
66     down at his notes. ))
```

Extracts 4.1 and 4.3 are entextualizations of the same discursive practice, but the differences between them are obvious. Extract 4.1 is a representation of 12 turns at talk, whereas Extract 4.3 is 66 lines of dialogue. Extract 4.1 reproduces only the verbal resources used by the participants, whereas Extract 4.3 attempts to represent the nonverbal resources used by the teacher, especially the direction of his gaze, the orientation of his torso, the position and movement of his body, and the relevant objects within the classroom environment. The entextualization in Extract 4.1 represents oral language as if it were written, using the graphemic conventions of punctuation and spelling, whereas in Extract 4.3 an attempt is made to entextualize some of the prosodic elements of the participants' talk by repurposing punctuations symbols to indicate pitch movement and variations in volume and length of vowels and consonants. The representation of the syntagmatic structure of the talk in Extract 4.1 is simple: One word follows another and one turn at talk follows another. In contrast, the transcriber of Extract 4.3 has attempted to entextualize silences between words and between turns at talk, overlaps between turns, and occasions when one turn latches onto a previous turn with no hearable silence between the two. An attempt has also been made to indicate the temporal relationship between nonverbal action and the sequence of talk.[11]

Why should an ethnomethodological analysis of this oral practice require so much greater detail of representation than a systemic functional analysis? One answer was given by Markee and Stansell (2007), who argued that, in CA, analysts make their original data available to consumers so that "critical readers should have the means independently to critique researchers' interpretations of primary data" (p. 27). That argument, however, would apply equally to an SFG analysis, as most systemic functional analyses focus more on the paradigmatic organization of utterances than on their syntagmatic structures. No, the richness of detail in an ethnomethodological analysis is necessitated by the procedures listed earlier. Social action and interaction are mediated by all human semiotic systems, not just language, and, because of an analyst's emic indifference to theories of communication and social interaction, any verbal and nonverbal actions may be taken as documents of an underlying pattern or regularity. Equally, prosody may index social action just as much as lexicogrammar does, and the sequential organization of talk may be as relevant as its paradigmatic organization of utterances. Most importantly, perhaps, these separate systems of lexicogrammar, sequential organization, prosody, gesture, and embodied action may interact, such that social action may be indexed by the confluent operation of different systems or by disjunction among them.

In a CA of talk-in-interaction, the fundamental question to ask about the data is "Why this now?"—a single question that in effect represents three procedures:

This—Characterize and specify an object in the talk-in-interaction that an analyst attends to. "This" may be a document of a presupposed underlying pattern.

Now—Any point in a conversation is a "now": a place in the sequential development of the interaction. Its place in the sequence is as much a part of its meaning and function as "this" itself.

Why—How is "this" functioning? Answering this question does not mean divining the intentions of the speaker but involves finding patterns of similar "this's" and inducing some conclusion about an underlying pattern. An

answer to this question may be supported by considering how other participants treat the utterance, especially if they orient to any deviant action.

One interesting thing about Extract 4.3 is the transition between speakers.
The teacher T holds the conversational floor during most of this 45-second
transcript, but various students take turns throughout. What my analysis focuses
on—the "this"—is the transition between a turn by the teacher and a turn by
a student. Speaker transitions occur on several occasions: In lines 1–3 at the
beginning of the extract, student C completes a turn, which is followed by a
turn by the teacher; in line 7, C latches a question onto the teacher's turn in
lines 3–7, which is followed by a turn by the teacher beginning in line 9. There
are hearable silences between the end of student C's turns and the beginning
of the teacher's turns, but there is no silence before C takes a turn in line 7.
After this rapid alternation of speakers, the teacher produces a long turn from
line 9 through line 59. During his turn, several unidentified students take short
turns, but there are no hearable silences before their turns in lines 35, 39, 53,
and 56, nor are there silences before the teacher retakes the floor immediately
after the students' turns. Toward the end of the extract on lines 57–60, student
D asks the teacher a question, but waits to do so for 0.8 seconds after the end
of the teacher's turn in line 57. In lines 61–63, the teacher has no hesitation is
dismissing D's question with an overlap before D has finished.

Transitions between speakers happen in this extract, as they do in most
conversations, and because speaker alternation is such a common feature of
talk-in-interaction, it has been studied extensively. Three aspects of speaker
transition have been described: how units in interaction of turn-taking are
constructed (Ford, 2004; Sacks, Schegloff, & Jefferson, 1974; Young & Lee,
2004), how participants identify moments at which transitions take place (Ford
& Thompson, 1996; Streeck, 1995), and how the selection of next speaker is
made (Sacks et al., 1974). Each of these aspects of participants' management
of speaker transition in Extract 4.3 reveals an underlying structure of social
relations.

Sacks et al. (1974) asked how participants know when to end one turn-
at-talk and when to begin another. They answered the question by invoking
the notion of the turn-constructional unit (TCU). Such a unit may be a unit
of the lexicogrammar, of intonation, or a pragmatic unit (a complete idea)
and, as Ford and Thompson (1996) noticed, these units often coincide to make
a complex TCU. The use of this resource can be seen by the participants'
actions in Extract 4.3. In line 7, C's turn "if he's three feet away, would he be
smaller?" is a complete lexicogrammatical unit of two clauses, which ends on

a final rising intonation and forms a complete pragmatic unit of a request for information:

```
 7→ C: =if he's three feet away, would he be smaller?
 8      (2.0)
 9   T: ⌈nuh-. well, ↑think about it.
10      ⌊((T raises his R arm with his index finger in the
        air.))
```

The transition from C's talk to the teacher's response in line 9 is thus accomplished by both participants recognizing the boundary of a TCU. The 2-second pause between C's and T's turns on line 8 is not, in itself, part of the transition mechanism because there are other transitions in Extract 4.3 in which speakers do not pause between turns. In the transition between D's and T's turns in lines 60–61, for example, T begins his turn before D has reached the conclusion of a clause, in the middle of a tone unit, and before D has completed his request for information:

```
60→D:   so then it would be one quarter, would⌈n't it?
61→T:                                          |I don't know.
62                                             ⌊((T drops his R
63      hand and turns to face the class.))
```

As Streeck (1995) suggested, transitions between speakers occur at places when participants *project* the completion of the TCU, projecting not only the form of the next word but also the completion of larger lexicogrammatical, intonational, and pragmatic units. Projection is thus an important part of what participants do when listening to talk in progress, and the place in an ongoing turn when participants are able to project the completion of the TCU is called a transition-relevance place (TRP).

The question of how to select the next speaker was answered by Sacks et al. (1974, p. 704) by means of a procedure that I paraphrase as follows:

1. If the current speaker selects the next speaker, then that party has the right and obligation to speak.
2. If no next speaker is selected, then self-selection may (but need not) occur. The first starter acquires rights to the turn.
3. If no next speaker is selected, then current speaker may (but need not) continue.

The current speaker may select the next speaker in a variety of ways, one of which is by the production of the first part of a sequence that participants orient to as having two parts, the second part of which is produced by a different speaker. Adjacency pairs that conversationalists have described include question and answer, call and response, request and response, and others. Orientation to a sequence of actions like these does not imply any obligation on the part of another speaker to produce the typed second part of the sequence; instead, the sequence of actions is best considered as a normative frame of reference. The degree to which participants orient to the norm can be examined by investigating the consequences when participants deviate from it. Other means by which the current speaker selects next include nonverbal means such as gaze and orientation of the upper body as well as normative speaker-transition procedures in institutional discourse.

Institutional discourse of a teacher-fronted classroom is both structured and improvised. The discourse is, in one sense, beyond the control of individual speakers and is, at the same time, within their control. It is a means by which institutional norms are enforced and a moment in which the institution itself is recreated. This appears throughout Extract 4.3, when one individual may select the next speaker and may continue their turn at any time. In the teacher's long turn in lines 9–34, for instance, there are several occasions at which another participant in the classroom could self-select as next speaker. There are complex TRPs in the teacher talk at the end of line 9 "well, ↑think about it." and in lines 23–27 "so I have to look up at an angle about that much, right? (.2)," yet at neither of those places does a student take a turn. Students do so only when they are selected by the teacher, indexing their orientation to the sequential norms of question-answer and the gestures and gaze of the teacher. Examples of these transitions are in line 35,

```
34        does my height get different? no.
35   ?:   °no.°
```

line 39,

```
36   T:   ⌈I look smaller because I'm farther away, right?
37        ⌊((T drops his R hand and turn his head to gaze at
          the
38        students.))
39   ?:   yeah.
```

and line 53.

```
48        ⌈they're still going at the same- (0.5) angle, aren't
49        |they.
50        ⌊((T continues to step backward away from the wall toward
51        the center of the room moving his hand rapidly to and fro
52        in front of his eyes as he moves.))
53  ?:    yeah. =
```

Teacher and students are not always constrained by the current-speaker-selects-next norm of institutional discourse, however. There are occasions in Extract 4.3 when students do self-select. On two occasions, students C and D self-select with questions: in line 7,

```
 3  T:   ⌈well as he moves
 4        ⌊(T gazes at C.))
 5        ⌈away, =
 6        ⌊((T moves back out of the light of the OHP.))
 7 →C:    = if he's three feet away, would he be smaller?
```

and line 60.

```
57  T:   ⌊I look smaller cuz I'm farther away.
58        ⌊((T turns his head to gaze at the class.))
59       (0.8)
60→D:    so then it would be one quarter, would⌈n't it?
```

In line 56, a student attempts but fails to produce a full turn:

```
53   ?:   yeah. =
54   T:   = ee::: ((imitating high pitch sound of a ray gun)) so I
55        must be the same height.
56→  ?:   ⌈you s-
```

The transition between a turn by the teacher and a turn by students is different from the transition from students to teacher. There is no hearable silence after the completion of a turn by the teacher and the response by students, whereas two questions by the students are both followed by pauses before the teacher's response. The first 10 lines of Extract 4.3 show the pauses clearly in lines 2 and 8:

```
 1    C:   if he moves, how far he is away.
 2→       (1.5)
 3    T:   ⌈well as he moves
 4         ⌊((T gazes at C.))
 5         ⌈away, =
 6         ⌊((T moves back out of the light of the OHP.))
```

```
7     C:   =if he's three feet away, would he be smaller?
8→         (2.0)
9     T:   ⌜nuh-. well, ↑think about it.
10         ⌞((T raises his R arm with his index finger in the
           air.))
```

In the last few lines of the transcript, however, a question asked by student D results in a transition with no pause between student D's question and the teacher's response:

```
60→D:   so then it would be one quarter, would⌜n't it?
61→T:                                          │I don't know.
62                                             ⌞((T drops his R
63      hand and turns to face the class.))
64      ⌜but I don't wanna spend many more time on this.
65      ⌞((T raises his R hand in a gesture of refusal and looks
66      down at his notes.))
```

Why does this different pattern of speaker transition occur? Recall that the procedures of ethnomethodological CA involve investigating the consequences when participants deviate from a recognized and shared social order. The transition between student D and the teacher at the end of the extract differs from the transitions between student C and the teacher at the beginning of the transcript. The teacher provides substantial responses to the substance of C's questions, whereas he refuses to provide a substantial response to D's question, saying simply "I don't know." Although all three questions from students result in turns from the teacher that are heard as answers, only the teacher's responses to C provide information that is relevant to C's requests. The teacher provides no information relevant to D's request for confirmation that the image of the teacher's height would be one quarter of his real height and, in fact, the teacher goes on to say that he does not want to spend any more time on the matter. Although all three events are question-answer pairs, the lack of pause and the overlap in the transition between D and the teacher index a violation of the expectation that a student's request for information will be fulfilled.

What can be concluded about speaker transition in this classroom? The first thing to note is that speaker transition happens and it happens in a systematic way. Teacher and students recognize units in talk and attempt transitions at moments when they perceive units to be complete or when they can project their completion. The moments of transition are at or near complex TRPs as defined by Ford and Thompson (1996). At these TRPs, selection of next speaker happens generally by the teacher selecting a specific student or generic students to speak, but the teacher often continues his current turn. On three occasions, students self-select, and when they do so, they always select the teacher as the next speaker. A student-selects-teacher transition and a teacher-selects-student transition differ, however. When the teacher selects students, they respond immediately, but when a student selects the teacher, hearable silence precedes a substantial response from the teacher; alternatively, the teacher cuts off the student's turn on the occasion when he chooses not to provide a substantial response. Asymmetry between the conversational roles of teacher and students in this extract is one way in which the participants bring into concrete reality the abstract institution of school and is, at the same time, a way in which they spontaneously construct institutional power.

Nonverbal Resources

Throughout this book, I have argued that language is but one of several semiotic systems through which people do social action and acts of identity; yet, in this chapter my presentations of a systemic functional analysis of text and a conversational analysis of talk-in-interaction have focused largely on aspects of talk and language—the means by which lexicogrammar instantiates choices of meaning at different levels in SFG and the ways in which social actions are performed through turn-taking in CA. Language as a resource for meaning-making and talk-in-interaction is clearly not the only resource that participants employ in order to do social work in discursive practice, and C. Goodwin (1979, 1981, 1984, 1995, 1997, 2000, 2007) has shown in detail how semiotic resources such as gaze, gesture, and positioning of participants' bodies relative to the environment combine with linguistic action to create embodied participation frameworks in which discursive practices are done. C. Goodwin's work is briefly reviewed here before revisiting the interaction in Extract 4.3, this time as multimodal action.

C. Goodwin (1979), in a brilliant analysis of one short utterance in a multiparty conversation, showed how the gaze of participants is integral to the construction of a participation framework and how changing patterns of gaze do work to change footing. A change of footing, as Goffman (1981) wrote, "implies a change in the alignment we take up to ourselves and to the others present as expressed in the way we manage the production and reception of an utterance" (p. 128). These changes can be seen in the online construction of the utterance that C. Goodwin examined: "I gave up smoking cigarettes one week ago today actually." This is produced by John, who with his wife Beth, have invited Don and his wife, Ann, to dinner. Neither John nor Beth has seen

Don for some time, and John has reason to suppose that Don has not heard about John's giving up cigarettes. The relationship between the movement of a participant's gaze and the talk-in-interaction is shown by C. Goodwin (1979) in a simple transcription system:

> A line indicates that [the participant] is gazing at some particular recipient. The precise point at which his gaze first reached the recipient is marked with a left bracket. A series of dots indicates that the speaker is moving his gaze toward some recipient, while commas mark a movement away from some recipient. (p. 99)

The system is used in entextualizing Extract 4.4.

Extract 4.4. Changes of footing

```
1    John:   ...., ,.........    ⌈Don,,        ⌈Don_____
2            I gave, I gave u⌊p smo⌈king ci⌊garettes::.=
3    Don:                        ..⌊X_____
4            = Yea:h,
5    John:   ...... ⌈Beth_____...... ⌈Ann_____
6            I-uh: ⌊one- one week ag ⌈o t'da: ⌊y. acshi ⌈lly,
7    Beth:                          |                  |
8    Ann:                   ........ ⌊Beth    ........ ⌊John
9            Rilly? en: y'quit fer good?
```

John's talk is transcribed on line 2 and his gaze is transcribed on line 1. C. Goodwin describes John's belief that his utterance is newsworthy to his guests and, with his gaze, John addresses Don as the recipient of the news. In line 5, John augments his utterance by remarking that today is the one-week anniversary of his giving up cigarettes. C. Goodwin argues that John's wife Beth is aware of when John gave up cigarettes but that John believes she may be unaware of the anniversary and so, with his gaze in line 5, John addresses Beth as the recipient of the news that today is the anniversary of that date. The relationship between a speaker's utterance and gaze as shown in these four lines is captured by C. Goodwin in the rule that "the gaze of a speaker should locate the party being gazed at as an addressee of his utterance" (p. 99). A second rule that C. Goodwin proposed is that when a speaker gazes at a recipient, the speaker should make eye contact with that recipient (p. 104). In line 3, Don appears to follow that rule. Lines 5–8, however, appear to violate that rule because, in line 7, despite John's work to design his utterance for his wife as the addressee, she does not make eye contact with him. C. Goodwin used the ethnomethodological procedure of identifying and analyzing deviant behavior to investigate the consequences when participants deviate from a recognized and shared social order. He did so by pointing out that Ann, who was at first not addressed by John as recipient of the news of the one-week anniversary, nonetheless recognizes that Beth is the intended addressee and directs her gaze at Beth, thus acknowledging, according to C. Goodwin, Beth's deviant behavior. When Beth still does not make eye contact with either John or Ann, John turns his gaze to Ann, who offers herself as John's addressee by returning his gaze at the end of his turn and by taking the next turn (line 9) to comment on John's original action of quitting, which, to her, was newsworthy rather than the anniversary, which to her was not.

C. Goodwin's analysis showed that the participation framework of a face-to-face, multiparty interaction and the status of participants as addressees or auditors can change very rapidly, and close interaction of talk with gaze of speakers and hearers is the means by which changes of participation status are accomplished. C. Goodwin extended his work on embodied participation frameworks in a number of publications throughout the following years (C. Goodwin, 1981, 1984, 1995, 1997, 2000, 2007), of which his essay on "Participation, Stance, and Affect in the Organization of Activities" (C. Goodwin, 2007) is perhaps the most nuanced. In this essay, C. Goodwin described the embodied participation framework of a father and his daughter as they work on her homework together; Goodwin showed how their gesture, language, and structure in the environment combine to create a discursive practice. Although less detail of the visual aspect of the classroom interaction is provided in Extract 4.3 than is available in C. Goodwin's analyses, it can also be seen as a multimodal practice in which the teacher's embodied actions are essential to his pedagogical work.

The teacher's gestures and bodily movement in Extract 4.3 are closely coordinated with his talk. In lines 9 and 10, for example, his gesture of raising his finger is coordinated with his instruction to the student to reconsider:

```
9   T:  ⌜nuh-. well, ↑think about it.
10      ⌞((T raises his R arm with his index finger in the air.))
```

Throughout his long turn from line 9 through line 59, his use of deictics "here" in line 15, "that" in line 23 "so I have to look up at an angle about that much", and "this" in line 27 "cuz I'm this height" is coordinated by gestures or movements of his body. What appears most central to the teacher's presumed pedagogical aim of explaining reflection in a plane mirror is his embodiment of rays of light in lines 47 through 55:

```
43     now look at the rays from my eyes, ⌈ee::: ((imitating
44     high pitch sound of a ray gun))      |(0.5)
45                                          ⌊((T moves his R hand
46     rapidly to and fro in front of his eyes in the direction
47     of the wall. ))
48     ⌈they're still going at the same- (0.5) angle, aren't
49     |they.
50     ⌊((T continues to step backward away from the wall toward
51     the center of the room moving his hand rapidly to and fro
52     in front of his eyes as he moves. ))
53 ?: yeah.=
54 T: =ee::: ((imitating high pitch sound of a ray gun)) so I
55     must be the same height.
```

The teacher's embodiment of the physical process of reflection of light in a plane mirror is very different from the way that the same concept is presented in the textbook in Extract 4.2. The teacher's embodiment of the process casts him and his students in the role of human participants in the physical process of reflection in a plane mirror. The textbook, on the other hand, maintains a distance between the reader and the phenomenon by casting the reader in the role of a third-person observer. One could say that the textbook helps construct the reader as objective observer, whereas the teacher helps construct his students as subjective participants, which one of his students characterized as presenting "things you can see."

Discursive practice encodes, as Ochs (1986) observed, sociocultural knowledge. Extracts 4.2 and 4.3 encode sociocultural knowledge about the discipline of physics. We may then ask: How do the systematic choices made by the teacher and the textbook writer socialize the students and readers to the discourse community of physicists? The teacher's embodiment of the process casts his students in a subjective role, whereas the textbook writer casts his readers as objective observers of phenomena. Many analyses of written scientific register in English (e.g., those studies of research articles summarized in Swales, 1990) have identified the same features as those found in Extract 4.2. Scientific objectivity is constructed in these texts by means of the use of passives, third-person verbs, nominalizations to encode processes, and a high frequency of technical vocabulary. More recent work on the spoken discourse of lab meetings, however, has shown that in the course of making sense of scientific research, practicing scientists blur the distinction between the scientist and the physical world to "construct a referential identity which is both animate and inanimate, subject and object" (Ochs, Gonzalez, & Jacoby, 1996, p. 328). In this respect, the teacher's embodiment of the physical process of light reflection ("I look smaller cuz I'm farther away") is a very similar strategy to that adopted by the practicing physicists studied by Ochs et al. ("When I come down I'm in the domain state"). Thus, the teacher's choice of an embodied, participatory approach, rather than being a popularization of the objectivity of the textbook, may be a reflection of the discourse of practicing scientists.

Chapter Summary and a Look Ahead

The approaches to the analysis of talk-in-interaction by researchers whose work I reviewed in chapter 3 were, I argued, quite shallow. I hope in the present chapter to have provided the necessary depth for understanding the ways in which the stuff of talk and embodied action reflect and construct context. The techniques that have been developed for describing talk and action are sophisticated, and there are extensive literatures on participation frameworks, SFG, ethnomethodological CA, and embodied action. In the present chapter I have only been able to demonstrate a few of the ways that they can be used in the analysis of a discursive practice and to provide some pointers to some of the original studies. Nonetheless, a thorough understanding of the stuff of talk and embodied action demands painstaking analysis of the verbal, interactional, and nonverbal resources employed by participants in a discursive practice. Analyses of discursive practices in formal learning situations are provided in the unit on "Describing Discursive Practices" in Young (2008a). In the present chapter, I have cataloged the verbal, interactional, and nonverbal resources that participants employ in discursive practice and I have bracketed the list with a discussion of participation framework. In this closing section, I briefly revisit each one and discuss how they provide complementary perspectives on discursive practice.

Participation framework, originally proposed by Goffman (1979), is a specification of all participants whose presence is relevant to a discursive practice, both speakers and hearers, both official and unofficial, both ratified and unratified, both present and nonpresent. During a single discursive practice, the status of participants (their footing) may change from moment to moment as they and others change their attention and orientation. Understanding the statuses of participants goes beyond analysis of the transcript of the interaction, which, as Ochs (1979) pointed out, represents a theory of the practice and, as Urban (1996) argued, is an extextualization of an oral practice that removes it from its original context. It involves close attention to the gaze, the embodied actions of official participants, and their social and ecological environment. An analysis that goes beyond the transcribed words of official participants also means that the participation framework of a practice cannot be analyzed using the tools of CA alone.

The current popularity of CA and especially the attention that analysts are now beginning to pay to nonverbal as well as interactional resources has arisen for several reasons. One reason is that technology is now available that allows close analysis of the ongoing flow of talk-in-interaction and the confluence of gesture, gaze, and talk. Another reason is that, with its epistemological roots in ethnomethodology, CA has been able to show that achievement of meanings through becoming is as much, if not more, important in understanding social life than a static interpretation of meanings as given. For all its importance and the depth of its insights, however, CA is limited by its dependence on a transcript, sophisticated and multilayered though the transcript may be. As I argued in chapter 2, analysis of context beyond the transcript is necessary in order to understand talk within its cultural context, within its ever-shifting frames of participation.

All this going-beyond leaves us with the question of what to do with language itself. Although throughout this book I have argued against putting language (and especially language in its written decontextualized form) at center stage in the description of human interaction, it would be foolish to ignore the purposes for which participants employ linguistic resources. Whereas most formal theories of language have taken the functions of language in interaction as secondary or even ignored function altogether, the function of language is central to the enterprise of SFG and that function is the instantiation of meanings. Participants in interactions create meanings, meanings that are not only the denotational and indexical meanings of logical semantics but also social identities and relationships among participants, stances, and emotions. The fundamental mapping in SFG of context on metafunction and the systemic choices among meaning paradigms along the way to instantiation in lexicogrammar shows most clearly the relationship between language and context.

These approaches—systemic functional analysis, ethnomethodological CA, and the analysis of participation framework—are the methods that are used in the description and analysis of discursive practices in the remaining chapters of this book. In these chapters, analysis by these methods of discursive practices in teaching, learning, and assessment provides a fresh understanding of teachers', learners', and testers' activity.

Notes

1 Radio program "Fresh Air" from WHYY, March 18, 2008. Audio available from NPR.org.

2 Translation: "Something you should have asked is in which cases we speak
   Quichua here in the United States. Of course because you can have a normal
   conversation, but there are other situations when we use it, such as we see a
   beautiful girl and we say *oooh aligu nachu* [nice huh?]. That is, we are seeing them
   in front of us but since they don't know the language, then [. . .] it's as you say,
   sometimes we use [Quichua] as a code, for selling, for admiring a girl or to tease a
   guy, or to say that someone is coming, for all of this we use Quichua more as a
   code when we are at work."

3 Chomsky (1986) argued that it is impossible to describe the structure of natural
   languages using context-free phrase structure rules such as S $\rightarrow$ NP VP and VP $\rightarrow$
   V NP because they would allow the production of ungrammatical sentences with
   intransitive verbs such as "John upped." Grammars, therefore, according to
   Chomsky, must be context-sensitive. Context, however, for Chomsky involved
   constraints on particular lexical items like the complementation of verbs. It did not
   refer to the sociocultural context with which we are concerned here.

4 Why the rather unwieldy term "metafunction?" Halliday and Mattiessen (2004)
   responded: "We could have called them simply 'functions'; however, there is a long
   tradition of talking about the functions of language in contexts where 'function'
   simply means purpose or way of using language, and has no significance for the
   analysis of language itself [. . .]. But the systemic analysis shows that functionality
   is **intrinsic** to language; that is to say, the entire architecture of language is arranged
   along functional lines. Language is as it is because of the functions in which it has
   evolved in the human species. The term 'metafunction' was adopted to suggest that
   function was an integral component within the overall theory" (pp. 30–31).

5 In systemic theory, a distinction is made between "realization" and "instantiation."
   Realization is the relationship between different levels of a multilevel semiotic
   system and *instantiation* is the relationship between the semiotic system itself and
   the observable events of sound and writing.

6 The classroom conversations reproduced in Extracts 4.1 and 4.3 come from the
   project "The Socialization of Diverse Learners into Subject Matter Discourse,"
   Jane Zuengler and Cecilia Ford, Principal Investigators. The project was part of the
   Center on English Learning and Achievement (CELA), supported by the U.S.
   Department of Education's Office of Educational Research and Improvement
   (OERI Award #R305A60005). The views expressed here are my own and do not
   necessarily represent the views of the U.S. Department of Education, of CELA, or
   of the project's principal investigators.

7 In SFG shorthand, the caret symbol ($^$) placed between elements indicates a
   sequential arrangement and the plus symbol (+) in a clause divides Theme from
   Rheme.

8 Although, in one of its senses, "obey" is a behavioral process verb, I have
   interpreted its function here as indicating the relationship between the rays of light
   and the law of reflection.

9 *Ethnie* is a French term used by Smith (1987) to describe a prenational ethnocultural group.

10 Block's (2006) analysis of the interaction between Carlos and his workmates reported in chapter Two is an example of the indexical meaning of Carlos's action—his silence.

11 Conventions used here for entextualizing talk-in-interaction are taken from Jefferson (1984) with additions by Ford and Thompson (1996) and are explained in the Appendix.

CHAPTER FIVE

Language Learning and Discursive Practice

In his contribution to a symposium at the World Congress of Applied Linguistics in Essen, Germany in 2008, Johannes Wagner framed the question of learning in Practice Theory with three questions: What is learned? Whose learning? And whose participation? In this chapter I take those three questions as ways to begin describing and explaining learning a discursive practice. As I have argued elsewhere (Young, 2007, 2008b; Young & Miller, 2004), with its emphasis on socially constructed knowledge, discursive practice is an approach in which language learning is viewed not only as the changing linguistic knowledge of individual learners but also primarily as learners' changing participation in discursive practices: What is learned is not the language but the practice.

Focusing on practice rather than language does not at all mean that language development does not occur or that it is not interesting; it is simply a question of focus and of framing the question of cognitive and social development as a larger process of which language learning is a part. In chapter 3, I reviewed several key studies exemplifying ways of analyzing context, and in all of these studies, language was a part and language development will continue to be a part of the answer to Wagner's question: What is learned? However, second language (L2) development by learners in these studies was not considered in isolation from contextual factors. The features of context that the authors of the studies considered to be central to learning include the following: the participation statuses of learners and their interlocutors (Liu, 2000), the institutional constraints imposed by a political authority (Toohey, 2000), learners' attention to and emotional responses to the languages they were learning (Garret & Young, 2009), and the cultural interpretations of history and society that were presented to them (Baquedano-López, 1997/2001; Conteh, 2007; Gebhard, 2002/2004; Shameem, 2007). Although language was certainly a focus in all of these studies, in no case was language development construed as the sole and ultimate outcome of a complex process.

This widening of the scope of investigation into the phenomenon of L2 development goes beyond what is normally considered language learning in second language acquisition (SLA). In a view that may be considered representative of mainstream SLA, the development of a learner's linguistic knowledge as indexed by the learner's production, comprehension, and social use of an L2 is an outcome of apperceived input, the learner's affective responses to the input, the learner's prior knowledge, and the learner's attention to the input (Gass & Selinker, 2008). In this conception of learning in SLA, the emphasis is on the getting or gaining of knowledge or skill—a focus on learner-internal and psycholinguistic factors. The kind of learning that I wish to engage here, however, is the answer to Wagner's first question: What is learned? It is obvious that language is learned, but the key studies that I reviewed in chapter 3 suggest that what is learned is much more than language.

In the present chapter I elaborate on the claim that what is learned is not the language but the practice. I will examine how this claim has been explicated in several theories of learning. I first engage with Language Socialization and review the main claims of how a first language (L1) socializes children and adults to the culture of their home community. I argue that those claims must be modified for adult Second Language Socialization and show that the consciousness of L2 learners is a site of struggle between identities in which the symbolic values of age, gender, status in a hierarchy, nationality, and professional skill differ between L1 and L2 communities. Understanding Second Language Socialization thus requires an understanding of community, and I argue against using the speech community as a model because there are communities of practice in which a stylistic repertoire is shared, but not a language; also, there are other communities of practice in which one group has severely limited knowledge of the other group's language. Asking how learning happens leads me to embrace Situated Learning and engagement of learners in legitimate peripheral participation as the model of learning that I adopt, and I review the two metaphors for learning as acquisition and participation. Framing learning as changing participation requires what Garfinkel (1967) called "documents" of the phenomenon and I conclude the chapter with a review of some extensive documents of learning.

Language Socialization

The view adopted by many linguistic anthropologists is that learning a language is part of a much larger process of becoming a person in society. The approach taken by these scholars has come to be known as *Language Socialization* and was first articulated by Schieffelin and Ochs (1986). In a later overview, Ochs (2002) defined Language Socialization as follows:

The discipline articulates ways in which novices across the life span are socialized into using language and socialized through language into local theories and preferences for acting, feeling, and knowing, in socially recognized and organized practices associated with membership in a social group. (p. 106)

Although most of the research in Language Socialization has focused on the socialization of children in societies in which the language they learn is dominant (Kulik, 1992; P. J. Miller, 1982; Schieiffelin, 1990; Watson-Gegeo & Gegeo, 1986; and the studies collected in Schieffelin & Ochs, 1986 are representative), the methods and interests of Language Socialization researchers have been adopted by researchers in the related fields of bilingualism (Bayley & Schecter, 2003) and SLA (reviewed by Duff & Hornberger, 2008; Watson-Gegeo & Nielsen, 2003; Zuengler & Cole, 2005). For L2 learners, especially adult sojourners and transmigrants, the important insights of Language Socialization as a theory of L2 learning have been stressed by Roberts (2001): "Language socialisation rather than language acquisition better describes how learners come to produce and interpret discourse and how such learning is supported (or not) by assumptions of society at large about multilingualism and second language learners" (p. 108). The connection in Language Socialization theory between language and culture and the value of that connection for understanding L2 development was also stressed by Kasper (1997), who wrote, "Language socialization theory has a particularly rich potential for SLA because it is inherently developmental and requires (rather than just allows) establishing links between . . . the macrolevels of sociocultural and institutional contexts and the microlevel of discourse" (p. 311).

As Ochs (2002) wrote, Language Socialization answers the question of what is learned in a straightforward way: Through language, what is learned are the beliefs and attitudes of members of a community toward ways of acting and feeling in specific discursive practices. Those who approach a new language thus do so not simply by learning a system of new ways in which to express and interpret their native ways of acting and feeling, but also by learning the preferences and theories of a new community. For newcomers, this may or may not require adopting a new subjectivity, but it does mean realizing the differences and similarities between a learner's perspective (particularly feelings, beliefs, and desires) and those of members of the new community—which Kramsch and others have termed "critical cross-cultural literacy" (Kramsch, 1996, 1997; Kramsch & Nolden, 1994). What is learned by children and newcomers is how members of a community acknowledge and respond to displays of knowledge and emotion and the ways that actions and identities are interpreted in the community.

Explaining how discursive practices encode societal values and socialize participants to social and cultural values is a question of pragmatics and envisages a function for language that goes far beyond the representation of factual information. Children and newcomers learn how to act in certain social contexts not only by explicit instruction but also by interacting with others and observing their language and actions. The connection between language and action is brought into relief when two or three communities are compared, which Ochs and Schieffelin (1984) did in their comparison of adult-child interaction in White middle-class Anglo-American communities and among the Kaluli people in the southern highlands of Papua New Guinea. Most of the research on child development in White middle-class Anglo-American communities has focused on the interaction between a single infant and a single caregiver, a dyadic interaction that is considered to be primary within this social group. In addition, the caregiver's language has been described as a simplified Baby Talk register (Ferguson, 1977), and many believe that the purpose of Baby Talk is to simplify speech in order to aid the infant's comprehension. In contrast, Schieffelin's (1990) research showed that Kaluli mothers organize interaction among three or more participants in which the infant is oriented away from the mother and the Kaluli adults do not simplify their speech when addressing the infant because they believe it will inhibit the child's speech development.

Because interactions between infants and caregivers in these two communities are so different, what the White middle-class infant and the Kaluli infant learn of discourse and culture also differs; for example, learning the tactics of turn-taking in a dyadic interaction—including selection of next speaker and recognition of transition relevance places in an ongoing turn—is a very different task from learning the tactics of turn-taking in a multiparty interaction. The construction of social identities by means of the interaction for the infant and caregivers also differs. In White middle-class dyadic interaction, the individual child and adult co-construct clear and reciprocal identities, whereas in the multiparty Kaluli interaction, individual roles are more complex.

The interpretation of SLA as Second Language Socialization has been made by a number of scholars, whose work has been conveniently categorized by Zuengler and Cole (2005) according to the institutional contexts of learning. The socialization of children in kindergarten and elementary school was studied by Kanagy (1999), Willett (1995), He (2003), Watson-Gegeo and Gegeo (1986), and Moore (1999). In Kanagy's study, American English-speaking children were enrolled in a Japanese immersion program, whereas Willett reported a case study of four learners of English as a second language in a mainstream first-grade class in the United States. Another study of children in classrooms in the United States was carried out by He, who observed the socialization of young Chinese American children to their heritage culture through heritage language instruction. The studies by Watson-Gegeo and Gegeo and by Moore were ethnographic studies of children learning in non-Western settings. Watson-Gegeo and Gegeo studied why children in the Solomon Islands who speak Kwara'ae, the largest indigenous vernacular in the Solomons, have had problems with academic achievement in English-medium schools. Moore studied the differences between community and school language practices in the Mandara Mountains of Cameroon and concluded that discontinuities between community classroom practices had serious consequences for classroom acquisition of French.

Second Language Socialization in high school was studied by Duff (1996, 2002), Harklau (2003), and Rymes (2001). In Duff's (1996) study, she reported her observations in a school in Hungary during the period shortly after the fall from power of the Hungarian Community Party and the transition to a multiparty system in 1990. One practice that Duff focused on was formal assessment of student by oral recitation called *felelés*, which she reported became less frequent as the society outside the classroom changed. In her 2002 study, Duff described a Canadian high school class with a large proportion of students speaking English as a second language. This study revealed the contradictions and tensions in classroom discourse and in a teacher's attempts to foster respect for cultural identity and difference in a linguistically and socioculturally heterogeneous discourse community. Harklau studied how the identities of adolescent immigrant students are shaped in U.S. schools, and in her study of an alternative school in Los Angeles, Rymes analyzed how the institutional context facilitated the telling of certain kinds of personal narratives and, in turn, the possibility for students to imagine new life trajectories through talk.

The studies of Second Language Socialization in schools cited above provide insights into how learning certain discursive practices in a new community creates learner subjectivities that are in tension with the discourse practices in their home language communities. Second Language Socialization, however, should not be seen as a process of apprenticeship through which the newcomer is gradually inducted into accepting the practices and values of a new society. As Rampton (1995) and Roberts (2001) have stressed, encounters between newcomers and native speakers are not simply opportunities for transmission of existing interpretations and cloning of native identities, but they are sites where social identities are constructed, where interlocutors are positioned and position themselves.

Perhaps the most detailed study of the battle for subjectivity that learners wage between identities in their L1 and identities in the L2 is Siegal's (1994, 1996) study of White Western women studying Japanese in Japan. The women were sojourners in Japan, not immigrants, and, in part for this reason, the conflicts between their L1 and L2 identities were highlighted. In her study, Siegal (1994, 1996) described the discourse pragmatics of four women in conversational interaction in Japanese, focusing in particular on honorific language and appropriate discourse registers. She found that socialization of the women to Japanese society through their use of Japanese was tied to what they experienced as a conflict between their gender and status identities in Japan and in their home communities. As one of them reported:

> I don't think I've found my Japanese persona yet, who I am when I am speaking Japanese—I was listening to this lady speaking on the telephone in a little squeaky voice <imitates voice> it's like, no, I don't think I can do that, it's not for me—um—I don't know. (Siegal, 1994, p. 331)

In Siegal's 1996 article, she analyzed a conversation between one of the women, Mary, and her Japanese academic advisor, a professor at Hiroshima University, where Mary was taking an intermediate course in Japanese. At the time of Siegal's study, Mary was 45, single, and a teacher of Japanese as a foreign language at a high school in New Zealand. Twenty years earlier, Mary had lived in Japan with her family and had studied Japanese with a tutor. She scored at the advanced level on a Japanese language placement test administered by Hiroshima University but chose to study in an intermediate class because she believed the advanced class would be too difficult. Siegal also described Mary's demeanor: "Tall, with strikingly short cropped platinum blonde hair, Mary was well traveled and socially adept; she applied her social skills in Japanese situations. She talked to people wherever she went" (Siegal, 1994, p. 178). In her home community of New Zealand, Mary's position (her social identity in relations with others, her occupation, her age, her gender, and her social class) was established by possession of what Bourdieu (1991) has termed "capital":

> The position of a given agent in the social space can [. . .] be defined by the position he occupies, that is, in the distribution of the powers that are active in each of them. These are, principally, economic capital (in its different forms), cultural capital and social capital, as well as symbolic

capital, commonly called prestige, reputation, fame, etc., which is the form assumed by these different forms of capital when they are perceived and recognized as legitimate. (p. 230)

In the social field of interaction with her advisor at Hiroshima University, however, Mary's position was quite different. She was a student and a woman, and she recognized that these forms of symbolic capital in Japan had different meanings than back home. Siegal reported that Mary attempted to create a humble and polite demeanor, which she believed to be appropriate for her in Japan, by adopting a communicative style in Japanese that she termed her "shuffle" style. This was created symbolically by Mary introducing herself with the humble distal form of the verb "be" *de gozaimasu*, by covering her mouth when she laughed, by uttering the hesitation marker *ano* when she expressed opinions, by providing frequent *azuchi* (response tokens of active listenership), and by often speaking in a higher than normal pitch. By behaving in this way, especially in interactions with Japanese men in the workplace, she believed that she was projecting an appropriately feminine demeanor.

In the conversation with her advisor, Mary adopted many of these behaviors that she considered appropriate (expected of her) in the new culture. Having just returned from a trip abroad, she brought a gift for her advisor's son and continued throughout the conversation to adopt her shuffle style in Japanese. However, there were many aspects of the conversation that Siegal identified as pragmatically inappropriate for a student in interaction with an academic advisor. First, it was Mary who controlled the topics of the conversation, which moved from (a) presenting the gift, to (b) obtaining her advisor's *hanko* (official stamp of approval) on a university document, (c) giving her advisor information about a conference, (d) presenting him with an article in his area of expertise, (e) informing him that she will be leaving Japan to attend conferences in the United States and Canada, (f) discussing her ability in Japanese during which she got him to say that her language has progressed, and, finally, (g) ending her conversation by discussing the tutors her advisor had chosen for her to work with over the year. In this sequence of activities, it was Mary, with the acquiescence of her advisor, who decided what was talked about, how long the topic lasted, and how the transition to the next topic was managed.

A second aspect of their conversation that Siegal (1996) discussed is that Mary never used honorific language in addressing her advisor or in talking about her tutors. Honorific language in Japanese or *keigo* is by no means simple, and honorific terms are found on nouns, adjectives, verbs, and adverbs. Use of honorific language is determined by a complex combination of factors, such as social status, rank, age, gender, and even favors done or owed. The absence of honorifics in Mary's Japanese, although it may have been due to the fact that as an intermediate learner she had not mastered the complex forms, was also a way in which she fudged the symbolic meanings of rank, age, and gender in the interaction with her advisor.

Two other aspects of Mary's Japanese are identified by Siegal (1994) as particularly inappropriate. At the end of the conversation, she thanked her advisor with *chotto dōmo, sumimasen, arigatō gazaimasu*, which she produced in a high-pitched cheerful "singing" tone of voice with the final two words uttered as a musical phrase. Siegal (1994, p. 367) remarked that this kind of singing voice is an imitation of service personnel such as may be found in department stores. It indexes cheerfulness, but it is not the appropriate demeanor with which to end an encounter with an academic advisor. Finally, Siegal analyzed Mary's possibly face-threatening use of *deshō*. This form is an epistemic modal with a wide range of semantic and pragmatic functions in Japanese. Its unstressed form is sometimes used with rising intonation to seek confirmation from the person addressed. In this case, it indexes the speaker's lack of certainty, imprecision, and indirectness. It is often used by women in conversation with other women to index harmony and agreement. The use of *deshō* to a superior should be avoided, however, because the speaker appears to be asking for confirmation of something that the superior is assumed to know. In Mary's conversation with her advisor, her use of *deshō* appeared to be particularly inappropriate and even face-threatening when she presented her advisor with information about a conference and with an article in his area of expertise. Combined with lack of honorifics, Mary's use of *deshō* can be interpreted as her attempt to position herself as her advisor's social equal because she, like him, attended professional meetings and read professional literature.

From a conventional interpretation of Language Socialization, Mary's performance in the conversation with her advisor could be interpreted simply as pragmatic failure. She had apparently not been fully socialized to the linguistic implications of her role as a female student at a Japanese university. However, her positioning as a sojourner in Japanese society is, I argue, more complex. Mary's subjectivity was a site of struggle between identities in which the symbolic values of her age, her gender, her status in a hierarchy, her nationality, and her professional skill differ between her L1 and L2. In managing that struggle, Mary both accepted certain aspects of her new identity as a female Japanese student while at the same time resisting her loss of identity as a respected

teacher of Japanese in New Zealand. Her experience is aptly described as a
battle for subjectivity by Weedon (1997):

> In the battle for subjectivity, and for the supremacy of particular versions
> of meaning, which is part of that battle, the individual is not merely the
> passive site of discursive struggle. The individual, who has a memory and
> an already discursively constituted sense of identity, may resist particular
> interpellations or produce new versions of meaning from the conflicts and
> contradictions between existing discourses. (p. 102)

In Mary's case as a sojourner in a society that Siegal (1994) admitted has
few expectations of the linguistic or pragmatic achievements of foreigners, the
battle for subjectivity had perhaps few negative outcomes. In other contexts,
however, such as that of immigrant groups or ethnic minorities in predominantly
monolingual societies, the outcome may be far more serious for the fate of the
language learner who does not accept an imposed interpretive framework. As
Philips (1985) stressed, in public education of minorities, losing the battle for
subjectivity has serious consequences for educational achievement and sows
the seeds of discrimination because teacher and student do not meet on an
equal basis and work out between them what is meaningful. It is the teacher
who interprets and defines what is meaningful, what is of value, what is true,
and what is false.

Community

Essential to the theory of Language Socialization are the practices, discourses,
and ways of knowing and feeling in a *community*. In the studies reviewed in
the previous section, community has been interpreted as a place—a host community for immigrants or the community imagined in a distant nation-state by
foreign language learners. However, the notion of community is much broader
than these geographical localities and should be taken to include households,
neighborhoods, peer groups, schools, workplaces, professions, religious organizations, recreational gatherings, and other institutions. In fact, the notion of
"community" itself has been defined in different ways by different scholars.
Membership in a community is closely related to doing the same things that
other members of the community do, and one of the most frequent indexes
of membership is languaging—using the same language or language variety
in the same way as other people. As Patrick (2002) has written, the idea of a
community has been very important in the history of linguistics because it has
been invoked in order to explain the apparent fact that groups of people are able

to communicate because they speak the same language. The *speech community* is a concept that helps to explain a connection between psychology and sociology: how what seems to be a psychological fact—an individual's knowledge of a linguistic system—connects with a social fact—interactive communication using that system among a large group of people.

In discussing speech community, Saussure (Saussure et al., 1966) invoked Rousseau's (1766) idea of a social contract by members of a community to accept the arbitrary nature of the relation between word and meaning and to do nothing by individual action to change that relationship. Underlying Saussure's theory is a community that is homogeneous in the sense that every member accepts the same arbitrary semiotic conventions. A very similar interpretation of speech community was accepted by Bloomfield, who wrote "A group of people who use the same set of speech signals is a *speech community*" (1933, p. 29). Homogeneity is also fundamental to Chomsky's approach to linguistic theory, which is concerned with "an ideal speaker-listener, in a completely homogeneous speech-community, who knows its language perfectly" (1965, p. 3). Claiming that a speech community is homogeneous has at least two advantages. Politically, it simplifies the connection between community and language, and this corresponds to a view of the nation-state as a single entity: We can conveniently assume that all Koreans speak Korean, all Poles speak Polish, and all Saudis speak Arabic. For a language learner, the advantage of considering a speech community as homogeneous is that, despite the many social and dialectal varieties that exist within a single speech community, there is a single well-defined object to study: the standard language.

The disadvantage of considering a speech community as homogeneous is, of course, that it is not true. People within the frontiers of the same nation-state speak different varieties of a language, whose grammar, vocabulary, and pronunciation vary geographically and socially; and, in many countries, different groups of people speak different languages. The geographical boundaries of nation-states rarely coincide with the boundaries of languages. This was recognized some years ago by European linguists who used the German term *Sprachbund* ("language area") to describe parts of the world where a number of different languages are spoken that mutually influence one another and where languages cross national boundaries. Geographical boundaries do not make languages and languages alone do not make communities. There is a sense, however, in which communities are defined not by similarities of linguistic form but by discourse pragmatics—how people use their languages. People who speak different languages may, nonetheless, share similar discourse pragmatics (which Ochs, 1996, has termed the Universal Culture Principle) in such discursive practices as greetings, judgments about what topics are acceptable in polite conversation, or how to organize turn-taking. In the model of *Sprachbund*, parts of the globe where practices and discourse pragmatics are shared across language boundaries have been called a *Sprechbund* or "speech area."[1]

In the modern world, with frequent movement of people across national boundaries, the concept of community has become much less bound to physical location. Members of a virtual community, for example, may have very little face-to-face contact and still create a community by shared uses of language in computer-mediated communication. In addition, use of language is only one way in which individuals create a community. As Erickson (1992, 2004) pointed out in his study of a dinner-table conversation among members of an Italian American family, rhythmic coordination of talk with gesture, posture, gaze, and activity is a crucial part of identifying a group of individuals as a community.

If L2 learning involves socialization to (or at least critical recognition of) the discursive practices of a community and if communities are not necessarily defined by their physical location or by a shared language, in what other ways can community be defined? An answer to that question has been provided by Wenger (1998), who extended the meaning of community beyond location and language to what he termed a *community of practice*. Morgan (2004, p. 6) provided the following example of a community of practice that unites two individuals across geography and language "barriers": the French Hip Hop artist MC Solaar and the American Hip Hop artist Guru.

> In the prelude to their music video "Le Bien, Le Mal—The Good, The Bad," MC Solaar telephones Guru to arrange a meeting. [...] MC Solaar is in Paris and speaks to Guru in French using *verlan* – urban French vernacular that incorporates movement of syllables and deletion of consonants. Guru is in New York and uses hip hop terminology and African American English ... as he talks to MC Solaar.

Paris

MC Solaar: C'est longtemps depuis qu'on a vu Guru Gangstarr.
            (It's been a long time since we've seen Guru from Gangstarr.)
            C'est pas cool, s'il venait a Paris?
            (It will be fly [very cool] if he comes to Paris.)
Friend: Ouais.
            (Yeah)
MC Solaar: On essait de l'appler
            (Let's give him a call.)

New York

Guru (on phone):   Hello – who dis? Solaar! What up Man? Yeah!
No I'm comin' man. I know I'm late Yo! Hold up for me
al(r)ight. Baby! I'm on my way now al(r)ight! Peace!

At the end of the conversation, Guru leaves to meet MC Solaar and
descends stairs into a New York subway. When he ascends the subway, he
is in Paris!

What evidence is there of community in Morgan's description of this short
interaction? It is certainly different from a speech community because the
two artists live in different parts of the world and speak different languages,
but it can be interpreted as a community of practice. According to Wenger,
a community of practice is formed by three essential dimensions: (a) mutual
engagement in activity with other members of the community, (b) an endeavor
that is considered to be of relevance to all members of the community, and (c)
a repertoire of language varieties, styles, and ways of making meaning that is
shared by all members of the community. Wenger illustrated how these three
dimensions are related in a community of practice in Figure 5.1.

Mutual engagement is certainly a feature of the interaction between MC
Solaar and Guru. Both are involved in the production of a music video and,

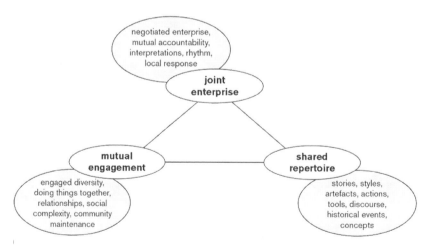

Figure 5.1 Dimensions of practice in a community of practice (Wenger, 1998, p. 73,
Figure 2.1). From Wenger, E. (1998). *Communities of practice: Learning, meaning, and
identity.* Cambridge, UK & New York: Cambridge University Press. Reproduced with
permission.

although this project may be of limited duration, while they are doing it together they are certainly mutually engaged. The question of joint enterprise is whether, beyond their mutual engagement in the production of the music video, they share goals in a larger undertaking. That undertaking is the production of Hip Hop music, which both artists do, sometimes independently and, on this occasion, together. What distinguishes Hip Hop from other communities is a shared repertoire and, in fact, the *Sprechbund* is a particularly useful concept for describing Hip Hop. Hip Hop has stylistic characteristics like rapping, rhyme, and beatboxing, but these styles can be performed in different languages and, in some cases, independently of language. Other features of Hip Hop also extend beyond language boundaries and include musical style, clothing, and association with minorities. Although Hip Hop transcends national boundaries, the idea of a Hip Hop community has been invoked by Alim (2004), who reminded us of the traditional relationship between language and nation by referring to the shared repertoire as "Hip Hop Nation Language." There is, of course, no geographical entity called Hip Hop Nation, and Hip Hop Nation Language is a collection of styles "spoken" in so many different places that it has been defined by Cran and MacNeill (2005) as "a universoul-sonic force being adopted and adapted by youth around the planet, in countries as distant and diverse as Mexico, Cuba, France, Bulgaria, Ghana, Pakistan, Japan, Australia and many more."

I take Hip Hop as an example in order to demonstrate that although a common language is not necessarily a dimension of a community of practice, a shared repertoire of styles is. In many communities, however, a shared language *does* form part of a shared repertoire, although not every member of the community may have access to the same communicative resources in the language. This is often the case in intercultural communication, and where individuals are not mutually engaged in a joint enterprise, the lack of community may lead to misunderstandings and discrimination against one group. This is not the case, however, in contexts in which communities of practice have developed around mutual participation in a joint enterprise, even when members have differential access to a shared communicative repertoire. Sunaoshi (2005) described just such a community, whose members include Japanese technical advisers and American workers on the production floor of a Japanese manufacturing company operating in the American Deep South. In the company's plants in the United States, workers stamp panels for automobiles using the dies that the company manufactures. All of the managers, engineers, and technical support personnel are sent from Japan to the U.S. plants, where they train local workers inexperienced in die modification and panel production. In one main area of the plant, Japanese support personnel and their American co-workers work on fixing dies, while in another, they work together to stamp panels using powerful presses. Because all Japanese and American co-workers are involved in the production of automobile panels and in fixing problems with the stamping process when they arise, they participate in a joint enterprise.

Mutual engagement of the Japanese and American co-workers is described by Sunaoshi (2005) in a series of five vignettes in which Japanese and American co-workers are engaged in talk aimed at resolving issues in the die stamping process. In these vignettes, the Japanese support personnel demonstrate limited proficiency in English, but participants compensate for these limited linguistic resources by creative use of nonlinguistic resources, including paralinguistic elements, gaze, gesture, body positioning, and artifacts. Both facets of the communication can be seen in Extract 5.1, in which Rob, an American worker in the Die area of the plant, brings up the need to order more grind wheels because there is only one remaining. He reports his concern to Hashida, a Japanese supporter. Sunaoshi's description of the interaction continues:

Extract 5.1 When do we get more grind wheels?

Rob reports to Hashida that Glen in the Tools department said it would take one month for [the grind wheels] to arrive. Rob also knows that Okano, the team leader of the Die area, has perhaps ordered more as well. Since 1 month is obviously unacceptable, they decide to ask Okano to order them directly from the vendor, who can ship them more quickly. The extract continues up to the point where Hashida finds out that it will take 1 month and shares his disbelief with Rob[2]:

1	Rob:	grind wheels?
2	Hashida:	Yeh
3	Rob:	uh: Glen ordered + two hundred.
4	Hashida:	two hundred?
5	Rob:	{yesterday} { }
6	Hashida:	a: yesterday?
7	Rob:	{yesterday} { }. + today maybe Okano order also.
8	Hashida:	{ } uh + four/ four hundred?
9	Rob:	I don' know I'll talk to Okano-*san*,
10	Hashida:	{eh}
11	Rob:	see how many he ordered
12	Hashida:	uh: + {*ha:* [yeah]}. {*ha:* [yeah]}. + but: from Japan?=

```
13      Rob:    =from Japan maybe.      he says one month.
14   Hashida:                      ah              one mon[th?
15      Rob:                                         [one
        mo/(I know){ }{ }{ } I said eh      no good we
        only have one
16   Hashida:                                  yeah
        oh yeah
```

(Sunaoshi, p. 196)

Rob and Hashida have no difficulty in communicating that more grind wheels have been ordered, and both understand that perhaps two separate orders for a total of 400 have gone in. They also both understand that it will take one month for the grind wheels to arrive from Japan, which is too long because there is only one grind wheel left at the plant. They achieve the task of understanding the problem and a shared sense of dissatisfaction at the length of time that the order will take to arrive despite their linguistic limitations. In Sunaoshi's (2005) close analysis of this and four other interactions, she attributes successful intercultural communication to the positioning of the two parties in the vertical hierarchy of the company, their recognition of each other's skills, their shared work knowledge and goals, and the time they have spent together (Hashida has spent considerable time as a technical supporter). In other words, their shared knowledge of historical events, social positioning, and task-oriented discourse are what function as a shared repertoire in the community of practice. Much less importance is given to Rob's knowledge of Japanese and Hashida's knowledge of English.

Situated Learning

In the preceding pages, I have argued that Second Language Socialization involves socialization of individuals to a community of practice and, in fact, within Practice Theory's emphasis on socially constructed knowledge, what is learned is not primarily language but local practices associated with membership in a community. A community of practice is formed by mutual engagement of individuals in an endeavor that is considered relevant by members of the community, and one dimension of that endeavor is a repertoire of communicative styles that is shared by members. A theory of learning appropriate to entering a community of practice was put forward by Lave and Wenger (1991), who maintained that learning is a situated activity that has as its central defining characteristic a process they called *Legitimate Peripheral Participation*. This term describes the incorporation of a learner into activities of communities of practice, beginning as a newcomer—a legitimated (recognized) participant on the edges (periphery) of the community of practice—and moving through a series of increasingly expert participant statuses as the learner's knowledge and skills develop.

The contexts of learning described by Lave and Wenger (1991) involve adults participating in five new communities: Mayan-speaking midwives in Mexico, tailors in Liberia, quartermasters in the U.S. Navy, meat cutters in American supermarkets, and nondrinking alcoholics in Alcoholics Anonymous. Through these documents of learning, Lave and Wenger described the processes by which newcomers become members of these communities, processes that may include some formal schooling but mostly involve personal and physical involvement of both newcomers and old-timers in a formal or informal apprenticeship. In addition to these studies of adults, Situated Learning theory has also been adopted by developmental psychologists as a framework to understand learning by children (Goodnow, Miller, & Kessel, 1995).

Situated Learning theory is a means of framing learning that is particularly appropriate for Practice Theory because the unit of analysis is not the learner in isolation but a unit that P. J. Miller and Goodnow (1995) termed "person-participating-in-a-practice." In a definition that recalls the presentation of discursive practice in chapter 2, practices are defined by B. D. Miller (1995, p. 77) as people's routine activities, linked both to the societal structures within which people operate and to the meanings that people give to their activities. In practices both societal structure and meaning intersect, and they are the basis for transformation and change in societal structure and meaning. In other words, practices are the everyday pivot between societal structure and the individual.

There are three important consequences of this definition. The first is that practices are recurrent, and because of their routine recurrence, they are not neutral to members of a community, who regard practices as having value and meaning within the community. Second, practices are goal-directed; that is, participation in practices may further social goals of participants and the communities within which practices have meaning. Finally, although cultural practices are open to observation, understanding practice is not the same as describing behavior; rather, analysis of a person-participating-in-a-practice involves understanding the meaningful action of a participant in a social context.[3] In their discussion of child development, P. J. Miller and Goodnow (1995, pp. 8–14) provided five characteristics of situated learning of cultural practices, which I have rephrased here to characterize development at any stage of the life cycle:

1. Practices provide a way of describing development in context, without separating the learner from the context of learning and without separating development into separate domains such as the learning of facts, the learning of skills, or the learning of actions.

2. Practices reflect or instantiate a social and moral order. This characteristic of Situated Learning is also at the heart of Language Socialization, in which learning to talk in a certain way involves socialization to the values of a community. Practices are also, as Ortner (1984) has pointed out, the mechanism of cultural reproduction: "Much of systemic reproduction takes place via the routinized activities and intimate interactions of domestic life" (p. 156).

3. Practices provide the route by which newcomers come to participate in a culture. As we have seen in the discussion of Second Language Socialization earlier in this chapter, however, participation in practices does not simply involve reproduction of the culture but may also be a means by which it is transformed. At the same time, participation by newcomers is conditional on the coparticipation of other powerful participants (most often, experts or old-timers). Because of the power and status differentials in any newcomer/old-timer interaction, participation by a newcomer is not necessarily progressive and may be resisted by old-timers.

4. Practices do not exist in isolation. As P. J. Miller and Goodnow (1995) phrased it, "Development may be regarded as a process of learning about options, limits, and blends that are acceptable to oneself or to others" (p. 12). Learners are not given the freedom to choose among an unlimited number of perspectives but are usually constrained by a dominant ideology, a hegemonic culture in which the values of powerful participants become the commonsense values of all. One example of the power of a hegemonic culture over consciousness was given in chapter 3, where I reported Shameem's (2007) research on how teachers in a Fijian elementary school were mystified by the dominant ideology to believe that they were using more Fiji Hindi in their teaching than in fact they were.

5. Participation in practices has consequences for an individual's identity and social role, and these are mediated by the affective expressions of individuals. Research in Language Socialization into the learning of local ways of feeling has shown how affect plays an important role in learning and how learning to express affect is an important part of socialization (Clancy, 1986; Eisenberg, 1986; P. J. Miller, 1982). A relevant example of identity construction through affect was reported by Schieffelin (1979) in her research on Language Socialization among the Kaluli people of Papua

New Guinea. Kaluli children learn social roles by making and responding to requests based on a strategy of appeal. In Kaluli, the address form "adɛ" is used when making a request (usually for food) and invokes in the addressee a socially appropriate sense of pity for the requester. The "adɛ" relationship is considered to be appropriate between siblings, in which the younger child makes a request of the older child. Schieffelin described it as follows:

> In establishing the *adɛ* relationship in daily interactions, the passage of food is frequently from older sister to younger brother. The younger brother comes to feel "owed" and begs what the sister has. The older sister has been taught to respond to this type of appeal and give, while demanding little in return. Thus to deny her younger brother is a serious breach of the expectations he has about the *adɛ* relationship. (p. 18)

The consequences for both younger brother and older sister of participating in this recurrent practice are the socialization of Kaluli children to accept the importance of responding to appeals for help and food. Through this, they are socialized to the deeply held Kaluli fear of loneliness, which is seen as nonassistance, no one to share food with, the state of being without a relationship to another.

Almost all applications of Situated Learning theory have been used to explicate learning by adults and children of practices in their home communities. In addition to the studies of adult learning reported in Lave and Wenger (1991) and collected in Chaiklin and Lave (1993), Goodnow et al. (1995) collected four studies of children and adolescents in different practices. Schweder, Jensen, and Goldstein (1995) described sleeping arrangements among high-caste families in rural Hindu India and families in urban middle-class White America and showed how the moral and social values of the two communities were reflected and created by family sleeping practices. Rogoff, Baker-Sennett, Lacasa, and Goldsmith (1995) reported their observations of two troops of girl scouts participating in the annual Girl Scout cookie sale in Salt Lake City. They related the girls' participation to the development of the institutional practice of cookie sales. B. D. Miller (1995) reported the identity conflicts experienced by adolescent children of Indian immigrants to the United States, which were expressed in their choice of dress and hair style. Nunes (1995) reviewed research on the display of mathematical abilities by people in different practices, of which she provided two examples. One was Lave's (1988) report of adults in California who were able to solve some mathematical problems much better in the supermarket than on a mathematics test and a second was Nunes, Schliemann, and Carraher's (1993) study of Brazilian children, who displayed clearly superior problem-solving ability in either real or simulated shop situations in comparison with other contexts for solving mathematics problems. Nunes's conclusions that an individual's ability (or competence) in mathematics is displayed differently in different practices has important implications for the assessment of cognitive abilities, which will be explored further in chapter 6.

Very few studies of L2 development have been conducted within the framework of Situated Learning theory and most of those published have described computer-mediated communication (e.g., Hayes, 2006; Zhao, 1996). The few published studies that have framed L2 development in face-to-face interaction as Situated Learning include Brouwer and Wagner (2004), Hellermann (2006, 2007, 2008), and Young and Miller (2004). The last named is a longitudinal study of English as a second language (ESL) writing conferences, which I will review here. The view that Young and Miller take is of learning as a situated, co-constructed process, distributed among participants. They performed a close discourse analysis of dyadic interactions between tutor and student to understand patterns of interaction. From this perspective, learning was manifested as progress by both participants along trajectories of changing engagement in a discursive practice, changes that lead the student from peripheral to fuller participation and growth of identity.

The discursive practice that Young and Miller (2004) reported is part of a writing conference between a student of ESL and his American tutor. Writing conferences are one-on-one meetings in which tutors offer feedback for writers at all stages of composition. The conferences that Young and Miller analyzed took place once a week over a period of 4 weeks. Before each writing conference, the student had written a draft of an essay on a topic assigned by the teacher and, during revision talk, the tutor and student identified problem areas in the student's writing, talked about ways to improve the writing, and revised the essay. The first conference took place after the student had written a first draft of an essay on the topic "The Most Important Person in My Life" and the student continued to work on the same topic over subsequent weeks.

The discursive practice of *revision talk* was unfamiliar to the student and, at first, he participated mainly by uttering receipt tokens in response to his tutor's talk. Over a period of 4 weeks, however, he participated more fully in the revision talk, and his tutor changed her participation in ways that allowed for learning and fuller participation on the part of the student. As Hanks (1991) suggested, the tutor's changing participation over time provided the "matrix for learning" (p. 22).

One feature of the practice of revision talk was the following sequence of actions performed by the participants in all writing conferences:

1. ATTEND: Display attention to the student's paper.
2. IDENTIFY: Identify a problem in the student's paper.
3. EXPLAIN: Explain and/or justify the need for revision.
4. DIRECT: Direct the student to produce a candidate revision.
5. CAND REVISION: Say or write a candidate revision.
6. DIRECT WRITE: Direct the student to write the candidate revision.
7. WRITE: Write the revision.
8. EVALUATE: Evaluate the revision.

In the first instance of revision talk in the student's first writing conference, his participation was peripheral, as illustrated in Extract 5.2.

Extract 5.2 The student's peripheral participation in the first instance of revision talk

```
 1  T:  mhm? [okay we'll talk about-]
 2  S:       [(do it) (.) yeah     ]
 3          (1.3) ((Tutor looks at the checklist.))
 4  T:  the supporting detai:ls?
 5  S:  yeah.
 6  T:  next.
 7          (0.7)
 8  T:  because you still need some help
 9          he:re, ((Tutor taps paper twice on ''here''.))   IDENTIFY
10          with your main idea.
11  S:  ((Student shifts his head slightly forward
12          and down to the paper to which tutor is          ATTEND
13          pointing.))
14  S:  yeah.
15  T:  u:m, the people who helped to raise me,
16  S:  yeah.
17  T:  u:m it's u:h (.) it's a goo:d a:::h
18          a good subject,
19  S:  yeah.
20  T:  but it's too::: tsk general.                         EXPLAIN
21  S:  yeah.=
22  T:  =all right? you nee:d to narrow it,
23  S:  yeah.
24  T:  to make it more specific.
```

```
25 S:  °yeah.°
26 T:  and- so: the people who helped raise
27     me, you:'re 'n talking about one              EXPLAIN
28     person, ri:ght?
29 S:  yeah,
30 T:  and- [who:'s]
31 S:       [his- h]is name.
32 T:  yeah. =
33 S:  =yeah. [(Same)]
34 S:  ((Student turns to look at paper.))
35 T:       [and-  ] and you're talking abou:t
36     (.) the pastor.
37 S:  yeah.=
38 T:  =right?
39 T:  you can say maybe:, ·hh one of the
40     mo:st important people:::,               CAND REVISION
41     (0.4)
42 T:  who helped to rai:se me:,
43 S:  °yeah.°
44 T:  wa:s my pastor.
45 S:  °yeah,°=
46 T:  =okay?
47     (0.5)
48 T:  does that make sense?
49 T:  it- it's a little more specific.=
50 S:  =ah- >°(I see) ye:s.°<
51 T:  so: could you rewrite that for us,          DIRECT WRITE
52     and see:,
53     (0.2)
54 T:  go ahead an- and rewrite this,
55     and then we'll look at your supporting
56     details. could you rewrite it? why
57     don't you put it right down here.
58     (0.6)
59 T:  °oops° ((Tutor clicks her pen.))
60 T:  °main idea.°
61 S:  °mhm.°
62     (2.6)
63 T:  °sh- you can write it right down here.°
64     (0.4)
```

```
65  T:   take your time.
66       (1.7)
67  S:   Mhm
68       ((Student writes revision.))              WRITE
69  S:   I can write it, the people who have
70       raised me, is my pastor.
71  T:   ·hh alright?                              EVALUATE
72  S:   yeah.
73  T:   um he helped raise you,
74  S:   yeah.
75  T:   but do you thi:nk um do you think
76       he was the mo::st important?
77  S:   yeah.
```

In the student's first experience of revision talk, his peripheral participation is noticeable in two features of the interaction: the participation framework and the participants' management of turns. Participation framework, as defined by Goffman (1981) and discussed in chapter 4, refers to the combined statuses of participants in an interaction, statuses that may change from moment to moment. In Extract 5.2, one way of identifying the participation statuses of participants is by considering how each participant contributes to the actions that constitute the practice. When considered in this light, the participant statuses of tutor and student, although complementary, are very different. First, the actions constituting the revision talk are performed almost entirely by the tutor. In lines 8–10, she identifies a problem in the student's draft and then, in lines 20 and 26–28, explains to him why she believes that a revision is needed. She does not ask him to produce a candidate revision but instead produces one herself in lines 39–40 and then, in lines 51–62, directs him to write the revision. He does so in line 68, and his revision is then evaluated by his tutor.

In this first conference, not only does the tutor perform almost all of the actions comprising the sequential organization of revision talk, but she also appears to take a different and more powerful role than the student; for example, the tutor makes frequent use of *you* and *your* to index the student and features of his papers in lines 8–10. The student, however, never uses *you* to index the tutor. The tutor's use of *you* helps to construct her institutional role as tutor in these interactions, demonstrating her license to identify the student's problems and successes in his writing. The absence of *you* in the student's utterances positions him not as an equal but as the recipient of the problem identification and the suggestions for revision.

One of the most noticeable features of this first occasion of revision talk is the student's minimal utterances, which are almost all limited to *yeah*. Most of the instructor's turns are completed with falling and often final-falling into-nation, which helps establish potential turn transition-relevance places (TRPs) within the turn-taking system (Sacks et al., 1974). TRPs occur at points of potential turn completion and allow for a change of speaker. In this first in-stance of the practice of revision talk, however, these TRPs do not seem to create a strong relevance for speaker transition; that is, the student can claim a turn at the TRPs, but he is not obligated to do so. His minimal responses of *yeah* are continuer tokens that yield the right to speak to the interlocutor (Schegloff, 1982). Although it seems that the student's minimal participation is constructed, in part, through the tutor's lack of elicitation of fuller turns from the student (in particular, the absence of a directive to produce a candidate revision), his *yeah* utterances show him as complicit in producing the tutor's extended turn. His continuer tokens show he is engaged in the interaction and, as Schegloff noted, these tokens can signal the listener's recognition that the speaker is producing an extended turn. Thus, student and tutor co-construct the asymmetric production of turns in this first occasion of revision talk. The student's peripheral participation is legitimated through the tutor's production of an extended turn.

Extract 5.3 The student's fuller participation in the third instance of revision talk[4]

```
 1 T:  °in Vietna:m, which has a system        ATTEND
 2      that is still° huh ba(hh)ckward.        IDENTIFY
 3      and there are (1.0) uncomplete,
 4      (1.0)
 5      °right here you want to say incomplete.° CAND REVISION
 6 S:  this this very strong?                   EXPLAIN
 7      it might be [behind.   ]                CAND REVISION
 8 T:              [backward?]
 9      it is pretty stro::ng hhh.
10 S:  yeah,
11 T:  it is- I I would suggest that you put
        behind.
```

```
13 S:  yeah,
14 T:  i(hh)nstead of backward.=
15 S:  =yeah I-
16 T:  cuz backward [means comple:te]ly
17 S:               [I think-     ]
18     I think so.
19 T:  go ahead, [you can] change that if        DIRECT WRITE
20     you want.
21 S:            [yeah.]
22     ((Tutor slides paper slightly toward student.))
23 T:  huh [huh huh]
24 S:      [huh huh]
25     (7.0) ((Student marks his paper.))          WRITE
26     ((Tutor continues reading quietly.))        EVALUATE
27 T:  °there are traffic signal control signs,
28     okay u:m°
29     (1.0)
30 S:  I- I- [incomplete (          )]            CAND REVISION
31 T:        [what can you put he:re,]
32 S:  (uh)
33 T:  yeah [it's in]complete,
34 S:       [yeah. ]
35 T:  instead of uncomplete. [huh huh] huh
36 S:                         [yeah. ]
```

Two weeks later, however, during revision talk in the third writing conference, there is evidence of the student participating more fully. In Extract 5.3,
taken from this conference, the tutor very quietly reads aloud a sentence from
the student's paper (lines 1–3). As she does so, both the tutor's and the student's
gazes are directed at the student's paper, displaying their attention to revision
talk. The tutor seems to have initiated a problem identification when she breaks
off her reading of the student's sentence and produces a laugh token (line 2)
just before uttering *backward*, as written in the student's paper. Her production
of the first syllable of *ba(hh)ckward* is marked by more breathy laughter. This
brief break in her reading and the laughter tokens suggest that she has encountered something unexpected and humorous while reading the student's paper.
After this minimal and potentially ambiguous problem identification, the tutor
continues reading the next clause in the student's paper. She again initiates a
problem identification, this time more overtly, when she pauses before and after

uttering the word *uncomplete* (line 3). She then produces a candidate revision by commenting that he should write *incomplete* (line 5).

Despite only a brief break in the tutor's reading and minimal laughter when she utters *backward* (line 2), the student seems to recognize that this perturbation in his tutor's turn signals a problem identification. He produces an explanation of the problem when he utters, "this this very strong?" (line 6). Although he initiates this action, he utters it with a soft, tentative voice and quickly glances over at the tutor upon uttering *strong*. Both his glance and his rising, questioning intonation suggest that he intends to elicit the tutor's confirmation that his explanation is correct. Even though she does not confirm his explanation, the student produces a candidate revision, offering the word *behind* as an alternative to *backward* (line 7). The tutor indicates her return to the problem when she repeats *backward* in overlap with the student's utterance of *behind* (lines 7–8). She then shows agreement with his explanation that it is *pretty strong* (line 9) and demonstrates alignment with his candidate revision by suggesting *behind* as a substitute for *backward* (lines 11 and 13). The tutor comments that he could change the word and slides the paper toward him, offering both verbal and nonverbal directives to write the candidate revision (lines 19–20 and 21). The student produces the written revision (line 25), and the tutor continues to read the next sentence of the student's paper. No overt evaluation is uttered, but, in this case, the participants seem to have oriented to its absence as a positive evaluation because the revision talk on that problem is not recycled.

As the tutor quietly reads the next sentence from the student's paper, the student references the second problem the tutor had identified earlier (line 5), repeating the tutor's candidate revision *incomplete* (line 30). The student's utterance of this second candidate revision, although a repetition of the tutor's earlier utterance (line 5), indicates his awareness that a revision is needed after a problem has been identified. It is interesting that although the tutor appears to have moved on to a different problem (line 30), she nonetheless utters a positive evaluation of his candidate revision and confirms his suggestion that he should change *uncomplete* to *incomplete* (lines 33 and 35).

Unlike the student's peripheral participation in revision talk in the first conference, two weeks later in this third conference, the student produces an explanation for the need to revise, a candidate revision for the problem word *backward*, and he repeats the tutor's candidate revision for the problem word *uncomplete*. The student's performance of these actions points to his fuller participation in this third instance of revision talk. As Hanks (1991) described it, the tutor provides a matrix for learning the sequential structure of the practice by producing the actions in a sequence appropriate to the practice and by modeling performance of seven out of the eight actions in earlier occurrences of revision talk. In so doing, she enables the student to participate more fully in revision talk.

Further evidence of the student's fuller participation in the practice can be seen in the fourth conference four weeks after the first (Extract 5.4). In contrast to the turn management adopted by the student and tutor in the first conference, in the fourth conference the student produces no continuers, and he participates more fully in the revision talk. There is also a shift in the prosodic and syntactic shape of the tutor's turns that provides a matrix for fuller participation by the student; for example, the tutor produces a turn structure (line 5) that is particularly powerful in eliciting the student's participation in revision talk. Koshik (2002) has called the kind of utterance that the tutor produced "a designedly incomplete utterance," or DIU, and noted that these utterances are designed to position students' responses as the completers. Thus, DIUs can be seen as utterances that assist students in producing revisions themselves, but they also allow both the tutor and student to co-construct a candidate revision.

Extract 5.4 The tutor provides a matrix for student's fuller participation in the fourth instance of revision talk

```
 1  T:  yup, and is this (.) sa:ve that you wrote here?
 2  S:  save.
 3  T:  this right here sa:ve (0.8) is a ve:rb?
 4      (1.0)
 5  T:  but- (.) you wa::nt,
 6      (1.0)
 7  S:  adjective.=
 8  T:  =an adjective, [so-   ]
 9  S:                 [safe. ]
10  T:  safe.
11  S:  ((Student pulls paper toward himself and puts pen to
12      paper to begin writing.))
13  T:  oh, I'm sorry, it's an adverb, cuz you're talking about
14      walking and bikely:? biking? so it's an a:dverb.
15  S:  m[mm]
16  T:   [so] what is it going to be:.
17      (0.3)
18  S:  safely.
19      ((Student lowers body toward paper and begins to
        write.))
```

```
20   T:   safely.
21   S:   huh huh
22   T:   yeah::.
23   S:   ((Student slides paper back toward tutor.))
24   T:   °okay great.°
25        (1.8)
26   T:   safely a::nd,
27   S:   easily.
28   S:   ((Student slides paper back toward himself and begins
          writing.))
29        (2.0)
30   T:   °great.° see you're finding all your own mista:kes.
          that's grea:t.
```

In Extract 5.4, taken from the fourth conference, the tutor utters a statement but with rising intonation (line 3), and her stretched pronunciation of *sa:ve* and *ve:rb* allows her to highlight these words. The rising intonation of *verb* along with its stretched production, followed by the contrastive conjunction *but* (line 5) suggests that the tutor is seeking something different from *verb*. However, she does not complete the clause signaled by *but*. Instead, she utters the transitive verb *wa::nt* with a stretched vowel and falling-but-continuing intonation (line 5). By not supplying the missing object of *want*, the tutor produces a DIU, thereby seeming to select the student to supply the object. After a brief pause, the student utters *adjective* (line 7), completing the clause by supplying the missing object of *want*, and uttering a word that also provides a contrasting word category to *verb*. Another example of a DIU can be found just a few moments later when the tutor produces the first half of a coordinated adverb phrase *safely a::nd* (line 26). The student then co-constructs this candidate revision utterance by completing the adverb phrase with the word *easily* (line 27).

The student's display of greater awareness of when it is appropriate to produce a written revision is evidenced by his nonverbal participation and his increased verbal participation. Even though the tutor produces no verbal or nonverbal prompts directing the student to write a revision, after the student utters a candidate revision (line 9) he immediately pulls his paper toward himself and begins writing the revision (lines 11–12). On two subsequent occasions, he performs the same action after verbalizing yet another candidate revision (line 18); he then slides the paper back toward the tutor after completing this written revision (line 23).

The appropriateness and success of the student's verbal and nonverbal participation in this fourth conference are reflected in the expressions of pleasure on the faces of the student and the tutor. They both smile frequently, and the tutor utters several positive assessments throughout the revision talk (lines 22 and 24), culminating in her high praise (line 30) of the student's ability to find all of his own mistakes.

There seems to be clear evidence that the tutor and student co-construct the student's fuller participation in revision talk. The tutor selects the student to produce fuller turns by uttering DIUs or direct questions (line 16), and he participates by completing the turns. Furthermore, at the appropriate moment in the sequence of actions, the student pulls the paper toward himself and writes revisions instead of waiting for a directive from the tutor to do so. The student's fuller participation in the management of turns, including his nonverbal actions, demonstrates his learning of the practice of revision talk and his socialization to the institutional expectations of the tutor.

The theory of Situated Learning has been exemplified in this section by studies of adults and children learning new practices, and many studies have been carried out by anthropologists, developmental psychologists, and sociologists. Several studies have investigated learning a discursive practice by an L2 learner, of which I have reviewed one. All of these studies have been of either a single learner or small groups of learners because the unit of the theory is "person-participating-in-a-practice"—a way of describing development that does not separate the learner from the context of learning. In many cases, researchers have analyzed a practice by showing how the practice instantiated societal structure and moral values of a community and how those values are recreated by the individual participants. In all cases, however, the relationship between learners and old-timers in a community is central to the analysis, either as an impediment to development or, in most cases, as a way of facilitating it. The transformation of a learner's identity by participation in practices has also been touched on, as in the transformation of the learner in Young and Miller's (2004) study from listener to active coparticipant who is "finding all [his] own mistakes" altercast by the positive affect of his tutor.

Researchers who have studied situated learning have described the context of learning in detail, the change in the observable actions of old-timers and newcomers over time, and changes in the means of participation. Rogoff (1995) has distinguished among community, interpersonal, and personal planes of analysis and has located forms of change on each plane: changes in the learner's participation on the personal plane, changes in the relationship between participants on the interpersonal plane, and historical changes in technologies and institutions on the community plane. If learning is change on three different planes, then it is necessary to consider how to expand the definition of learning. This is the topic of the next section.

Metaphors for Learning

Although the verb "learn" has been used frequently in this chapter, it is prudent at this point to reflect on its meaning. If at first blush the meanings of "learn" and "learning" appear to be simple, common usage obscures a wealth of semantic complexity. I start with two dictionary definitions: The *Oxford English Dictionary* (OED) defines "learn" as "To acquire knowledge of (a subject) or skill in (an art, etc.) as a result of study, experience, or teaching," and in *Webster's Third New International Dictionary, Unabridged*, "learn" is defined as "to gain knowledge or understanding of or skill in by study, instruction, or experience." Both dictionaries provide definitions in two parts: *what* is learned (knowledge or skill) and *how* it is learned (by study, instruction, or experience). Let us consider the two parts of those definitions separately.

First, *what* is learned? The distinction between knowledge and skill that is made in both definitions has a long history, going back at least to Aristotle, who recognized three ways of knowing: *theoria, praxis*, and *techne* (Cole, 1995). *Theoria* is concerned with knowing for its own sake and is the most abstract form of knowledge applied in mathematics and philosophy; *praxis* is a more practical form of knowing aimed at performing well in the social spheres of ethics, politics, or business; and *techne* (or *poeisis*) is closer to the OED's definition of skill in an art—the productive knowledge of craftsmen, artisans, and workers in any field who produce goods or services. The distinction between *praxis* and *techne* is that *praxis* involves the knowledge of how to adapt rhetoric (public performance) to different contexts, whereas *techne* is the know-how of techniques of performance, including organizing ideas and coming up with arguments. Aristotle's distinction among different kinds of knowledge applies to the kinds of knowledge that an individual commands as well as the kinds of knowledge that characterize different groups in society. In an individual's knowledge of an L1 or L2, all three kinds of knowledge co-exist. The distinction between *theoria* and *techne* is paralleled in the modern distinction between declarative and procedural knowledge, between knowing *that* and knowing *how*, exemplified in the distinction in Young and Miller's (2004) study between the student knowing *that* adjectives take different forms from verbs in English and knowing *how* to suggest a candidate revision. Praxis is the part of an individual's knowledge that relates performance to social context, an example of which is Siegal's (1994) recognition of a weakness in her own L2 praxis of taking the role of a Japanese woman.

Different kinds of knowledge are also ways in which classes are distinguished in a society. Marx (Engels & Marx, 1941), in his critique of what he saw as Feuerbach's identification of *praxis* and *theoria*, distinguished between a philosophy of action and a philosophy of contemplation, famously concluding that "Die Philosophen haben die Welt nur verschieden *interpretiert*; es kömmt drauf an, sie zu *verändern.*"[5] In terms of social classes, those who contemplate the world and phenomena as *theoria* must have the leisure to do so, whereas at the other end of the social scale, *techne* or the knowledge of material production is characteristic of those who produce goods or provide services. Intermediate between the two is the social class of those who recognize a dynamic interaction between *theoria* and *techne* and how each can inform the other. In his famous aphorism, Marx was describing the difference between *theoria* and *praxis* as characteristics of social classes, inferring that because of their knowledge of *theoria* but ignorance of *praxis*, a social class of intellectuals is incapable of bringing about social change.

Because the three kinds of knowledge are found in all individuals and, at the same time, characterize different social classes, the kind of knowledge that is identified with a powerful social group constitutes a dominant system of values, a hegemonic culture in which the knowledge values of powerful participants become the commonsense values of all. Practical knowledge is thus undervalued in a community in which abstract knowledge characterizes a powerful social class. An example relevant to L2 learning and teaching would be the value of knowledge of grammar as an abstract system over the practical social knowledge of using that system in communication; alternatively, social skills may be valued more than productive skills in a community in which *praxis* is the kind of knowledge prized by the dominant group.

The second aspect of the dictionary definitions of "learn" is that both the OED and Webster's specify *how* knowledge and skills are learned: by individual study, by a teacher's instruction, or by personal experience. These describe the process of learning, and much recent debate in education and child development has centered on the process and culminated in contrasting views of the process.[6] Sfard (1998) has characterized these contrasting views as "two metaphors for learning": the *acquisition metaphor* and the *participation metaphor*, which have been reworded by Larsen-Freeman (2008) for the field of applied linguistics as *learning as having* and *learning as doing*.

Framed by the acquisition metaphor, the growth of knowledge through learning has been viewed as concept development. Concepts are basic units of knowledge that can be accumulated incrementally in the same way that material goods can be accumulated, and concepts can be gradually refined and combine with other concepts to form richer cognitive structures. The view of L2 learning as a cognitive process residing in the mind-brain of an individual learner has been espoused by Long and Doughty (2003) and is the frame in which theories of second language processing developed by Krashen (1982), McLaughlin (1990), and Pienemann (1984, 1998) are interpreted. This metaphor, as Sfard (1998) wrote, "makes us think of the human mind as a container to be filled with certain materials and about the learner as becoming an owner of these materials" (p. 5).

The metaphor of learning as participation is summarized by Rogoff (2003): "Human development is a process of people's changing participation in sociocultural activities in their communities" (p. 52). This is a learning theory that takes social and ecological interaction as its starting point and develops detailed analyses of patterns of interaction in context. Framed in this perspective, language learning is manifested as participants' progress along trajectories of changing engagement in discursive practices. Such changes lead from peripheral to fuller participation in a community of practice and growth of self-identity. Considering learning in this light means recognizing a process very different from knowledge acquisition. Learning activities are never considered independently of the social context in which they take place—a context that, as I have often argued in this book, is rich and co-constructed by learners. In addition, as was illustrated in the discussion of Situated Learning, learning does not occur in a single individual. It is not the development of an individual's cognition that is observed but interaction between an individual and a complex sociocultural environment that affects an individual's learning and is, in turn, influenced by it. The environment includes both the other participants in the interaction and the tools that are available to the individual. In the participation metaphor for learning, cognition is distributed because "people think in conjunction and partnership with others and with the help of culturally provided tools and implements" (Salomon, 1993, p. xiii).

The path of learning as changes in participation is quite different from the incremental process framed by the acquisition metaphor. The participation metaphor characterizes learning as becoming a participant in a community, developing from peripheral participation to full use of the interactional and linguistic resources that are available as a veteran member of the community. As was illustrated in chapter 4, interactional and linguistic resources are configured in ways that are specific to a discursive practice, and this makes it inappropriate to view the participation metaphor for learning as the accretion of skill in one specific resource, be that linguistic or interactional. There are certainly differences in the interactional competence of novice and veteran members of a community of practice, but those differences cannot be represented on a trajectory of accretion.

The two learning theories presented earlier in this chapter—Language Socialization and Situated Learning—are obviously theories of learning that are framed by participation as their primary metaphor. Neither of the two metaphors for learning that Sfard (1998) presented should be considered exclusive, however. The goals and processes of learning, the role identities of student and teacher, and conceptions of what is to be learned and what knowing it means differ from one learning context to another and, equally, both metaphors provide complementary insights into a single learning process. Comparisons among the ways that the goals of learning, the learning process, the participants in learning, knowledge, and the end results of learning are mapped by the two metaphors are summarized in Table 5.1.

Laying out the two metaphors for learning side by side allows us to see the weaknesses of one metaphor from the perspective of the other. One example of how the two metaphors complement each other can be seen in interpretations

Table 5.1 A comparison of the acquisition and participation metaphors for learning based on Sfard (1998, p. 7)

Acquisition metaphor		Participation metaphor
Individual enrichment	What is the goal of learning?	Community building
Acquisition of something	How does learning take place?	Becoming a participant
Recipient (consumer), (re-)constructor	Who learns?	Peripheral participant, apprentice
Provider, facilitator, mediator	Who teaches?	Expert participant, preserver of practice/discourse
Property, possession, commodity (individual, public)	What is knowledge?	Aspect of practice/discourse/ activity
Having, possessing	What is the end result of learning?	Belonging, participating, communicating

Note. Copyright (1998) by the American Educational Association; reproduced with permission from the publisher.

of the role of the teacher. In the acquisition metaphor, where knowledge is viewed as the possession of an individual, that individual's task as a teacher is to provide knowledge to learners and to evaluate their acquisition of that knowledge according to criteria of which the teacher is guardian. The situation viewed from the participation metaphor is rather different, however, because, as Barnes (1976) wrote, "It would be a mistake to think that what a teacher teaches is quite separate from how he teaches" (p. 139). In other words, students are learning to participate in a discursive practice at the same time they are acquiring knowledge of a subject. The social context of transmission of knowledge is one in which an identity as knower is created for the teacher, and very different identities are created for the students. If, moreover, the students' knowledge is evaluated by criteria established by the teacher, then knowledge is quite literally power, and what the students are learning in addition to official knowledge specified in a curriculum are values and attitudes toward people who have knowledge. In other words, what is being learned and implicitly taught is a social hierarchy in which a knower is in a higher position than a consumer of knowledge.

Another example of the value of comparing learning in the two metaphors and the dangers of choosing just one is what Sfard (1998) considered to be a weakness of the participation metaphor. The emphasis on knowledge as an aspect of practice and of learning as becoming a participant in a practice in the participation metaphor strongly emphasizes the context-bound nature of learning as participation. What learners learn is to participate in one practice. However, is that learning—that participation—portable[7] to other practices? Framed by the acquisition metaphor, porting knowledge from one situation to another and using it in the new context is not problematic because knowledge is abstracted from the situation in which it is acquired. However, if what is learned is how to participate in a given practice, what are learners to do when they encounter a different practice? In one view of participation, the dependence of learning on context is far too great to allow learners to port resources and a participation framework from one context to another. To a certain extent, this must be true, of course. When we find ourselves participating in a completely novel practice, we often try to participate in ways that we have learned in other practices. However, are practices so different one from another that some practices are completely new, and when we find ourselves in a new and different context, we are at a loss? This is surely not the case. Life is not full of surprises and, in fact, the essence of learning is being prepared to deal with new contexts that we encounter tomorrow. If learning occurs in a participation framework, then that framework has a structure, and elements of structure can be found, albeit in different configurations, in different contexts. It is a question that merits further investigation which aspects of participation in one context are portable to a different context.

The questions of what is learned and how it is learned are thus worth spending considerable time on, and attempting to answer them goes far beyond what seems at first sight so obvious. The kinds of knowledge described by Aristotle lie at the heart of a debate in modern cognitive science about the nature of knowledge. What I have argued in this section is that questions about knowledge itself are not merely questions about individual cognition but are also questions about the kinds of knowledge that characterize different groups in society and the power that one group exerts over others by virtue of the kind of knowledge that members of that group value. Knowledge is concepts, knowledge is resources, and knowledge is power. Getting knowledge or learning is also a process that can be framed in two ways. Does getting knowledge mean acquisition—a process that ends in an individual possessing something—or does getting knowledge mean participating—the end result of which is belonging to a community of practice? Sfard (1998) cautioned that devotion to one particular metaphor can lead to unreasonable models of learning and undesirable practices of instruction. In other words, the two metaphors for learning are two different and complementary ways of understanding the same phenomenon. The acquisition metaphor may be more familiar, but the participation metaphor is more recent, and I have therefore taken more pains to present it, but that does not mean that either one is superior. As Sfard concluded, "the sooner we accept the thought that our work is bound to produce a patchwork of metaphors rather than a unified homogeneous theory of learning, the better for us and for those whose lives are likely to be affected by our work" (p. 12).

Documents of Learning

Given that views of learning are subject to very different interpretations about what is learned, who is learning, and who is participating in the learning process, in this section I consider the documentary evidence of the underlying phenomenon. As I discussed in chapter 4, Garfinkel (1967) embraced the documentary method of interpretation of social phenomena, which involves treating any observable action as a document of a presupposed underlying pattern. In the present chapter thus far, I have reviewed a series of documents of learning in which learning was construed as L1 or L2 socialization in a community of practice. After an investigation of what exactly characterizes a community of practice, the conclusion I arrived at was that it is characterized by (among other things) a shared repertoire of styles but not necessarily a common language. Framed within Situated Learning, a shared repertoire of styles has been interpreted as practices—people's routine activities that combine both the societal structures within which people operate and the meaning that people give to their activities. Within Situated Learning, documents of learning that were reviewed included descriptions of five practices that provide contexts for development: family sleeping arrangements, Girl Scout cookie sales, hair styles and dress, and display of mathematical abilities in shopping and school. The only document of learning by an L2 speaker that was examined was Young and Miller's (2004) study of revision talk in ESL writing conferences.

In this final section of this chapter, I present a document of learning that is more extensive and has been analyzed in greater detail than any that have been presented thus far. Nguyen (2003, 2006, 2008) studied the development of communicative skills in the counseling performed by three inexperienced pharmacists with patients at independently owned pharmacies during the course of the pharmacists' internship.[8] In her study, Nguyen focused on two young students of pharmacy who had completed their formal training at a School of Pharmacy in the American Midwest. Part of their training involved learning to perform patient consultations: conversations with patients that take place at the pharmacy counter at the time when patients pick up medication. These consultations are intended to provide patients with the most health benefits from their medications. As Nguyen (2008) wrote,

> Patient counseling is crucial to the success of pharmaceutical therapy, and current federal law and most states' regulations in the United States mandate pharmacists to counsel patients about the drugs they receive in order to prevent and manage potential problems with the drugs.
> (p. 526)

After completing their formal training at the School of Pharmacy, the students worked as interns under the supervision of an experienced pharmacist in a community pharmacy. Nguyen's analysis focused on two pharmacy interns, Jim and Mai, and their conversations during patient counseling over a period of 8 weeks.

The documents of learning that Nguyen (2003, 2006, 2007) presented are particularly appropriate for several reasons. First, Nguyen's unit of analysis is fully contextualized because it is what P. J. Miller and Goodnow (1995) termed a "person-participating-in-a-practice." Second, the practice of counseling a patient in a pharmacy consultation is well defined. It is a recurrent, goal-directed sequence of actions using a particular technology and particular systems of knowledge. Third, the practice of patient consultation reflects and instantiates a particular social order, with norms that have been recognized by societal laws and mandates. Nguyen's method of analysis is also appropriate because she described the interactional and verbal resources that the student pharmacists employed in the practice, using the analytical procedures of Conversation Analysis (CA) and Systemic Functional Grammar (SFG) described in chapter 4. Nguyen's data are longitudinal, and her documents of learning consist of descriptions of changes in how the two student-pharmacists deployed interactional and verbal resources over the 8-week observation period.[9] It should be noted, however, that there is one aspect of Nguyen's study that does not parallel other studies of Situated Learning. Unlike Young and Miller's (2004) study, for instance, which documented learning as distributed between two individuals (the student and his tutor), Nguyen's data involved observations of the same student-pharmacist interacting with *different* clients. It was thus not possible to view the participation of the clients in learning because the same client did not appear in different consultations.

Nguyen (2003) analyzed different discursive aspects of the practice. She looked first at how the two student pharmacists sequenced the actions in the consultations, focusing in particular on the ordering of the pharmacists' advice to their patients and their reference to the prescribing doctor's instructions and how smoothly the pharmacists transitioned from one action to the next in the consultations. She then considered how far the pharmacists elaborated their instructions and their discussion of the symptoms and prognoses of their patients' diseases and the frequency with which the pharmacists used technical terms and unpacked them in nonspecialist language. The third aspect of the practice that Nguyen examined was how the pharmacists constructed participation structures for themselves as experts and as members of the same social group as the patients. Finally, one aspect of the practice that Nguyen analyzed but in which she found no evidence of change over time was the system that participants used to allocate turns-at-talk. Throughout the period of observation, the pharmacy students employed the same range of interactional resources to claim the floor, to maintain their turns-at-talk, and to allocate a turn to the next speaker. Because of the extent and depth of Nguyen's analyses, they cannot be reproduced in full here. In two subsequent essays, however, Nguyen elaborated on two aspects of the practice in which documents of learning are particularly clear, and it is these that I review.

In her 2006 article, Nguyen analyzed changes in the participant status of the pharmacy intern Jim in patient consultations. She showed how, in patient consultations, Jim displayed expertise in pharmacology but was initially insensitive to context. In later consultations, Jim achieved a different interactional style by which his expertise was deployed only at appropriate moments in consultations with particular patients. The different participation statuses that Jim deployed, Nguyen termed *novice expert* and *experienced expert*, which she defined as follows:

> Unlike the novice expert, the experienced expert is someone who not only has access to professional knowledge, but also 'no longer relies on analytic principles (rules, guidelines, maxims)', and 'has an intuitive grasp of each situation and zeroes in on the accurate region of the problem without wasteful consideration of a large range of alternative diagnoses and solutions' (Benner, 1984, p. 31). (p. 148)

The first example of the participation status of novice expert is in Extract 5.5, in which Jim provides information about the side effects of a medication without apparently attending to the patient's lack of uptake.

Extract 5.5 Side effects of a heart medication (from Nguyen, 2006, pp. 151–152)[10]

```
81        (0.7) Pt nods
82   Ph: Um when you take it you be sure you're either sitting
          down or lying down,
83        (0.2)
84   Pt: It's the [↑headache.
          Pt makes up-down vertical nod
85   Ph:           [Cause-
86→  Ph: Yea:h. Cause the way it
          Pt looks down at purse
          works, (.) it will uh (.)
          Pt looks up at Ph
          it makes some of your blood vessels dilate and
          Ph makes tube shape with hands
          that will help the blood flow to the heart and
          Ph makes hand gesture downward
          that's how it helps the pain,
87   Pt: Oh, O [kay,
          Pt nods, takes money out
88   Ph:       [Chest pain.
89        (.)
```

```
90→ Ph: And also (.) um when the
           Pt looks at money in purse
           blood vessels dilate it
           Pt takes more money out
           causes the headache. so:
91         (0.6)
92→ Ph: Some people might even have problems with fainting=
           Pt looks up
           =so ↑that's why they want you to sit down.
93    Pt: Okay. hhh. That's how. Good.
           Pt nods
94         (1.5)
95→ Ph: So you can do that once,
           Pt counts bills and coins
           (0.2) and wait five minutes, (.) and if you still have
           pain
           Pt looks up
           then do it again, (.)
           Pt nods
           Wait another five minute and do it a third time,
           Pt makes a quick nod
           and after five minutes after the third pill, if you're
           still having chest pain [you should either call
96    Pt:                          [Just go.
           Pt nods, chops hand in the air, and looks down at
           money
97    Ph: nine one one or have somebody take you to the emergency
           room.
98    Pt: Okay.
99    Pt: hhhh. if I have [chest pain
100   Ph:                [And then:
101   Pt: I'll probably go to the emergency room anyhow,
102   Ph: There is trouble.
           Ph smiles
103   Pt: Yeah.
104        (1.0)
```

In Extract 5.5, Jim—a novice pharmacist in the fifth week of his internship at a community pharmacy—displays his expert knowledge despite the patient's apparent lack of interest in his advice-giving. At the beginning of the extract, in turn 84, the patient describes a side effect, headache, associated with the medication, but Jim does not acknowledge this information and continues to explain in turns 86–88 the way that the medication will relieve chest pain, using technical vocabulary such as "blood vessels dilate." After Jim's lack of uptake, in turn 90 the patient begins an action that is not normally associated with advice-giving and normally occurs at the end of the consultation: She orients to the money in her purse in preparation of payment for the medication. During this action by the patient, Jim does not design his extended turn 95 to match the patient's action but continues to display his professional knowledge. Although Jim is providing advice about how to administer the medication, he shows no awareness of the patient's lack of uptake until, in turns 96–101, they both agree that it is necessary to go to the emergency room if chest pain continues. In this consultation, Jim displays his technical expertise independently of the local conditions of the interaction but, as Nguyen wrote, the co-construction of the identity of an *experienced expert* may involve withholding professional information rather than displaying it in a context where the recipient is not receptive.

In contrast, three weeks later during Jim's internship at the same community pharmacy, he displays technical knowledge only when it is sequentially appropriate and he also aligns himself with the patient's stance toward a previous medication. Extract 5.6 is evidence of the change in Jim's participant role from novice expert to experienced expert.

Extract 5.6 Side effects of a laxative (from Nguyen, 2006, p. 153)

```
108 Ph: If it tastes bad, ↓it probably doesn't have a good
        taste, (.) you might wanna put in like a lemonade, or
        something like that, [it usually will (0.2) take the
        Ph grimaces, waving hand laterally
109 Pt:                      [((breathy)) Ah:.
110 Ph: edge off a little bit, °but it's°=
111 Pt: =Yes. The last time (.) that I tried this, it was just
        a gra:y (.) [thing,
112 Ph:             [Yeah.
113 Pt: But that's not as ba:d as some.
114     (0.2)
115 Pt: I mean. heh.
116     (0.7)
117 Pt: So that's good,
118 Ph: Better than Magnesium,
        Ph puts bottle into bag, smiles
        (.) Citrate?
```

```
119 Pt: hhhh.
120     (.)
121 Pt: That's kind of a nice sort of (medicine). It helps your
        body
        Ph walks toward other counter
        balance just very much ( ).
122 Ph: A little bit more harsh.=
        Ph turns body toward patient
123 Pt: =Oh. yeah.
124     (2.6) Ph comes back to counter with stapler
125 Ph: Yeah the- Magnesium Citrate,
        Ph staples receipt to bag
        it's more of a stimulant sort of a, (.) effect, this
        works a little bit differently, it k- it causes your
        body to draw fluid into the large intestine and that
        softens the stoo:l, (.) [a little bit
126 Pt:                          [Mhmm
        Pt nods
127 Ph: rather than being a laxative [it's more of a stool
        softener,
128 Pt:                                      [Ahhh.
        Pt nods
129 Pt: ↑A:hhhh,
130 Ph: But it also have some laxating effects, it doesn't
        draw- so it does draw quite a bit of
        Ph raises eyebrows
        water in.
131     (0.2)
132 Ph: So:. I think it will help you.
        Ph straightens bag up
133 Pt: Then I'll keep my water intake high then.
134 Ph: Yeah.
        Ph makes quick double nods
```

In turns 108–110 of Extract 5.6, Jim aligns with the patient's stance toward the taste of the medication by describing what he believes it to be and by suggesting a way to improve it—an alignment with patient's stance that was absent three weeks earlier in his internship. The consultation continues in turn 111 with the patient recalling the taste of another medication that she had used, which she refers to as "a gray thing." Jim then goes on to give the previous medication its official name of "Magnesium Citrate" and again aligns with the patient's negative reaction to the taste. In this instance, however, Jim provides a direct assessment of the taste of the medication that he is dispensing by saying in turn 118 that it is "better than Magnesium Citrate." In the following turns 125–132 comparing the effects of Magnesium Citrate with the medication that he is now dispensing, Jim's display of expertise emerges sequentially after the patient has raised the topic in turn 121. The difference between Jim's displays of expertise in Extract 5.6 and in Extract 5.5 is significant because, as Nguyen wrote, "His use of technical expressions at this particular point in this particular meeting thus suggests a *selective* display of expert behaviors, a clear contrast to his consultation three weeks earlier" (p. 153).

Nguyen (2006) goes on to show how during his internship Jim developed other skills in patient consultations, including his responses to patients' challenges, the development of a shared perspective with his patients toward medication and toward the technical language provided in the patient information slips that are provided with every prescription. As his participation status as novice expert developed, Jim was able to utilize interactional and verbal resources more skillfully, both in displaying his expertise and in maintaining a stance of alignment with his patients—both of which are, according to Nguyen, important attributes of an experienced expert.

In the second document of learning that I have extracted from Nguyen's research (Nguyen, 2008), she shows how another student pharmacist, Mai, changed the sequence of actions during patient consultations and how she achieved smoother transitions between actions. A template of actions in patient consultation includes two actions that form part of a sequence of advice-giving. The pharmacist refers to the doctor's prescription, including how frequently the medication should be taken and for how long, and the method by which it should be administered. The pharmacist also provides his/her own advice to the patient without referring to the doctor's prescription. These two actions are usually performed by experienced pharmacists in a fixed sequence: The doctor's instructions are given first, followed, if necessary, by an elaboration by the pharmacist. By referring to the doctor's instructions (in many cases, indexing the instructions by gesture and by referring to the doctor by name or simply as "they") the pharmacist creates a participation structure for the doctor as author of the words that the pharmacist utters. The doctor's status is also principal, whose position is established by the words uttered and creates a context for the instructions that the pharmacist gives. Extract 5.7 is an example of how those two actions occur in sequence in a patient consultation from Mai's sixth week as an intern in a community pharmacy. The medication is a topical steroid cream.

Extract 5.7 Doctor's and pharmacist's instructions (from Nguyen, 2008, p. 536)

```
29 Ph: .hhh uhm the instructions here is to
       points to bottle label
       apply twice daily or three times daily,
30     (.)
31 Ph: Okay, so you can go- (0.2) two to three times, [depending on
       how you feel,
       hand gesture outward away from bottle
32 Pt:                                                [Okay,
                                                       nods
33 Pt: Mmhm,
       Nods
34 Ph: Usually you wa- (.) after you've put it on you wanna to make
       sure (.) to leave it on for about twenty minute to half an
       hour, make sure that it absorb, .hh and
                                    twist cap to open bottle
       ↑all you need is just like a <thin film> over it.
35                                  Pt nods
```

The doctor is invoked as author by Mai in turn 29 of Extract 5.7 by reference to "the instructions" and by pointing to the label on the medication.[11] Mai then, in turn 31, repeats the instructions about how often to use the medication and provides further advice on how to administer the cream in turn 34. In the consultation reproduced here, the doctor's instructions precede Mai's repetition and advice, and the patient's only responses are verbal and gestural receipt tokens in turns 32, 33, and 35. However, Nguyen cited an earlier consultation performed by Mai in which the pharmacist does not precede her own advice by reference to the doctor's prescription. In this case, Nguyen reported, "there were several instances of interactional trouble which were evident in the patient's lack of immediate receipt of the pharmacist's advice" (p. 536). Perhaps as a result of Mai's experience of interactional trouble that occurred when she changed the sequence of doctor's instructions and pharmacist's advice, over time she changed toward a less problematic sequence, specifically invoking the doctor as author before giving her own advice.

Another aspect of sequence organization that changed throughout Mai's internship was the way in which she transitioned between actions. As Nguyen

(2008) remarked, in practices in which participants are familiar with the sequential organization of actions, they can project what will happen next, and when one action ends, the next action emerges rhythmically. In the early weeks of Mai's internship, she appeared unsure of the sequential organization of the practice and her transitions were markedly disfluent; later in her internship, Mai's initiation of the next action in the sequence that made up the patient consultation changed to be more fluid. Extract 5.8 is from Mai's second week in the community pharmacy and illustrates her problematic transitions.

Extract 5.8 Mai's problematic transition during week 2 of her internship

```
29   Ph: Uhm. (.) What did your doctor say that
         holds bottle up in mid-air
         you take this one ((creaky)) for:,
30       (.)
31   Ph: °Did he say°?
32       (.)
33   Pt: U::h. Ei dee dee?
34   Ph: °Ei dee dee°,
         Nods
35→      (1.0) Ph about to write on paper, shifts it sideways,
         then slightly lifts receipt label and lets it drop. Pt
         looks down at counter area
36→  Ph: So basically this um- (0.3)
         gazes down
         ↑Usually most people once they've
         gazes up at Pt
                      Pt looks up
         start this uh they will have probably have to (.) you
         know be on it for a while,
37   Pt: Okay,
         nods
```

In turns 29–34, Mai asks the patient about the illness for which the doctor had prescribed the medication, and the patient replies that it was A.D.D. (Attention Deficit Disorder). In turn 34, Mai acknowledges receipt of this information, but she appears to be unsure as to how to proceed. In turn 35, Mai shifts her gaze from the patient to the paper in front of her, on which she seems about to write but does not. In the following turn 34, she turns her gaze away from the paper on the desk in front of her and gazes at the patient. The patient appears just as unsure about the progress of the interaction, as his gaze follows Mai's, first down to the paper between them and then returns to direct his gaze at Mai only in turn

36, after Mai has begun a new action of describing for how long the medication should be taken. Over the length of her 8-week observation, Nguyen (2008) noticed developing fluency of transitions between actions in Mai's consultations until, in the eighth week, all transitions were accomplished smoothly with clear initiation of a new action after the conclusion of the current action. Extract 5.9 from the eighth week exemplifies a smooth transition from Mai's identification of the pain medication in turn 9, the patient's acknowledgement in turn 10, and an inquiry about the nature of the pain for which the medication was prescribed in turn 11.

Extract 5.9 Mai's fluent transition during week 8 of her internship

```
9        Ph:    .hhh Okay? So your medication today i:s
                Ph holds bottle and points on label
                Acetominophen? and Codeine?=
                =so it's Tylenol number three,
10              (.) ((Pt nods))
11→      Ph:    °Tks°. What type of pain do you have °there°.
12       Pt:    I have bad knees and I'm having knee replacement
                surgery.
13              (.)
```

The documents of learning that I have shown in this section are changes over time in the actions and deployment of interactional resources by two student pharmacists participating in the practice of patient consultations. The practice of patient consultation is recurrent, has clear goals, and instantiates a social order in which the participant relationships among the prescribing doctor, the pharmacist, and the patient are clear and hierarchical. The changes that have been documented are in Jim's context-sensitive display of technical expertise and his greater alignment with his patient's stances and in Mai's sequential organization of actions in the consultation and her transitions between actions. Longitudinal observation of the interactions between the student pharmacists and their patients and a close CA of representative consultations has shown changes by which these two novices adopt an interactional repertoire, which is one important dimension of the community of practice in which they are becoming members.

Chapter Summary and a Look Ahead

In the theories of Language Socialization and Situated Learning that I have reviewed in this chapter, Wagner's question of what is learned has been answered.

Within these theories, language learning is understood to include not only acquisition of knowledge about language but also development of ways in which language and other semiotic systems are put to use in the service of socialization to a new culture and participation in a new community. Although most documents of learning within these theories have been studied by anthropologists and developmental psychologists, the principle of documenting learning by studying a person participating in a practice is now beginning to be adopted in studies of L2 learners. This is way overdue, as has been remarked by some SLA researchers. In their comprehensive review of L2 pragmatic development, Kasper and Rose (2002) observed that contemporary SLA research had not moved much beyond the stage two decades earlier when Schmidt (1983) introduced his study of the communicative abilities of Wes by commenting that "What is new, in fact, just beginning, is systematic study of the actual acquisition of communicative abilities by nonnative speakers" (p. 138).

Close observation of changes in participation in discursive practices has allowed documents of learning to reveal changes in participant status and by inference changes in cognition. The methods of CA and SFG have proved invaluable in documenting the changes on which an understanding of learning can be founded. What it has also revealed is the answer to Wagner's second question, Whose learning? (Which is almost identical both in sound and meaning to the question Who's learning?). Just as for methodological reasons, the study of sentences in isolation has preceded the study of language use in context, so the study of an individual learner has been preferred over the study of other participants in learning interactions. Those other participants—the teachers and the political frameworks in which learning occurs—are now beginning to be studied as agents and subjects of change themselves. This issue will be addressed in full in the following chapter, but here it is sufficient to say that to ignore other participants in learning is to isolate the learner and to assume that all the learner's changes of participation and cognition arise from a simple interaction between input and existing knowledge. As Larsen-Freeman and Cameron (2008) have argued, language learning is not the taking in of linguistic forms by learners but the constant adaptation of learners' linguistic and interactional resources. Learners adapt resources in the recurrent performance of a practice with different participants and they reconfigure those resources to meet the demands and affordances of unfamiliar practices. It is the participation framework of the practice that affords the possibility for coadaptation and colearning by all participants because what is learned is not the language but participation in the practice.

Notes

1 The German term *der Sprachbund* is built from the nouns *die Sprache* (language) and *der Bund* (bond or alliance), thus the use of the term in sociolinguistics to mean a group of languages that are structurally similar because of their geographical proximity. The first part of the contrasting term *der Sprechbund* is the verb *sprechen* (to speak) and thus *Sprechbund* has been used in English to refer to shared ways of speaking that go beyond language boundaries. Both Hymes (1972) and Romaine (2000) attributed the term *Sprechbund* to the Prague School linguist Jiří V. Neustupný.

2 Sunaoshi's transcription conventions are as follows: "+" indicates a short pause; 'underline' indicates stress on underlined words; "{ }" indicates a head nod; " = " on adjacent lines indicate overlap; "*ha:* [yeah]" indicates the speaker uses Japanese and its English gloss.

3 The Polish film-maker Krzysztof Kieślowski also maintained that observing behavior was easy, but the spring of meaningful actions is not directly observable: "The realm of superstitions, fortune-telling, presentiments, intuition, dreams, all this is the inner life of a human being, and all this is the hardest thing to film" (Stok, 1993, p. 194).

4 Italics in Young and Miller's transcription indicate that the speaker is reading aloud. Other conventions are explained in the appendix.

5 Translation by Carl Manchester at http://www.carlmanchester.net/marx/: "Philosophers have only *interpreted* the world in different ways. What is crucial, however, is to *change* it."

6 The controversies in the field of education between a cognitive view of learning and an appreciation of learning as changing participation were debated in *Educational Researcher*, volumes 24 and 25, published in 1995 and 1996.

7 Sfard (1998, pp. 9ff) used the term "transfer" to mean carrying knowledge across contextual boundaries. Because of the rather different meaning of "transfer" in SLA, I have preferred to use the verb "port," to call the process "portability," and to discuss whether knowledge is "portable" from one practice to another.

8 Nguyen's study did not address L2 learning because her subjects, Jim and Mai, were both highly fluent English speakers. Nguyen (2005) described them as follows: "Jim was a male Caucasian American. He was from the Northern Middle West of the US and was in his early twenties. [. . .]. Mai was a female Vietnamese American. She came to the U.S. when she was young and spoke English with practically no foreign accent, except for some minor pronunciation mistakes that were noticeable only in the playback of the recorded conversations" (p. 24).

9 Another longitudinal study of the development of interactional resources by learners is Brouwer and Wagner's (2004) study of learners using Danish on work-related tasks.

10 The transcription conventions that Nguyen used are standard CA conventions explained in the Appendix. In addition, she used *Text in italics* to transcribe nonverbal actions occurring at about the same time as the talk in the line immediately above. "Ph" is the pharmacist and "Pt" is the patient.

11 Criteria for identifying the nonpresent doctor as participant are those proposed by Hanks (1996a) and discussed in chapter 4.

Language Learning   ISSN 0023-8333

CHAPTER SIX

Contexts of Teaching and Testing

In the chapters preceding this one, the case has been made that an approach to language learning that foregrounds language and pays only passing attention to the social, cultural, and political contexts in which people use language is inadequate. Building on the theoretical framework for learning discursive practices discussed at some length in chapter 5, in the present chapter I argue for the important role of context in understanding language teaching and language testing. The focus of learning in Practice Theory is a person participating in a practice, and practices are human activities that are recurrent, have specific verbal and interactional architectures, and form the everyday pivot between society and the individual. As I argued in chapter 5, learning a new practice is a process in which we participate throughout our life span as we move from one community of practice to another. The process of learning a second language (L2) is a similar process to entering a new community of practice—whether that community is a conventional classroom, a virtual community online, a workplace community, or a community in a different part of the world.

Although the process of learning remains my central concern, in this chapter I examine two different contexts in which we find documents of learning: teaching and testing. The teaching of discursive practices in an L2 has been approached in different ways. One way is to analyze the verbal and interactional architecture of practices that people do in a community and attempt to reproduce that architecture as a pedagogical exercise. This approach I call the pedagogy of practice and it has been a way of grounding L2 instruction in discursive practice. With its exclusive focus on internal architecture, however, the pedagogy of practice has ignored the function of practice as pivot between the individual and society. This is the concern of critical pedagogy. Critical perspectives are evidenced in the descriptions of classrooms by Baquedano-López (1997/2001), Gebhard (2002/2004, 2005), Shameem (2007), Toohey (2000), and others; in these classrooms, pedagogical practices are subject to ideology and political control, and through their participation in pedagogical practices, learners are positioned in privileged or subordinate roles.

The second context in which documents of learning may be found is in the assessment of learning, and here my point of departure is the report by Nunes (1995) and Nunes, Schliemann, and Carraher (1993) that an individual's ability is displayed differently (and thus assessed to be different) in different practices. Considering language assessment as a discursive practice has several important consequences. Above all, the verbal and interactional architecture of the practice of assessment must be described and then compared with the performance that the assessment is intended to measure. Much progress has been made in the procedure known as evidence-centered test design to establish clear relationships among the inferences an assessor wants to make about a candidate, what needs to be observed to provide evidence for those inferences, and the features of the practice that evoke that evidence.[1] However, testing, like teaching, does not occur in a social and political vacuum, and much attention has been directed in recent work by Shohamy (1998, 2001a, 2001b, 2004), McNamara and Roever (2006), and Leung (2005; Leung & Lewkowicz, 2006) to the political purposes that language assessments serve in multicultural societies. Critical approaches to language assessment highlight the functions and consequences of language tests as instruments to sort individuals and to control access to a desired status and to economic resources. A practice approach to language pedagogy and assessment thus complements a practice approach to language learning by explicating these two contexts of use.

The Pedagogy of Practice

Practicing Speaking

Classrooms in which second or foreign languages are taught are sites of complex interactions among students and teachers. These interactions have been the subject of intensive study by teachers, curriculum specialists, discourse analysts, and others, and several descriptions of practices frequently observed in language classrooms have been published. One example of classroom practices was published by Hall (2004), who recounted her year-long observation and analysis of a first-year Spanish-as-a-foreign-language classroom at a suburban public high school in the United States. I review Hall's study here because she described a discursive practice that socialized students into a particular classroom community and constructed for them identities as language learners. The classroom community that Hall studied was one in which communicative skills, abilities, and understandings of the target language helped define students as members, although they did not necessarily define students as members of any Spanish-speaking community outside the classroom.

The classroom community that Hall (2004) studied comprised one teacher and 15 students who were studying Spanish for the first time. The students were taking the Spanish class as part of their preparation to go on to college. Hall termed the most common activity in the classroom community "Practicing Speaking," which she described as follows:

> First, it was, not surprisingly, the teacher who took primary responsibility for beginning the activity, orchestrating its development and ending the activity. She provided most of the talk, decided what counted as a relevant topic and a relevant comment on the topic, and moved the interaction from student to student and contribution to contribution, deciding which communicative behaviors of the students were to count as part of the performance. (pp. 73–74)

The instructional practice of "Practicing Speaking" was thus constructed by the teacher, and it took place almost entirely in Spanish, with the teacher doing most of the talking. Extract 6.1 was recorded by Hall just two months into the school year and is an example that, according to Hall, typifies the practice.

Extract 6.1 "Practicing Speaking" in a high school Spanish class (based on Hall, 2004)[2]

```
1    T:   Ok aquí tenemos Coca Cola tenemos Pepsi Cola tenemos
          Fresca cómo se llaman
          (Ok. Here we have Coca Cola. We have Pepsi Cola. We
          have Fresca. What are they called?)
2    S1:  Budweiser
3    T:   Refresco refresco sí se llaman refrescos sí y aquí hay
          refresco. Rápidamente qué es esto
          (Soft drink soft drink, yes they're called soft
          drinks. Yes, and here there is a soft drink. Quickly,
          what is this?)
4    S2:  O::u
5    S1:  Uhum ice cream.
6    T:   Helado muy bien señor el helado
          (Ice cream, very good, Sir. Ice cream.)
7    S1:  Helado
          (Ice cream.)
8    T:   Clase qué es esto aquí
          (Class, what is this here?)
```

```
 9 S3:  Papas fritas
        (French fries.)
10  T:  Papas fritas muy bien señorita aquí clase
        (French fries. Very good, Miss. Here, class.)
11 S4:  Kweso
12  T:  Muy bien queso queso hay queso aquí
        (Very good. Cheese, cheese. There is cheese here.)
13 S3:  Mantequilla
        (Butter)
14 S2:  Uh mantequilla
        (Butter)
15  T:  Mantequilla mantequilla aquí
        (Butter, butter here.)
16 Ss:  (  )
17  T:  Limonada limonada muy bien limonada sí los refrescos son
        (  ) la limonada yo no considero limonada refresco no sé
        sí no yo no sé para mí (  ) [ok limonada. por favor
        (Lemonade lemonade. Very good. Lemonade. Yes, soft drinks
        are lemonade. I don't consider lemonade a soft drink. I
        don't know. Yes. I don't know. For me, it isn't for me
        [ok lemonade please
18 Ss:  [(  )
19  T:  Clase qué es esto
        (Class, what is this?)
20 Ss:  Ensalada
        (Salad)
```

In Extract 6.1, the teacher is pointing to an image projected over her head from a transparency. The image is of various food items displayed on a table. In the teacher's interaction with her class, she points to various food items on the image and asks in Spanish "¿Cómo se llaman?" (What are they called?) or "¿Qué es esto?" (What is this?). Her questions are not directed to individual students and, in many cases, she prefixes her questions by calling on the whole class, as in turn 8: "Clase ¿qué es esto aquí?" (Class, what is this here?). Individual students provide answers to her questions, sometimes in English and mostly in Spanish. Their answers are very short, consisting either of a single word such as "helado" (ice cream) or a phrase such as "papas fritas" (French fries) to name the object to which the teacher is pointing. After a student answers her question, the teacher's next turn is a positive evaluation of the student's answer in which the teacher provides the correct Spanish name of the food (turns 3, 6, 10, 12, and 15), even when the student has not provided it accurately in Spanish. The interaction between the teacher and students in turns 16–18 appears to be a discussion of whether "limonada" (lemonade) can be considered a "refresco" (cold drink or soft drink). After her positive evaluation of a student's answer, the teacher proceeds to ask the class to name another item of food on the projected image.

Hall's (2004) description of Practicing Speaking in the Spanish class is not limited to the talk transcribed in Extract 6.1 or other extracts from the teacher's conversations with her class over the year. In addition, Hall noticed that while the focal talk was occurring, there was considerable amount of what Goffman (1981) and M. H. Goodwin (1997) have called byplay: "subordinated communication of a subset of ratified participants" (Goffman, 1981, pp. 134). Hall described byplay in the class as follows:

> As the teacher talked to the large group, the students often interacted with their nearby seat mates. While there was occasional use of Spanish in these whispered side sequences, English was the predominant code. As long as the students interacted with each other quietly, and were not major distractions to the larger official instructional discourse, the teacher did not prevent them from doing so. Thus, there was usually a steady hum of background talk among the students throughout each class meeting. (p. 74)

The official name of the class that Hall (2004) described is a first-year high school Spanish class. However, what were the students learning? They did not seem to be learning the skills necessary to participate in a Spanish-speaking community outside the classroom because, as Hall commented, only the simplest conversational skills were required to participate in Practicing Speaking. All they had to do was to list, label, and recall Spanish words or simply wait for other students to do so. They did not have to monitor unfolding talk in order to detect or correct possible misunderstandings and, because most of the practice involved listening to the teacher, students could participate as much or as little as they wished. Instead, what students learned in Practicing Speaking was how to participate in the activities required of the teacher and to maintain their byplay at a level that did not result in unruly behavior that could have affected their grade in the class. Hall concluded:

> As long as the students did not get out of hand and overtly threaten the teacher's authority, they were allowed to create fairly comfortable spaces in their neck of the classroom, talking to neighbors, catching up on work for other classes, daydreaming, and in other ways living quietly along the border of the instructional practice. (p. 84)

Although the students apparently did not learn much that might serve them in Spanish-speaking communities outside the classroom, what they did participate in was the situated activity of school learning (Butterworth, 1992; Lave, 1992). Participating in the school-based practice of Practicing Speaking is just as much a Situated Learning activity as using Spanish outside the classroom, but the context of the practices are different. Through participating in the pedagogical practice of Practicing Speaking, students were socialized into a classroom community in which their identities as language learners and users of Spanish were defined by the teacher and the curriculum. The ideology that informed their identity included recognizing the unchallengeable power of the teacher and the importance of grades that would confirm their placement in the college preparatory track. What they learned was the practice of Practicing Speaking and only secondarily the Spanish language.

Practices Outside the Classroom

The practice that Hall (2004) described has its roots in the traditions and political necessities of public education in the United States, but the nature of the practice bears very little resemblance to practices in which students might participate outside the classroom. It does, however, help to achieve two important goals for the teacher and her students: By participating actively or peripherally in the practice and by not disrupting it, the students help to construct the teacher's role as authority in the classroom and to maintain their own roles as students. In contrast to this, if the goal of language instruction is explicitly related to students' performance outside the classroom, the nature of classroom practices must be different. Much work has been done by teachers, curriculum designers, and writers of teaching materials to analyze the needs that students might have after they finish their course of instruction. Often, such needs analyses or needs assessments are done informally by a teacher in order to tailor a course of instruction to a particular group of individuals, but, increasingly, needs analyses are conducted formally in preparation for the development of a new or revised curriculum or set of teaching materials. Needs analysis involves gathering information that will serve as the basis for designing a curriculum that meets the learning needs of a particular group of students. In the case of language programs, the information gathered may be language related or it may be related to the practices in which learners will participate. Once language or practice needs are identified, they can serve as the basis for designing teaching materials and classroom activities, as well as the design of assessments to test students' ability to perform tasks outside the classroom.

One example of a systematic needs analysis was performed by Iwai et al. (1998–1999) for the Department of East Asian Languages and Literatures at the University of Hawai'i at Mānoa (UHM). These researchers assessed the needs of students of Japanese at the University of Hawai'i by asking instructors and students in the Japanese language program to respond to questionnaires in which they evaluated how much they wanted to be able to perform certain activities in Japan or in Hawai'i at the end of their 2-year program of instruction in Japanese. A few examples of items from the student questionnaire are reproduced here:

> Please read each statement and indicate the extent to which you agree or disagree as follows: A = Strongly Agree, B = Agree, C = No Opinion, D = Disagree, E = Strongly Disagree
>
> At the end of the 2-year Japanese language program at UHM, I WANT TO BE ABLE TO perform the following IN HAWAI'I:
>
> 17) Engage in classroom discussion on current events and social issues.
>
> 23) Assist Japanese customers in a retail store (e.g., making suggestions, handling money, helping with lost and found items, giving directions)
>
> At the end of the 2-year Japanese language program at UHM, I WANT TO BE ABLE TO perform the following IN JAPAN:
>
> 36) Take a taxi (e.g., giving directions)
>
> 51) Go to see a doctor/dentist (e.g., describing symptoms)
>
> (Iwai et al., 1998–1999, pp. 85–86)

Performing a needs analysis in this way results in a ranked list of activities that curriculum designers can then use to develop teaching materials and classroom activities. In addition to the survey method adopted by Iwai et al. (1998–1999), other kinds of needs analyses involve observing students involved in tasks outside the classroom and noting the verbal and behavioral demands of the task. In certain cases, particularly in the development of curricula for courses of language for specific purposes, empirical analyses of learners' needs have adopted a taxonomy established in advance of the analysis. Munby's (1978) *Communicative Syllabus Design* was an influential set of procedures for establishing the resources needed to perform the activities specified in a needs analysis. The rationale for a needs analysis, as Johns (1991) saw it, is to discover the language and pragmatic characteristics of target situations and to use those discoveries as the basis for instruction to provide students with the specific verbal and pragmatic skills that they need in order to succeed in work or study beyond the language classroom.

Examples of teaching materials that are designed to address learners' needs in specific social situations are provided in textbooks such as *Stand Out: Standards-based English* (Jenkins & Johnson, 2002) and *Workplace Plus: Living and Working in English* (Saslow & Collins, 2001). Although these textbooks do not appear to be based on explicit assessment of learners' needs, they do address some of the activities that Iwai et al. (1998–1999) considered in their needs analysis. Interaction between customers and clerks in retail stores was one area that was investigated in the needs analysis and is presented in Unit 4 in Book 1 of *Workplace Plus*. This unit is titled "Your Customers" and provides materials for instruction in pragmatics, vocabulary, grammar, as well as critical thinking skills, math skills needed in retail transactions, and cultural information about interactions in retail stores in the United States. The verbal resources to be taught in this unit are categorized as "Workplace Skills," "Lifeskills," "Grammar," "Social Language," and "Vocabulary" and are summarized in Table 6.1. Within "Workplace Skills," the authors list a number of speech acts, including apologies and responding to requests. Speech acts such as complaints are also listed under "Lifeskills" but this category includes specific discourse topics such as clothes, colors, and sizes. Specific verbal objectives are included under "Grammar" and the verbal resources necessary to perform the speech

Table 6.1 Verbal pedagogical objectives for the "Your Customers" unit in *Workplace Plus* (Saslow & Collins, 2001, pp. vi–vii)

Workplace skills	Lifeskills	Grammar	Social language	Vocabulary
• Offers service • Responds to customer requests • Apologizes • Takes customer orders	• Talks about clothes, colors, and sizes • Asks for refunds and exchanges • Complains about merchandize • Fills out a merchandize return form	• The simple present tense • *This*, *that*, *these*, and *those*	How to • express likes and dislikes • state wants and needs • apologize • accept an offer • complain • offer a tentative answer	• Clothing, sizes, and colors

Note. Excerpts pp. vi and vii from WORKPLACE PLUS: LIVING AND WORKING IN ENGLISH by Joan Saslow and Tim Collins. Copyright © 2005 by Addison Wesley Longman. Reprinted by permission of Pearson Education, Inc.

acts and to talk about the topics listed in the earlier categories is the specific objective of "Social Language" and "Vocabulary."

In addition to the presentation of verbal resources, the authors of *Workplace Plus* also include cultural information about interaction between customers and clerks in retail stores. The objectives that they list for the "Your Customers" unit include facts about retail interactions in the United States with which learners from other cultures may be unfamiliar. These include the following: Salespeople are expected to help customers; salespeople apologize when they are unable to fulfill a request; customers can return unsatisfactory merchandise; customers should keep receipts as proof of purchase; and salespeople should follow company policy on returns. The verbal and cultural teaching objectives are presented in the context of dialogues such as Extract 6.2. This dialogue is accompanied by an illustration showing important nonverbal and verbal aspects of the context, including a sign announcing "Customer Service," a customer with the item to be returned, a receipt, and a salesperson entering information at a computer terminal.

Extract 6.2 Presentation of verbal and cultural resources in a dialogue. (Saslow & Collins, 2001, p. 54)

```
Customer: Hi, I need some help. I need to return this
          microwave oven. It's too large.
     You: I'm sorry. ... Well, no problem. Do you have
          the receipt?
Customer: Yes, I do. Here it is. Do you have any small
          microwaves?
     You: Yes, I think so.
Customer: Oh, that's good. Where are they?
     You: They're across from the coffee makers.
Customer: Great, thanks.
```

In the dialogue in Extract 6.2, the customer requests help in returning a microwave oven and the salesperson (identified as "You") responds to the request with an apology and a statement, "Well, no problem," which indicates that the store accepts returned merchandize. Cultural information is indexed by the salesperson's request for the receipt, which the customer provides, and by the visual depiction of the receipt in the accompanying illustration. Exchange of the receipt appears to provide a problem-free termination of the first part of the exchange, and the customer and salesperson then proceed to a second activity in which the customer, who apparently has forgotten where he had found the microwave that he is returning, asks to be reminded where the microwaves are located in the store. The salesperson responds to the customer's request by indicating the location of the microwaves, and the second activity terminates.

The presentation of this dialogue in *Workplace Plus* provides both a contextualization of some of the verbal and cultural objectives of the unit and at the same time attempts a simulation of a discursive practice that students may encounter outside the classroom. The goal of this example of L2 pedagogy is explicitly related to students' performance outside the classroom, but there are important ways in which the pedagogical simulation is (a) different from the discursive practice outside the classroom and (b) contributes to positioning students as disempowered in a monolingual community. The first issue arises from a consideration of what Hall (1999) has termed the "prosaics of interaction" and the second issue becomes clear when language pedagogy is viewed through a critical lens.

The difference between a pedagogical practice like the dialogue in Extract 6.2 and a discursive practice like returning an item to a store is that the two practices are sociocultural constructions that develop and maintain identities and ideologies in different communities of practice. The pedagogical practice reproduces a history of language pedagogy in which a linguistic model is provided in the form of a dialogue. In the dialogue, verbal and cultural objectives specified by the material writers in advance of its use in the classroom are presented. In doing so, the pedagogical practice develops and maintains identities of students in a classroom modeled on identities presented in the textbook. On the other hand, the discursive practice outside the classroom is a service encounter in which identities of client and provider are developed and maintained. Although the language presented in the pedagogical dialogue may or may not resemble the language used in the discursive practice in the community, *it is not the language by itself that positions the participants as client and provider*; it is the wider context of the interaction, its history as a practice, the participation framework, the emotions of the participants, their goals, their identities, the way in which the practice establishes subject positions, and the ideological context in which commercial transactions occur in the United States. The differences between a pedagogical practice and a discursive practice in the community outside the classroom are irreconcilable, and it is only because of the historical privileging of language over practice that teachers and textbook writers can believe that one can teach a practice by teaching the language of the practice.

Concept-Based Instruction
The way beyond the identification of language with practice in L2 pedagogy was sketched by Hall (1999), who maintained that L2 learners can attain interactional competence in part by the systematic study of discursive practices (which Hall called "interactive practices") outside the classroom, a study that she termed "the prosaics of interaction." Hall explained what she meant as follows:

> By standing outside of interactive practices that are of significance to the group(s) whose language is being learned, and analyzing the conventional ways that verbal resources get used, the movement that occurs between their conventional meanings and their individual uses, and the consequences that are engendered by the various uses, we can develop a far greater understanding both of ourselves and of those in whose practices we aspire to become participants. (p. 144)

The process of teaching and learning would then involve two pedagogical moments. In the first, learners are guided through conscious, systematic study of the practice, in which they mindfully abstract, reflect upon, and speculate about the sociocultural context of the practice and the verbal, interactional, and nonverbal resources that participants employ in the practice. In the second moment, learners are guided through participation in the practice by more experienced participants. These two pedagogical moments, Hall argued, facilitate the development of *interactional competence* in the second language, which she defines as follows:

> This competence involves such context-specific knowledge as (1) the goals of the interactive practice, the roles of the participants, and the topics and themes considered pertinent; (2) the optional linguistic action patterns along which the practice may unfold, their conventional meanings, and the expected participation structures; (3) the amount of flexibility one has in rearranging and changing the expected uses of the practice's linguistic resources when exercising these options and the likely consequences engendered by the various uses; and (4) the skill to mindfully and efficiently recognize situations where the patterns apply and to use them when participating in new experiences to help make sense of the unknown. (p. 137)

Systematic study of discursive practice involves the language teacher and learners in systematic observation of the practice in situ (when that is possible in an L2 context) or study of recordings of the practice available through broadcast media in a foreign language learning context. Systematic study of the practice does not require the teacher or learners to be skilled in ethnography or conversion analysis, but, as detailed in chapter 4, study and analysis of the practice should focus on the participation framework, and the verbal, interactional, and nonverbal resources employed by participants. In addition, as will be discussed later in this chapter, the roles of participants and the ways in which the practice reproduces and constructs broader societal values should be considered. Analysis of a particular practice is thus framed by a general theory of discursive practice, and it is this theory as applied to the interpretation of the practice that is the first pedagogical moment in teaching the practice.

There is considerable support for Hall's call for conscious and systematic study of practice by learners in the work of the Soviet psychologist Piotr Gal'perin and his theory of systemic-theoretical instruction (STI; Arievitch & Stetsenko, 2000; Gal'perin, 1969/1989, 1974/1989, 1976/1989; Haenen, 1996, 2001). Gal'perin was a contemporary of Vygotsky and shared with him many basic assumptions of cultural-historical psychology,[3] among which was the crucial role played by cultural tools such as language, concepts, and artifacts in the development and operation of the higher cognitive processes of attention, memory, and planning. Gal'perin focused on one particular aspect of the cultural mediation of cognition; namely, the quality of the cultural tools that crucially affect a child's cognitive development. He attempted to transform the cultural-historical approach to human development into a model for the teaching-learning process. Instruction, in Gal'perin's view, is the provision of efficient cultural psychological tools to learners so that they may solve problems in a specific domain. Comparing the kinds of cultural mediation available to learners in different types of instruction, Gal'perin concluded that the most efficient tool for learners was the provision of a general procedure that learners could use to solve any specific problem in a given instructional domain. For Gal'perin, the initial step in the procedure was construction of a "schema for a complete orienting basis for an action" (Gal'perin, 1974/1989, p. 70), which is in effect a theory of the domain of instruction. The new practice to be learned is first brought to the learner's attention, not in the small stages that characterize behaviorist instruction, but as a meaningful whole from the very beginning of instruction. Arievitch and Stetsenko (2000) provided a general description of the procedure as follows:

> In systemic-theoretical instruction, students acquire a general method to construct a concrete orientation basis to solve any specific problem in a

given subject domain. Such a general method involves a theoretical analysis of objects, phenomena, or events in various subject domains. The main feature of the analysis is that it reveals the 'genesis' and the general structure of objects or phenomena (the general make-up of things). In such analysis, students learn to distinguish essential characteristics of different objects and phenomena, to form theoretical concepts on this basis, and use them as cognitive tools in further problem solving. (p. 77)

According to Arievitch and Stetsenko, studies of the applications of STI with Russian children have been conducted in the domains of learning to write letters of the Russian alphabet, elementary mathematics, and learning the grammar of the Russian language. More recently, Negueruela (2003; Negueruela & Lantolf, 2006) designed a program of STI that he called "concept-based instruction" in Spanish as a foreign language for undergraduate students at an American university. The focus of instruction in Negueruela's program was verbal aspect in Spanish (usually discussed as the difference between the use of preterit and imperfect). The concept of verbal aspect in Spanish was presented to the learners as a conceptual unit in the visual form of the didactic flowchart reproduced in Negueruela and Lantolf (2006, p. 85) and Lantolf and Thorne (2006, p. 311). Learners were then encouraged to internalize the theoretical concept of verbal aspect by verbalizing it in either English (their first language [L1]) or Spanish, both through social speech and in private speech and writing. The function of verbalization in concept-based instruction is to focus learners' attention and to encourage selection and analysis, which leads directly to internalization and concept formation.

Although few studies of the effectiveness of concept-based instruction have been conducted on children (and fewer still on adults), there is considerable theoretical support for this approach to teaching in the collection of studies edited by Light and Butterworth (1992). These are studies of a top-down approach to learning based on a conceptual analysis of a learning problem and conscious attention to the general principles involved. One particular advantage of concept-based instruction that Gal'perin advocated was that a conceptual analysis of a specific problem encourages portability of the same analysis to other problems within the domain, whereas in bottom-up learning, learners are required to infer general principles from multiple examples and they must identify a new exemplar as similar to ones that they have already met. Thus, top-down analysis, provided by concept-based or systemic-theoretical instruction, encourages learners to transfer knowledge and skill from one context to others (Bassock & Holyoak, 1993; Detterman, 1993).

At the time of writing, no studies of concept-based instruction of discursive practice have been carried out, perhaps because such studies require that teachers and learners need access to a theory of discursive practice and an agreement on its essential characteristics. Given that work on a discursive practice approach to language learning and teaching is in its infancy, the lack of experiments in concept-based pedagogy is not surprising. However, there are certain aspects of instruction in a discursive practice approach that have been investigated, and one relevant area is the learning and teaching of discourse pragmatics in a study-abroad context. Kasper and Rose (2002) conducted a comprehensive review of the development of pragmatic competence in an L2 during students' residence in L2 communities. Many of the studies reviewed by Kasper and Rose provided comparisons between the effect of exposure to the pragmatics of native speakers during study abroad and the effect of classroom instruction in L2 pragmatics. Although methods of classroom instruction in pragmatics vary widely, all teaching approaches require some theoretical analysis of interaction, including concepts of relative status and/or social distance of interlocutors, degree of imposition of an action, and different conceptions of politeness in the L1 and L2 communities. To the extent that instruction in pragmatics provides learners with a theory of discursive practice in an L2 community, it is top down and concept based. On the other hand, exposure to interactions with native speakers of an L2 during study abroad provides learners with considerable empirical information and experience about discursive practice. Whether, through his bottom-up process, learners can attend to that information in order to learn the pragmatics of the new community and position themselves as members of a new community of practice *without previous instruction* is, in effect, a question about the effectiveness of concept-based instruction—a question that Kasper and Rose examined in considerable detail.

The studies that Kasper and Rose (2002) reviewed dispelled what they termed three "myths" about the effect of study abroad on learning pragmatics of an L2. They summarized the results of their survey in these words: "For developing pragmatic ability, spending time in the target community is no panacea, length of residence is not a reliable predictor, and L2 classrooms can be a productive social context" (p. 230). To reframe Kasper and Rose's findings for the present discussion of teaching and learning: Exposure alone to discursive practice in an L2 community is not an efficient instructional strategy, no matter how long or how intense that exposure is. A more efficient strategy is to encourage students to attend to the differences between the architecture of discursive practice in their home community and in the L2 community and to do so *in advance of immersion in the L2 community*—in other words, to encourage students to theorize about practice before they participate in it.

In the context of study abroad without concept-based instruction, learners face difficulties in participating in those practices that are superficially similar to practices in their own community but in fact have very different architectures. The serious cross-cultural misunderstandings that can result are eloquently described by Kinginger (2008) in her case studies of American students' experiences of study abroad in France. Kinginger recounted one particular vignette from the study-abroad experience that bears repeating in full because it reveals the source and the pain of cross-cultural misunderstanding, and a way to remedy it. Kinginger recounted the experiences of Beatrice, a 20-year-old American student majoring in marketing. During the spring semester of 2001, Beatrice was enrolled in a business-related program in Paris, where a home-stay arrangement was required. Beatrice had studied French throughout middle and high school and for four semesters at college. She had basic working proficiency in French and was a highly motivated student who had gained a very positive attitude toward French literature and culture from her teachers in high school and college. While in Paris, she lived with a French-Tunisian host family, who had two teenage daughters living at home. During her stay, Beatrice worked hard to improve her French mostly in activities with her host sisters, in conversations at home with the other members of the family, and while watching television at home. The vignette that illustrates Beatrice's painful misunderstanding of a French discursive practice is taken from her journal on March 11, 2003. Beatrice recounts an experience that she shared with her classmate, Olivia, who requested permission from their professor to absent herself from class so that, with her family, she could visit the site of the 1944 landings of the Allied forces on the Normandy beaches:

> Something absolutely unbelievable happened today that has managed to alienate me from every single French person I know. Today, Olivia asked our French teacher very politely if she could miss class next week to go with her parents to the beaches in Normandy—as her grandfather fought there during WW2. She would have to miss his class in particulier because that was the only day tours of the USA beaches were offered in English/ and her parents only speak English. Well our teacher flipped out on her basically telling her it was completely out of the question and how dare she ask something like that. It was by far the rudest thing I have ever witnessed. She's better than I am because if I had been she, I would have said something to the effect of "listen you asshole, he was fighting for you

and without people like our grandfathers you would be German now".
Olivia however said nothing but I told her to go anyway and I think she is
going to. Well when I told my French family—they said it was a bit rude
of her to ask that. Are you kidding me. The double standard of this is that
guys in our class skip and come late to class everyday and our prof. says
absolutely nothing. But Olivia, in trying to be polite is reprimanded and
her actions are considered rude. You have to be joking. I do not see what is
so wrong with going to the Normandy beaches and without the Americans
on those beaches that fought for them, the French would have become
German. (p. 71)

Beatrice's journal entry reminds me of the words of the captain of the
road prison in the 1967 movie *Cool Hand Luke*: "What we got here is . . .
failure to communicate." However, where is the failure? For Beatrice, the
failure rests with the professor, who fails to recognize a student's need to be
with her family and, what is worse, ignores the bloody sacrifices made by
her grandfather's generation for the liberation of France. For Beatrice's host
family, however, the failure lies with Olivia because she did not show the
respect that a student owes to a professor by asking to be absent from class.
Kinginger (2008) understood the difference between the French practice of
attending class and the expectations of American students and explains it as
follows: "French students typically do not request permission to be absent from
the university-level classroom, in part because, in contrast to the institutional
culture of [American universities], participation in class interpreted as seat-
time is typically neither monitored nor graded by teachers" (p. 71). Kinginger
went on to comment that if a student explicitly requests be absent from class, a
French teacher's likely interpretation of the request is that it shows the student's
blatant disrespect for the teacher's investment in the preparation to teach.

The different architectures of the practice of attending class in the United
States and in France were not apparent to Beatrice, presumably because she
had never received instruction in them. Kinginger (2008) wrote that Beatrice
did not entertain the possibility that she had encountered a rich point (Agar,
1994; Young & Halleck, 1998), which could reveal the reason behind the
apparent paradox of her professor's refusal to grant a student's explicit request
to be absent and the same professor's tolerance of unannounced absences by
other students in the class. Kinginger concluded: "Beatrice is a student who
might well have benefited from provision of guidance in the form of directed
reflection on the nature of language and of language learning, or of assistance
in interpretive framing of her encounters" (pp. 72–73). In her conclusion,

Kinginger agreed with Kasper and Rose's (2002) finding that without specific instruction in discourse pragmatics in advance of study abroad, exposure to the discursive practices of the new community does not provide opportunities for learners to acquire an appreciation of and expertise in those practices. In other words, Kasper and Rose's review and Kinginger's study provide indirect evidence that concept-based instruction is desirable if students are to learn the discursive practices of a new community and avoid the consequences of cross-cultural misunderstanding.

In discussing the pedagogy of practice in this section, I have considered the ways in which Practice Theory can inform teaching and learning in institutional contexts. The first example taken from Hall's (2004) study of a classroom practice called Practicing Speaking showed that organized talk in a classroom is itself a discursive practice, a recurrent goal-driven activity in which participants co-construct identities and which creates and reproduces the values and powers of an institution and of the society beyond the classroom walls. Practicing Speaking is, however, a pedagogical practice and bears only superficial resemblance to practices that second language learners may meet in the community outside the L2 classroom. Those similarities reside in the language—the Spanish vocabulary and grammar—but Hall showed that what the students learn is not the language but the practice. Turning their attention to life outside the classroom, teachers and curriculum designers can indeed analyze practices in which students may "need" to participate in an L2 community, but the classroom presentation of those practices in class is done by means of a simulation in a pedagogical dialogue. Although the language of the dialogue may resemble the language of the community practice, the differences between a discursive practice in the classroom and a practice outside the classroom are irreconcilable.

What is to be done? Hall (2004) proposed, and I agree, that students should study practices in a community of practice outside the classroom, either in situ or through video recordings of authentic community practices. The first stage in the teaching-learning procedure is then to construct a theory of the practice by considering how participants configure verbal, interactional, and nonverbal resources in order to construct a participation framework. An approach to theorizing the resources that participants in the practice employ would include a description of the following seven resources that are discussed in greater detail later in this chapter. The resources include the following: the identities of all participants in an interaction, present or not, official or unofficial, ratified or unratified, and their footing or identities in the interaction; the vocabulary and features of pronunciation and grammar that typify a practice; the ways in which participants construct interpersonal, ideational, and textual meanings in a practice; the selection of verbal actions in a practice and their sequential organization; the means by which participants select the next speaker and how participants know when to end one turn and when to begin the next; the ways in which participants respond to interactional trouble in the practice; and the opening and closing actions of the practice that serve to distinguish it from adjacent talk.

Configuration of these resources is only the beginning of a theory of practice, however. In the case that Beatrice reported of her friend's request to the teacher to absent herself from her class, the theory of seat-time in a French classroom is not simply a question of knowing how to configure verbal, interactional, and nonverbal resources in order for a student to successfully make a request to be absent from class. The theory must go beyond a description of *how* to participate to explain *why* participation is or is not possible. As we have seen in earlier chapters in this book, context of a practice includes its history, its institutional meaning, the power relations among participants, their symbolic and material resources, and the ideology or ideologies prevalent in the society. In order to build an adequate theory of the pedagogy of practice, these issues will be examined in depth in the following subsection.

Critical Pedagogy
Throughout this book, I have presented examples of how the teaching and learning process is reflective and constitutive of societal values that have much broader scope and greater political heft than classroom interaction. In discussing Language Socialization in chapter 5, I cited studies by Clancy (1986), He (2003), Ochs (2002), Rogoff et al. (1995), Schieffelin (1979), Watson-Gegeo and Gegeo (1986), and others showing that, in learning their L1, children learn ways of acting, feeling, and knowing that identify them as members of a community. The connections between discursive practice and the ways of acting, feeling, and thinking characteristic of members of a community of practice are by no means obvious, and the aim of critical studies is to demonstrate those hidden connections—including the connections among language, power, and ideology. The connections become clearer when two languages are involved and, in reviewing key studies in chapters 3 and 5, I argued that the individual identities of learners of an L2 are absorbed into and produced by the dominant ideologies within a society. Individual identities of learners are, in Althusser's (1972) term, *interpellated*, a process that occurs when learners recognize and acquiesce to their position within structures of ideology. Acquiescence is not the same as acceptance, however, because, as De Fina (2006) wrote, identities

are often contested in interaction but, when this happens, the contested identities "are based on ideologies and beliefs about characteristics of social groups and categories and about the implications of belonging to them" (p. 354). Turning to studies of classroom interaction reviewed in chapters 3 and 5, Conteh (2007), Duff (1996), Gebhard (2002/2004), Shameem (2007), and others have shown how the selection and organization of classroom practices and the beliefs of teachers are influenced by the prevailing political climate in the society of which the classroom is a microcosm. Classrooms are also locations in which the institutional culture of a school or a local education authority is reproduced and challenged as shown in the studies reviewed in chapters Three and Five.

These pivotal connections between the global and the local—socialization of children and newcomers to the culture of a community, the influence of ideologies on L2 identities, and the impact of societal politics and institutional power on classroom practices—are essential to a full understanding of discursive practice in language learning, teaching, and testing. As Wortham (2001) put it, in the classroom and in the world beyond the classroom, the contingent interactions of social life are the "empirical location in which broader theories and social patterns exist and get transformed" (p. 257). A critical approach to language pedagogy involves describing and analyzing pedagogical practices with a view to uncovering the ways in which participation in practice creates, reproduces, and provides opportunities for resistance to dominant power and ideology. The values of critical researchers are themselves open to a critical analysis. In some cases, a researcher's values may be fundamentally pessimistic; for example, some critical researchers may identify the sources of oppression and ground their analyses in the belief that we live in a fundamentally unjust world increasingly governed by the interests of multinational business. For others, critical research may be founded on the view that knowledge of the connections between local educational practices and societal ideologies may further an individual learner's resistance and struggle against the preponderant influence of harmful public policy. The position that I take differs from both of these: It is that of Foucault (1978; Foucault & Gordon, 1980), for whom power is not simply the institutional control of people by a powerful group, nor is it just a mode of thought control, nor does knowledge imply liberation. Power is exercised in every social interaction and its insidiousness lies in its very ordinariness. At his most explicit, Foucault wrote that "Power is everywhere; not because it embraces everything, but because it comes from everywhere" (1978, p. 93). For teachers, then, a Foucauldian critical analysis means that:

Everything in the classroom, from how we teach, what we teach, how we respond to students, to the materials we use and the way we assess the students, needs to be seen as social and cultural practices that have broader implication than just pieces of classroom interaction. (Pennycook, 2001, p. 139)

In other words, a critical approach involves asking how teachers and students orient to the everyday ordinariness of classroom practice and how L2 learners orient to being ordinary in a new community.

Examples of the ways in which a critical analysis of language pedagogy and the discursive practices of classrooms may reveal the connections between the global and the local are provided in the work of E. R. Miller (2006, 2009), Nelson (1999, 2004, 2008), and Benesch (1999). These researchers examined the role of societal ideologies in the construction of identities of L2 learners, particularly the dominant role of English in American contexts and the ideologies of gender and socio-sexual identity.

E. R. Miller (2006) investigated the attitudes of adult immigrant learners of English to the English language in the context of a contemporary debate in the United States about immigration. Issues in this debate, as summarized by the U.S. Congressional Budget Office (2006), include the status of recent immigrants, future policy toward immigrants admitted lawfully, policy toward those who have entered the country unlawfully, enforcement of immigration laws, and the role of the English language as part of the procedures toward becoming a U.S. citizen. Over a period of three years, Miller conducted an ethnographic study of people who had immigrated to a city in the American Midwest and had enrolled in free ESL classes offered by a social services agency in the city. Her data consisted of videotapes of classroom interactions in which Miller was the teacher and audio-taped interviews with focal learners. Miller investigated how the immigrants that she studied were positioned as individuals who lack the English language skills necessary to communicate with others and how they took on themselves the responsibility to be understood and to understand others. This sense of self-blame is expressed clearly in an interview with one of the students, Peng, a Chinese native speaker of Cantonese. The interview was carried out in Cantonese by another Cantonese speaker named Edwin and is reproduced in Extract 6.3. Edwin began by asking Peng about things Peng could do to help him communicate more easily.

In this interview, as E. R. Miller (2009) reported, Peng takes responsibility for the communication problems that he encounters at work, saying in turn 6 that the problem is his poor pronunciation. He does not question the underlying ideology of the dominance of English in a monolingual society in which people tell him to listen more and to take more risks when speaking this new language (turn 2). If we take a critical perspective on Peng's beliefs about the society in which he now lives, their source can be seen as inequities of economic opportunities and power between speakers of the dominant language and those who, like Peng, do not. In support of this perspective, Miller cited Grin's (2005) economic arguments in support of the maintenance of a dominant language by its native speakers:

> Native speakers of the dominant language are spared the effort required to translate messages directed to them by speakers of other languages, since the latter will have made the effort to utter them in the dominant language in the first place [and they] do not need to invest time and effort in learning other languages; this amounts to a considerable savings. (p. 456)

Extract 6.3 I have to depend on my son for everything (from E. R. Miller, 2009)

1 Edwin: 有無其他方式你學得會啲方法易啲有啲嘢可以幫助你既哩？
Is there any method that you think might help you, that can make it easier?

2 Peng: 都！人地啦我講就係多講多聽多，都敢講敢試。
Oh! People say to me, 'Listen more. Speak more. Dare to speak. Dare to try.'

3 咁宜家我單位即係照講人地講得唔明白呀。
When I am at work, sometimes people don't understand.

4 有時呀人講嘢人地就點講呢？既係我講嘢。我想講呢樣嘢，
人地既係人地以為我講 在第二样嘢就同我講第二樣嘢。
Sometimes when I speak to someone, they get a different meaning of what I am saying.

5 啦末，講講吓，就不麻不對題咁咁咁．即係咁樣啦。
Finally, I just give up what I wanted to say and I just say, 'okay okay.'

6 明白？即係咬字唔
You know? Because my pronunciation is no good.

7 Edwin: 明白明白明白！咁呀你諗住再take幾耐既係英文既班呢？
你諗住再會讀幾耐英文 班？
Yes, yes, I understand. How long are you going take English lessons? How long are you going to continue English lessons?

8 Peng: 哦……呢應該繼續讀落去啦！

Well, I must continue to learn, go on and on.

9 Edwin: 即係有話 ……學無止境, 即係有話諗住幾時完架勒。

So like the saying goes, 'There is no end to
study.' You will never stop learning.

10 Peng: 唔會唔會, 因因為 而家真係太太太差啦！

乜都旨意晒個仔所以, 就 …

Never, never. Be- because now my English is so, so,
so bad! Now I have to depend on my son for
everything. So, ...

11 Edwin: 有關係有關係。

I see.

The economic arguments in favor of maintaining the status of English as a dominant language in the United States form one basis for policies that advocate "English only" in the context of immigration by people for whom English is not their L1. This policy is promoted by organizations like English First, a national, nonprofit grassroots lobbying organization founded in 1986, whose goals are to make English the official language of the United States, to give every child the chance to learn English, and to eliminate costly and ineffective multilingual policies (English First, 2008). This is the political and economic context in which Peng and other immigrants learn English, a context that is clearly in the economic interest of those who speak the dominant language and results in immigrants like Peng blaming themselves for their lack of ability in English.[4]

The implications of societal attitudes toward English on the beliefs of language learners are clear. More subtle is how, by participating in pedagogical practices, learners' attitudes toward socio-sexual aspects of language, identity, culture, and communication are influenced. In English-as-a-second-language (ESL) classes in which students from a wide variety of language and cultural backgrounds come together, there are opportunities to construct and legitimize ideologies of gender and sexual identities. One of the pedagogical practices in which students' values and identities are compared with others is in the practice of classroom discussion. Nelson (1999, 2004, 2008) and Benesch (1999) reported two different discussions between teachers and classes of ESL learners in the United States on the topic of lesbian and gay identities. Nelson analyzed one classroom discussion that she observed in an ESL class at a community college and Benesch reported her own experiences as a teacher of an English-for-academic-purposes reading class at a university.

The class discussion that Nelson (2004) reported involved Roxanne, a female native-speaking American teacher with 20 years experience teaching ESL, and her 26 students, who were immigrants or refugees from countries in Africa, Central and South America, and Asia. Half of the students were women and half were men. The whole-class discussion was preceded by students working in small groups to discuss situations presented on a worksheet that the teacher had prepared as part of a unit on English modal verbs. Part of the worksheet is reproduced in Figure 6.1.

In an interview with the teacher after the class, Nelson (2004) asked her why she had included scenario number 3 about the two women. Roxanne replied:

> If a person's from this country [the United States] they're gonna visit that conclusion or speculation that the women are lesbians. And I think in

---

Speculations and Conclusions

Directions: For each situation below, think of 3 or 4 different possibilities to explain what is occurring.

Example: Those boys are hitting each other!

> *They must be fighting.*
> *They could be playing around.*
> *They might be pretending to hit each other.*

1. She is talking so loudly to that man.

2. I saw my friend José hugging a strange woman on the sidewalk last night.

3. Those two women are walking arm in arm.

[...]

Figure 6.1 Worksheet for a classroom discussion (from Nelson, 2004, Figure 1).

other countries you could talk for a long time before that particular thing
could come up for people. (p. 20)

She added, "the reason I did the whole worksheet was for No. 3" (p. 20).
In other words, what Roxanne was attempting was to introduce lesbian and
gay themes in her class discussion. Bringing the topic into public discourse,
Roxanne felt, would be desirable for her students and also for herself, but it
was not a topic on which she felt particularly comfortable. She believed that
she might get homophobic comments from some of her students and she was
not sure how she should respond. In the following comment, she revealed her
own apprehension:

> I want to let students know that even if I look nervous or blush, that I do
> want this conversation to happen [. . . because] I'm not comfortable with
> that topic being so uncomfortable for most of us in the world. The topic of
> two women in love or two men in love. (p. 21)

In the class discussion that followed student work in small groups on the
worksheet, Roxanne decided to allocate the final 15 minutes of class to a
discussion of item number 3, which generated a lively discussion engaging half
of the 26 students. During the discussion, some of the students contrasted the
cultural meaning in the United States of two people of the same sex holding
hands with the meaning of the symbol in their home countries. Raúl, a man
from Mexico, commented, "If I were in my hometown, we see two people walk,
two mens, holding hands. Afraid they're gonna get shot. (little laugh)" (p. 22).
Fabiola, a woman from Brazil, contrasted the meaning of the symbol in the
United States and Brazil, saying:

> I . . . be like long time here and when get back, you know back to my
> country again, I don't know 1 year after that or something like. And I'm
> gonna see my friends! I'm gonna HUG them and walking you know!
> (little laugh) And like, uh, you think people- maybe if you would do this
> here people say "Ah! Maybe they are gay!" (p. 21)

In response to Fabiola, Raúl admitted that the cultural meaning of the symbol
was mediated by the gender of the participants: "I think women will be different.
I mean you can see womens everywhere in the world. They can hug and, you
know, be kind of sissy" (p. 21).

After class, Roxanne reported that she was very pleased with the discussion
and felt that the students had benefited from the opportunity to discuss gay
and lesbian topics. The students that Nelson (2008) interviewed also felt very

positive about the class discussion. In this pedagogical activity, the teacher did not push her own viewpoint on same-sex relations; in fact, Nelson reported that Roxanne was unsure about her own sexual identity. As a teacher, she simply recognized that the topic was one of current relevance and invited her students to voice their own opinions, which they did with enthusiasm. Although Nelson (2004) reported that the "students were writing about lesbian/gay matters in their journals (which only the teacher read), none of them had yet raised these matters in front of their peers" (p. 23). By choosing to integrate the topic in a grammar lesson on epistemic modality, Roxanne had, in effect, moved the topic into a public universe of discourse. Nelson commented that integrating lesbian and gay themes in this ESL class was a means for topics that had been unspoken to achieve the status of ordinary topics of conversation in the class.

Roxanne's introduction of socio-sexual identities as an ordinary topic of conversation in the grammar class reported by Nelson (2004) contrasts with the way in which the same topic was introduced by Benesch (1999). Midway through a semester-long academic reading class, Benesch chose to have her class read a newspaper article about the murder in 1998 of Matthew Shephard, an openly gay 21-year-old student at the University of Wyoming who was fatally attacked near Laramie and subsequently died from head injuries. Russell Henderson and Aaron McKinney were convicted of kidnapping Shephard and murdering him.[5] Benesch's motivation for introducing this topic with her students was very different from Roxanne's. Benesch's approach was explicitly ideological. "I am committed to fighting injustice and inequality in society and the classroom," she wrote. "Therefore, when this hate crime was reported, I felt compelled to raise it with my students" (p. 577). Benesch provided a brief description of the class discussion that ensued after students had read the newspaper article about Shephard's murder. The description is designed to exemplify what Benesch termed *dialogic critical thinking*, which she defined as "expanding students' understanding beyond what they may have already considered to promote tolerance and social justice" (p. 573).

Dialogic critical thinking is designed to allow students to articulate their unstated assumptions and to consider a variety of views that may be held by other members of the class or by the teacher. The goal, however, is not simply to exchange ideas "but also to promote tolerance and social justice" (Benesch, 1999, p. 576). As the whole-class discussion progressed, Benesch (1999) noted three assumptions that students raised:

- Heterosexual men are justified in responding to homosexual men with anger or violence in order to assert their traditional ideas of masculinity.

- Some students expressed concerns about being perceived as gay or about becoming gay.
- Two male students said they did not show affection physically to their male friends in public because they feared being viewed as homosexual.

Benesch (1999) reported that during whole-class discussion, she acted as a facilitator and on two occasions intervened in the discussion with her own contributions:

> In the first intervention, I asked the students to question the assumptions on which many of their contributions seemed to be based: that homosexuals are primarily interested in making sexual overtures to and converting heterosexuals. [. . .] My other challenge was to ask the students to consider the social origin of their fears as well as alternatives to killing or beating up someone as a way of dealing with those fears. (p. 578)

The dialogic critical approach to teaching that Benesch's lesson exemplified resulted in a discursive practice that has broader implications than just a piece of classroom interaction. Her intention was explicitly ideological, and she believed that it had the intended effect on her students because she concluded that "the young men in my class who initially expressed contempt for homosexuals concluded that their scorn was based in fear and embarrassment" (p. 579).

These two teachers approached ESL classroom discussions of lesbian and gay issues from contrasting positions. Both appeared to believe that open public discussion of the issues is desirable because recognizing one's socio-sexual identity is an important part of self-knowledge. However, the discussions in the two classes were framed in very different ways—in Roxanne's class by an imaginary scene between two women and in Benesch's class by a newspaper report of actual violence perpetrated by men. Perhaps because of the different frames for the two discussions, Roxanne appeared unsure of her position in the discussion, whereas Benesch took pains to make her own position clear. In both classrooms, however, the discursive practice of whole-class discussion served the ideological ends of a powerful person, and in the context of the classroom that person is the teacher, whose power is discursively constructed by the practice of the discussion.

Power and Resistance

No matter how power is exercised in the classroom, no matter whether power is exercised in the service of ends that we admire or ends that we abhor, resistance to power is inherent in its exercise. Just as the power of the teacher in the Spanish high school class described by Hall (2004) created Practicing Speaking, so the resistance of many of the students in the class expressed itself in nonparticipation in the practice—in quiet talking to other students, in catching up on work for other classes, and in daydreaming. Another form of resistance was reported by Kinginger (2008) in Beatrice's journal entry and her complaints to her host family about the refusal of their French professor to allow Olivia to take time off to visit the Normandy Beaches with her family. As Foucault (1978) understood, resistance to power takes as many forms as there are forms of power, and resistance rarely results in a great Refusal or organized revolt. Did the students in Roxanne's class resist the opening up of public dialogue about lesbian and gay identities? Did the students in Benesch's class resist the ideology of tolerance and social justice toward Queer identities and lifestyles that their teacher was promoting? We do not know because expressions of resistance to dominant ideologies are rarely expressed openly. The students in the Spanish class talked quietly among themselves and Beatrice's anger at her professor was expressed privately in her journal. Their acts were not public, but they were acts of resistance nonetheless. Because a critical approach to language pedagogy involves uncovering the ways in which participation in practice creates and reproduces power, it also requires us to attend to students' resistance to dominant power and ideology, an approach that Canagarajah (2004) termed *critical learning*.

Grounding his analysis in the tradition of postcolonialism, Canagarajah (1997, 2004) showed that students' resistance to power is rarely expressed as an overt challenge to the source of power, often because power does not emanate from an individual subject; there are no headquarters to storm, no groups that control the apparatus of power. Who are the people exercising the power, creating the system of power, and why are they doing so? Because the source of power cannot be easily identified even in classrooms with a single teacher, resistance to power most often happens in private places, which Pratt (1991) and Canagarajah (1997) term "safe houses," defined by Pratt as "social and intellectual spaces where groups can constitute themselves as horizontal, homogeneous, sovereign communities with high degrees of trust, shared understandings, temporary protection from legacies of oppression" (p. 40). Safe houses in the classroom are asides or notes passed between students and private writing in textbooks and notebooks. Outside the classroom, safe houses are created in the school canteen, playground, or dorm rooms. There are safe houses in cyberspace, too, and Worth (2006, 2008) has described how students at an American university expressed their resistance to foreign language learning in an online chat.

Safe houses are proof of the relations of power that exist in the classroom because where there is power, there is resistance. Safe houses are a form of censorship—communication that is censored from observation and participation by the teacher—the logic of which Foucault (1978) described:

> One must not talk about what is forbidden until it is annulled in reality; what is inexistent has no right to show itself, even in the order of speech where its inexistence is declared; and that which one must keep silent about is banished from reality as the thing that is tabooed above all else. (p. 84)

How Does Practice Theory Clarify the Practice of Language Teaching?

I conclude the discussion of the pedagogy of practice with a question: How does Practice Theory clarify the practice of language teaching? An initial answer is that Practice Theory puts language teaching in context, where context is to be understood in broad terms—not just the physical space of the classroom, the learners and teacher present there, or the time of a lesson. The context of teaching includes the architecture of pedagogical practices, those recurrent goal-oriented activities in which learners participate in schools. An architecture of practice is a description of how participants configure verbal, interactional, and nonverbal resources in order to construct a participation framework for a practice.

The context of teaching includes the goals of pedagogical practices, which must be compared with the goals of participants outside the classroom. Although the verbal, interactional, and nonverbal resources used by learners in the classroom may resemble the resources used by participants outside the classroom, such a formal similarity does not imply that learners are doing what they "need" to do in the community outside the classroom. Learning a discursive practice does not mean simulating that practice in the classroom; it requires systematic study of the practice in the community in which it is practiced and appreciation of the social, cultural, and political foundations that create its meaning. Understanding those foundations inevitably requires an understanding of the relations of power in society and how societal power is created and reproduced in discursive practice. A critical approach to discourse will reveal those relations of power, and a critical approach to pedagogy will reveal how pedagogical practices create and reproduce the power of teachers, schools, and education authorities and how the same practices offer opportunities to construct resistance to power. One of the essential moments in which power is exercised is in the assessment of learning; thus, the contexts of teaching cannot be fully appreciated without an understanding of the contexts of testing, a topic to which I devote the remainder of this chapter.

Contexts of Testing

Schools inevitably reflect the values of the societies of which they are a part and assessments reflect those values. Some assessments are done informally by classroom teachers, others are done as part of a regular assessment process instituted by the school, and still others are mandated by policy-makers at the local, state, or national level. McNamara and Roever (2006) reviewed a variety of nationally mandated tests of language proficiency, including the Japanese senior high school entrance examination in English, the Common European Framework of Reference for Languages, and policy-driven assessment standards for language learning in the United Kingdom, Australia, Canada, and the United States. They concluded that the goals of these policies affect language learning at every level, including the goals of the curriculum, the teaching methods, and students' access to higher education. These tests and standards affect student learning principally by the theory of knowledge of an L2 that they promulgate—in other words, the *construct* of L2 knowledge that underlies language tests. When language testers and score users interpret people's scores on a test, they do so by implicit or explicit reference to the construct on which the test is based. Almost all of the constructs that underlie high-stakes language tests are theories of individual cognition that can be measured in one context (the test) and are stable enough to be ported to other nontesting contexts in which the language is used. As Chalhoub-Deville (2003) wrote, "context is important to the extent that it helps draw out" (p. 371) underlying cognitive abilities, and test results provide information about people's abilities that can be employed in other contexts.

Practice Theory, with its emphasis on the context of communicative interaction, provides a very different interpretation of the construct of L2 knowledge, an interpretation that can perhaps be best approached by considering how knowledge is displayed differently in different contexts. The research of Terezhina Nunes and her colleagues (Nunes, 1995; Nunes et al., 1993) on the display of mathematical ability by children in Recife, Brazil is relevant here because it shows how the individual differences that are created by test results are better understood as effects of the testing context. Nunes recognized that, in school, most computation exercises are mediated by written symbols on paper: Numbers are written down and computation is carried out from right to left across the page. She contrasted the practice of computation in school with the practice that is carried out outside school in street vending in which children from poor families in Recife are often involved. In this context, most computational operations are mediated orally by the vendor's private speech. In comparing the performance of poor and middle-class children on computational tasks, Nunes found that a much larger proportion of the poor children than the middle-class children failed in school arithmetic at the end of the school year. However, when the poor children were tested in outside-school contexts (street vending) and simulated tasks (a pretend shop), they performed significantly better than on paper-and-pencil computation exercises. Nunes (1995) explained the context-related difference in performance by the difference in the cultural-historical mediation of written symbols and oral language:

> Higher psychological functions are distinguished from basic functions because they are carried out through symbolically mediated actions. The symbols we use in mathematics are learned through our participation in cultural practices. (p. 95)

Middle-class children learn written mediation of arithmetic problems at school and at home, whereas those from poor environments learn a different form of cultural mediation—by oral language. Nunes (1995) argued that any test of an underlying ability involves measuring that ability in a particular context, a context that may impose a specific kind of cultural-historical mediation. Those students who have learned to use the mediation imposed by the test will do better than those who have learned mediation by other means, not because of a difference in underlying abilities but because of their different experiences with different cultural tools. As Nunes concluded, "We need [. . .] to prevent our psychological theories from taking the step from 'enabled by powerful tool' to 'a more able individual'" (p. 102).

Nunes's (1995) arguments about the cultural mediation of context in solving arithmetic problems can be applied to the assessment of knowledge of an L2. Assessment of a person's L2 knowledge in a specific discursive practice is challenging because from a person's performance on a test, not only do we wish to infer knowledge that is specific to the discursive practice of the test, but we also wish to know how the same person will do in other practices. Chalhoub-Deville (2003) discussed this dilemma at length and concluded that language testers need to develop theories that explain the interactions among "ability–in language user–in context" in order to relate test performance to nontest contexts.

Test Constructs

The general shape of the relationship between test performance and the construct underlying a test was laid out in several insightful articles by Messick (1989, 1996) and was revisited by Chapelle (1998). Chapelle distinguished among three perspectives on construct definition: A construct may be defined as a *trait*, as a *behavior*, or as *some combination of trait and behavior*. In a trait definition of a construct, consistent performance of a person on a test is related in a principled way to the person's knowledge and speech production processes; that is to say, a person's consistent performance on a test is taken to index a fairly stable configuration of knowledge and skills that the person carries around with them—and which that person can apply in all contexts. In contrast, in a definition of a construct as a behavior, the consistent performance of a person on a test is related in a principled way to the context in which the behavior is observed; that is to say, test performance is assumed to say something about a person's performance on a specific task or in a specific context but *not* on other tasks or in other contexts—unless these can be shown to be related to the task or context that was tested.

The contrast between definitions of a construct as a trait and as a behavior appears most obvious when multiple-choice grammar items designed to test linguistic competence are contrasted with open-ended performance assessments designed to test integration of multiple skills and knowledge in the performance of a complex task. In a trait definition of the construct of linguistic competence underlying a test composed of multiple-choice items, a person's performance on these items is taken to indicate knowledge of grammar that the same person can apply in different contexts. On the other hand, in a definition of a construct as a behavior such as essay writing underlying a performance test, an essay written by an individual writer is taken to indicate the performance of the same individual on that and other similar essay tasks. It does not, however, provide prima facie evidence of how the same individual might perform on other tasks—unless those tasks are related in a principled way to the essay task.

Clearly, neither definition of a construct as trait or behavior is satisfactory for theories of language in use because, as Bachman (1990) has emphasized, communicative language ability consists of *both* knowledge *and* "the capacity for implementing, or executing that competence" (p. 84) in different contexts of use. For this reason, it is desirable to consider the third of Messick's and Chapelle's definitions of a construct, which they refer to as the interactionalist definition. In an interactionalist validation of a test, a person's performance on a test is taken to indicate an underlying trait characteristic of that person and, at the same time, the performance is also taken to indicate the influence of the context (i.e., the task or situation) in which the performance occurs. The interactionalist definition is, in other words, a way to have your cake and eat it too: to infer from test performance something about *both* a practice-specific behavior *and* a practice-independent, person-specific trait. Moreover, the interactionalist definition of a construct refers not only to the trait and the context but also to some theory of how the two interact. In Bachman's (1990) model of communicative language ability, for example, traits interact with contexts by means of an individual's general strategic competence, which is understood as a means that a person has of assessing a situation as of one kind rather than another, of planning appropriate responses to the situation, and of executing the plans with a sensitivity to the shifting dynamics of the context.[6]

However, if interactionalist and behaviorist approaches to construct definition are to allow test users to generalize from performance in one context to another—that is, from the context of the performance elicited in the test to other nontest contexts—then what is needed is a theory that relates one context to another in a principled way. The question of generalizability of test results is identical to the question raised in chapter 5 about the portability of knowledge from one context of use to another. In the discussion in that chapter of the two metaphors of learning that Sfard (1998) contrasted, portability of knowledge was considered problematic for the participation metaphor but not for the acquisition metaphor. If knowledge is understood as a property of a person—some sort of possession—and learning is understood as getting or acquiring that property, then porting knowledge from one situation to another and using it in the new context is not problematic because knowledge is abstracted from the situation in which it is acquired. However, if knowledge is conceived as participation—as doing—and what is learned is how to participate in a given practice, what are learners to do when they encounter a different practice? Because learners *do* manage to participate in unfamiliar practices, the question arises of how far their participation is bound to a single practice. In theorizing interactional competence, Hall (1999) recognized the amount of flexibility that a person has in modifying verbal, nonverbal, and interactional resources within a single discursive practice and the likely consequences engendered by the modifications. Most relevant to the question of portability of resources is that interactional competence includes the skill to mindfully and efficiently recognize contexts in which resources are employed and to use them when participating in unfamiliar practices to help make sense of the unknown.

If a person's knowledge is displayed in a participation framework in a certain context, then because that framework has an architecture, elements of that architecture can be found, albeit in different configurations and in different contexts. What is needed is, as McNamara (1997) realized, a "close analysis of naturally occurring discourse and social interaction [to] reveal the standards that apply in reality in particular settings" (p. 457). Such an analysis of discourse and social interaction has been the objective of the explication of Practice Theory in this book. It is characterized by four features. First, analysis of language in social interaction is concerned with language used in specific discursive practices rather than on language ability independent of context. Second, it is characterized by attention to the co-construction of discursive practices by *all* participants involved rather than a narrow focus on a single individual. Third, analysis of social interaction identifies a set of verbal, nonverbal, and interactional resources that participants employ in specific ways in order to co-construct a discursive practice. Fourth, the problem of generalizability is resolved by identifying the particular configuration of resources that participants employ in a particular practice and, then, comparing the configuration of resources in that practice with others in order to discover what resources are local to that practice and to what extent the practice shares resources and a configuration with other practices.

Verbal resources include the register of the practice, defined as a recognizable repertoire of pronunciation and lexicogrammar that often occurs with high frequency in certain practices, the combination of which is associated with a specific activity, place, participants, or purpose. Another verbal resource that participants employ is certain kinds of meaning that participants create through the practice: the interpersonal metafunction through which participants influence others; the ideational metafunction with which participants describe, represent, and analyze experience; and the textual metafunction through which participants connect one part of a discourse to another.

The interactional and nonverbal resources that participants use to construct a discursive practice include some features of talk-in-interaction discussed in earlier chapters, including the selection and sequential organization of actions, the turn-taking system that participants use to manage transitions from one speaker to another, the ways in which participants repair interactional trouble, and the ways in which participants construct identities for themselves and others and, in so doing, construct a participation framework. In addition to these four resources, one further resource that was discussed by Levinson (1992) is the way in which participants construct boundaries of a practice. In order to identify a practice, it is necessary to distinguish it from other talk. This is done by means of locating the boundaries of the practice—the opening and closing actions in the sequence of a practice. Not all practices begin and end abruptly within a few moves and, in fact, boundaries of a practice may be vague, may be negotiated, or may be resisted by one or more participants; nonetheless, boundaries are essential in identifying discursive practices. In summary, then, we can describe a discursive practice by specifying the ways in which participants avail themselves of the following seven resources.

- Identity resources
  - *Participation framework*: the identities of all participants in an inter-action, present or not, official or unofficial, ratified or unratified, and their footing or identities in the interaction

- Verbal resources

  - *Register*: the features of pronunciation and lexicogrammar that par-ticipants frequently employ in a practice
  - *Modes of meaning*: the ways in which participants construct interper-sonal, ideational, and textual meanings in a practice

- Interactional and nonverbal resources

  - *Verbal actions*: the selection of actions in a practice and their sequen-tial organization
  - *Turn-taking*: how participants select the next speaker and how partic-ipants know when to end one turn and when to begin the next
  - *Repair*: the ways in which participants respond to interactional trouble in a practice
  - *Boundaries*: the way that participants open and close a practice and differentiate a given practice from adjacent talk

The configuration of these seven resources may be conceived as an interac-tional architecture unique to a specific discursive practice. However, the word "architecture" gives a very solid feel to the notion of a discursive practice al-though, as we have seen, practices are constructed, modified, and changed by participants on the fly, so it is more appropriate to consider participants as the architects and these seven resources as tools that they use to construct a practice. This framework for understanding the construct of L2 knowledge underlying a person's performance on a test is the interactionalist definition in Messick's (1989, 1996) and Chapelle's (1998) terms. The construct is local in the sense that it indicates the influence of the context in which the test performance was elicited. In addition, because the context involves other participants in addi-tion to the candidate (interlocutors in an oral test, the designer of the test, the item writers, an oral examiner, members of an examination board, and others), the performance of a candidate must be understood as co-constructed and the contributions of others must be considered—those others "whose behavior and interpretation shape the perceived significance of the candidate's efforts but are themselves removed from focus" (McNamara, 1997, p. 459).

At this point, some critics throw up their hands in confusion. The reaction of Chalhoub-Deville and Deville (2005) reaction is representative:

> Evaluating test-takers' performance according to this model offers a conundrum. Generally speaking, we administer tests to, assign scores to, and make decisions about individuals for purposes such as selection, placement, assignment of grades/marks, and the like. If we view language as co-constructed, how can we disentangle an individual's contribution to a communicative exchange in order to provide a score or assess a candidate's merit for a potential position? (p. 826)

However, the portability of resources from one discursive practice to another—in other words, the generalizability of an individual candidate's test performance—is within the scope of an analysis of context inspired by Practice Theory. The trait that an interactionalist theory of the construct considers is the configuration of verbal, nonverbal, and interactional resources employed in a test. However, that does not mean that every discursive practice is *sui generis*. That configuration must then be compared with the configuration of resources employed in other contexts.

One clear example of portability of resources is provided by Young's (2003) analysis of the resources employed by international teaching assistants (ITAs) in office-hour conversations with students. Young compared an office-hour conversation conducted by an ITA in the Math Department at an American university with an office-hour meeting conducted by an ITA in the Italian Department. By comparing the resources employed in the two office-hour conversations, Young concluded that there were enough similarities to describe a genre of office-hour conversation. This genre is characterized by: a problem-statement/problem-resolution script, an opening sequence that moves quickly to a statement of the problem, lexicogrammatical choices by both participants that mutually construct the ITA as an expert and the student as a novice, and a turn-taking system in which the ITA may take a turn at any time, may allocate the next turn to the student, and may deny the floor to the student by means of overlapping speech. However, interactional differences in office-hour interactions in the two disciplines were apparent in the topics that were chosen and in the way that topics were sequenced. Discipline-specific modes of reasoning were instantiated in these office-hours conversations by the way that topics arose, persisted, and changed in conversation and by the semantic relations between adjacent topics.

Other well-known comparisons of the interactional resources in different practices are the studies of oral L2 proficiency interviews collected by Young and He (1998) and reviewed by Johnson (2001), Lazaraton (2002), and Young (2002). These studies compared the interactional resources employed by participants in mundane conversations with those required for participation in oral proficiency assessments. The differences in the interactional architectures of the two practices are so apparent that Johnson titled her analysis of oral proficiency interviews *The Art of Non-Conversation*. He and Young (1998) concluded that the resources employed by an examiner and a candidate in the assessment practice of an oral proficiency interview are very different from those employed by participants in conversations between native and nonnative speakers. Prior to the analyses that Young and He published, the similarity between interviews and conversations was something that was taken on trust because few researchers had made any systematic comparisons between the two practices. However, the results of the comparisons carried out on practices in several different languages revealed that the interactional architecture of interviews is very different from the interactional architecture of ordinary conversation. Interviews, that is, are not authentic tests of conversation, and generalization from a person's performance in a testing context to their performance in a nontesting context is problematic.

In concluding this section, it can be seen that an approach to L2 testing that is inspired by Practice Theory requires much greater analysis of the discursive architecture of language testing practices and practices outside the testing room. This does not mean that generalization from test performance to nontest contexts is invalid. It does mean, however, that testers and applied linguists need to do much more work on the context of testing to elucidate the architecture of practices that language learners perform. As Anastasi (1986) stressed, "When selecting or developing tests and when interpreting scores, consider context. I shall stop right there, because those are the words, more than any others, that I want to leave with you: *consider context*" (p. 484, emphasis in original).

Critical Language Testing

If we wish to fully use Practice Theory to explicate the social context of L2 assessment, then the discussion in the previous section of test constructs and the generalizability of test performance is incomplete. At the beginning of that section, I argued that the work of Nunes (1995; Nunes et al., 1993) demonstrated the effect of cultural-historical context on students' performance on school-based tests of arithmetic. Nunes went further in her discussion of context to show the interaction between students' personal sense of identity and their test performance. She asked why working class children in her study who know so much oral arithmetic fail to master the schooled form of arithmetic mediated by written symbols. The explanation that Nunes provided was that:

> Children (along with their parents) who see no other future identity for themselves but being a rural worker come to reject school knowledge as not effective in practice, whereas those who start out well in school and seek a new identity do not value what they call "practical knowledge"—that is, oral arithmetic that works well for everyday needs. (p. 100)

Such an explanation of differential performance on school-based tests is grounded in the distinction made among ways of knowing by Aristotle. I recalled in chapter 5 that Aristotle distinguished among *techne*, *praxis*, and *theoria*, and in Nunes's commentary, "practical knowledge" can be interpreted as *techne*, whereas "school knowledge" is *theoria*, and these different ways of knowing index different social classes. Success in school as measured by school-based assessments involves *theoria*, not *techne*—in other words, written arithmetic not the oral arithmetic of the streets. At school, one way of knowing is favored and another way is disfavored, so, as one teacher asked Nunes: Why teach children oral arithmetic "when what they need to succeed in school and ascend the social ladder is written arithmetic?" (p. 100).

The social context of assessment thus involves an ideology of value, and in a society in which social groups are distinguished by access to economic resources, ethnicity, language knowledge, gender, or place of origin, the dominant social group exercises power by making their values accepted as norms by other groups. The power exerted by the dominant group is such that their values seem quite commonplace and unremarkable to others, so to contest them appears pointless. Those commonplace values are only brought to our conscious attention by breaching experiments that seek to examine peoples' reactions when accepted norms are violated. Consider one such breaching experiment in language testing. Most international students applying for admission to universities in the English-speaking world are required to take a standardized test of English proficiency—most often TOEFL in the United States and IELTS in Australia, Britain, Canada, and other countries. What would be the reaction of university admissions officers if an international student whose mother tongue is not English decided to violate the TOEFL/IELTS norm and submitted results from a test of the student's own devising? Perhaps the candidate had spent some effort to develop the new test and could submit information about its reliability and validity. Would the admissions officers accept it?

Only when tests are viewed from a critical perspective, does the broad impact of societal values become apparent. Shohamy (1998, 2001b) and McNamara and Roever (2006) have provided evidence that language tests are designed to carry out the policy agendas of those in power and this is achieved by establishing norms. Norms are principles or statements asserting or denying that something ought to be done or has value, and a norm is therefore a basis for comparison among test-takers. In multicultural societies or in tests of English as a lingua franca, the norms that are instantiated in the evaluation of test performances are critical in perpetuating the values of one social group as dominant.

The subject positioning of speakers of nondominant varieties of the standard language or of speakers of other languages involves accepting their own responsibility for the communication problems that they encounter, as E. R. Miller (2006, 2009) showed in Peng's orientation to being "ordinary" (i.e., *norm*-al) as a nonnative speaker of English in the United States. In language tests, too, lexicogrammatical norms are instantiated by the evaluation of a response to a norm as correct or incorrect. The norms used to evaluate test performance are those of the group that uses standard language, regardless of whether different groups adopt different forms. Examples abound in normative grammar of nonstandard English "errors" such as *anyways, you could of got one*, and *I could care less*. Those are all errors that were supposedly committed by native speakers of English, but the problematic status of the norms of standard (or is it "Standard"?) English becomes, like, ginormous when English functions as a lingua franca, as Seidlhofer, Breiteneder, and Pitzl (2006) have described it.[7]

Perhaps most problematic for language assessment in multicultural settings are the differences in discourse pragmatic norms between a socially dominant group and less dominant groups. Such differences are most often found in the contexts in which directness and volubility are evaluated positively and those contexts in which the same degree of directness and volubility are evaluated negatively.[8] Several ways of assessing pragmatics in an L2 are discussed by Röver (2005), including discourse completion items such as the following:

Ella borrowed a recent copy of Time magazine from her friend Sean but she accidentally spilled a cup of coffee all over it. She is returning the magazine to Sean.

Ella:..

Sean: "No, don't worry about replacing it, I read it already."

(p. 130)

The pragmatic ideology that this test item promotes is that (a) Ella should say something related to her action and (b) she should promise to replace the damaged magazine because of the rejoinder from Sean. In other words, the response of the party who has damaged the possession of another is entirely satisfied verbally. No action is required except verbal action, and yet there are occasions when a physical action may be more appropriate and more welcome by the injured party than any words, although the pragmatic ideology that such a test item promotes is that verbal action is sufficient.

A critical analysis of language testing practices thus brings to the forefront the social dimension of language testing, including speaker subject positions, lexicogrammatical norms, transcultural pragmatic conventions, and many other aspects of societal ideology. Practice Theory proposes that the practices of language testing occur in contexts that are much broader than the testing practice itself, including not only the designers and takers of a particular test but also the purposes for which the test is designed, the purposes for which people take the test, and the ends to which the results of the test are put. McNamara and Roever (2006) have stressed the importance of these broader political questions because the requirement to distinguish between *them* and *us* has increased in our intercultural societies and in our world of cross-border migration. The political dimension of language testing was famously recorded in the Book of Judges in the Hebrew Bible. Around 3,000 years ago in a war between Hebrew tribes, the Gileadites killed 42,000 Ephraimites who had crossed secretly into Gilead territory. The Ephraimites were given a simple language test: Pronounce the Hebrew word for "ear of grain" תלובש. The Shibboleth test was designed to distinguish the Ephraimites, whose dialect lacked a [ʃ] sound (as in shoe), from Gileadites, whose dialect did include the sound. Those who did not pronounce the [ʃ] sound were put to death.

As McNamara and Roever (2006) showed, many more recent versions of the Shibboleth test are recorded in the language assessment of immigrants, asylum seekers, and those who wish to become citizens. The political context of language testing is just as pertinent in more widespread but less fatal language testing enterprises that have resulted from the *No Child Left Behind Act of 2001* in the United States and the *Common European Framework of Reference for Languages* (Council of Europe, 2001). Both of these frameworks are designed to achieve policy goals and do so, as Foucault (1995) recognized, by "a normalizing gaze, a surveillance that makes it possible to qualify, to classify and to punish" (p. 184). Assessment within these frameworks is highly ritualized because in the frameworks are "combined the ceremony of power [. . .], the deployment of force and the establishment of truth" (p. 184) Just as Toohey (2004) described how some of the children that she studied were interpellated as "ESL," the heart of the procedure of assessment is "the subjection of those who are perceived as objects and the objectification of those who are subjected" (pp. 184–185). How are those ends achieved?

In the case of *No Child Left Behind* (NCLB), the policy is designed to improve education for all by allowing communities to distinguish between those schools where students do well on tests from those schools where students perform poorly and to direct financial resources to those schools with good testing results and, over the long term, to sanction those with consistently poor results. McNamara and Roever (2006) summarized the procedures involved in statewide tests of reading/language arts and mathematics in Grades 3–8 and at least once during high school. The subjects tested and the grades tested are mandated by NCLB, but states develop their own testing instruments. Aggregate results are reported at the school, district, and state levels for the entire student populations at the different grade levels. ESL learners, however, are one of the four groups of students whose scores are disaggregated from the population. Each school is required to make Adequate Yearly Progress in all parts of the assessment: scores of its entire student body and all its disaggregated subgroups on both reading/language arts and mathematics.[9] Evans and Hornberger (2005) argued that the consequences of NCLB for ESL learners have been mixed. On the one hand, added attention has been paid by school districts to their ESL students and small increases in funding of ESL programs have resulted because of the recognition in NCLB of ESL learners as one of the disaggregated groups who must also show adequate yearly progress. On the other hand, because students' achievement in foreign languages is not assessed in the NCLB framework, bilingual education programs are disappearing in the push to quickly develop students' proficiency in English. In addition, Rosenbusch (2005) has reported that NCLB has resulted in a decrease in instructional time for foreign languages, especially in schools with high minority populations. NCLB has, in effect, achieved what E. R. Miller (2006, 2009) documented in her study of immigrant language learning: the hegemony of English in schools and in the society.

The Common European Framework (CEF) was initially developed with the goal of facilitating the recognition of language credentials across national boundaries, and the framework promulgated one particular theory of language knowledge and the establishment of a progressive set of standards. It has rapidly become institutionalized throughout Europe, but, as Fulcher (2004) has argued, the impact of the CEF and the adequacy of its underlying construct are in need of debate because "for teachers, the main danger is that they are beginning to believe that the scales in the CEF represent an acquisitional hierarchy, rather than a common perception. They begin to believe the language of the descriptors actually relates to the sequence of how and what learners learn" (p. 260). In both the American and European cases, the establishment of a particular assessment framework has had a very significant effect on teaching and learning.

Because language assessments like these serve the purpose of distributing scarce resources such as jobs, higher education, and financial support to those who desire them, the question of how to distribute those resources fairly is by no means academic. The developers of language tests have indeed been aware of the necessity for internal equity in their tests, and there is a long and distinguished psychometric tradition of research in this area. Institutional testing agencies and professional associations of language testers have also responded to the need for fairness in the testing enterprise by the development of professional codes of ethics and institutional codes of practice. In many cases, however, such codes are responses to legal challenges to institutions or are intended to provide protection for members of the profession. Such measures undoubtedly reflect the concern of language testers for the fate of testing and test-takers in the community, but these concerns have been inward-looking and have so far lacked a foundation in description or research into the political consequences of language testing. It is only by taking a critical perspective on language testing and by implementing proposals such as those by Shohamy (2001a, 2004) for democratic assessment that those involved in testing can assume full responsibility for the tests and their uses.

Chapter Summary

I began this book by asserting that all talk happens somewhere, somewhen, and is produced by someone for some purpose. Practice Theory focuses attention on the where, when, who, and why of talk, and the methods of discursive practice provide ways of answering those four questions. In this chapter, I have applied those methods to the analysis of two important documents of learning in schools: teaching and testing. Hall's explanation of Practicing Speaking was an excellent example of how a pedagogical practice in an L2 classroom reproduces institutional power and the complementary roles of teacher and student but bears very little relation to practices in an L2 community outside the classroom. Even when teachers and textbook writers attempt to simulate in the classroom practices from an L2 community, the social context of the context of the classroom practice can never emulate the context outside. Teaching the lexicogrammar of an L2 practice does not teach the practice. What must be learned is not the language but the practice.

In this chapter, I have presented two ways of analyzing practices. In one way, by focusing on the configuration of verbal, nonverbal, and interactional resources that participants employ in a practice, it is possible to describe the architecture of a practice in terms of how those resources are configured by all participants. At the same time, by focusing on the relationship between a social interaction and the societal processes that occur beyond the time-space horizon of the interaction, the unique contribution of Practice Theory becomes apparent. Understanding practice requires conducting those two analyses and the pedagogy of practice requires bringing to students' conscious attention the internal architecture and the societal meaning of the practice. The discursive resources presented in chapter 4 are the means to understand the architecture of a pedagogical practice and a critical approach to pedagogy is the way to understand its societal meaning.

The presentation in this chapter of a practice approach to language testing followed a similar path to the discussion of language pedagogy. A practice approach encourages testers to do far more work to analyze naturally occurring discourse and the discourse of testing practices to decide the extent to which a person's performance on a test is generalizable to nontest contexts. Just as it is possible for "practicing speaking" in a Spanish as a foreign language classroom to bear little relation to speaking Spanish outside the classroom, so it is possible to get results from testing Spanish that are not generalizable to contexts outside the testing room. Only with the help of an interactionalist construct of L2 knowledge that, in a principled way, relates communicative resources to the context in which they are employed can a meaningful generalization be made from test results.

Language tests come from a long tradition of cognitive psychology and theories of individual difference that have characterized a person's performance on a test as an index of their cognitive ability. Testers have, until recently, been little interested in theorizing context, as McNamara and Roever (2006) emphasized:

> The situation or context is projected onto the learner as a demand for a
> relevant set of cognitive abilities; in turn, these cognitive abilities are read

onto the context. What we do not have here is a theory of the social context in its own right" (p. 32)

The ways of analyzing discursive practice presented in this chapter and the research in anthropology and sociology in which they are grounded are an attempt to provide that theory of social context.

Notes

1 Evidence-centered design views an assessment as an argument from observations of what learners say, do, or make in a specific context to inferences about what they know and can do in more general contexts. This perspective is then applied to test design (Kane, 1992; Messick, 1989; Mislevy, Steinberg, & Almond, 2003).

2 Hall's transcription conventions include a left bracket "[" to indicate the beginning of simultaneous talk and empty parentheses "( )" to indicate unintelligible talk. English translations are my own and are parenthesized in *italics* below each turn in Spanish.

3 The Soviet school of cultural-historical psychology originated in the 1920s and 1930s in the work of Vygotsky, his students, and colleagues. It prioritizes the role of cultural symbols such as language, concepts, and artifacts in the development and operation of mental activity. In the West today, many developments of the original theory have occurred and, especially within applied linguistics, there are many theories and research paradigms that relate mental functioning to social and cultural context. The term "sociocultural" has been applied so frequently to these approaches that it has begun to lose specificity. For this reason, in my discussion of the work of Piotr Gal'perin I have chosen to keep the original term of cultural-historical psychology (a translation of the Russian term культурно-историческая психология) for the school in order to distinguish Gal'perin's work from others. A good brief discussion of the terminology in this field is provided by Lantolf and Thorne (2006, pp. 2–3).

4 A more pertinent but less well-documented example of how linguistic dominance and language instruction are instruments of political power is the language policy of colonial policing. During the period of British colonial rule in Hong Kong, which ended in 1997, officers of the rank of inspector and above in the Royal Hong Kong Police Force were mainly expatriate native speakers of English from the United Kingdom, whereas the lower ranks were drawn from the native-born Cantonese-speaking populace of Hong Kong. Communication problems were common between the non-Cantonese-speaking officers and the non-English-speaking ranks. The dominance of English in the Royal Hong Kong Police was confirmed when English language instruction programs for Cantonese-speaking policemen were instituted.

5 See the Wikpedia article at http://en.wikipedia.org/wiki/Matthew_Shepard.
6 Bachman's description of strategic competence is very similar to Hall's (1999,
  p. 137) definition of interactional competence quoted earlier in this chapter.
7 The "errors" that I have cited and deliberately committed in this paragraph are taken
  from David Malki's cartoon strip *Wondermark* at http://wondermark.com/.
8 See the discussion of norms of interpretation in chapter 2.
9 The description of the implementation and the consequences of NCLB that I provide
  here is only an outline. Full details of the law are provided by the U.S. Department
  of Education's online document, *No Child Left Behind: A Desktop Reference*,
  available from http://www.ed.gov/admins/lead/account/nclbreference/reference.pdf.

Language Learning   ISSN 0023-8333

CHAPTER SEVEN

Prospects for Practice

This book has been my attempt to map out an approach to second language learning theory that has applications for second language teaching and testing. On the map, I have traced connecting lines between language and the contexts in which people use language. Although ways of describing language are well established by prestige and precedent, there is as yet no accepted way of describing context. There is no doubt that context is complex. It is a network of physical, spatial, temporal, social, interactional, institutional, political, and historical circumstances, and there is as yet no accepted way of drawing the lines between language and context. Descriptive studies of language begin with the question of what was said or what was written and, in this book, I have proposed five questions that lead to a description of context: When and where was an utterance said or written? Who said or wrote it? How and why did they do so? Answering those questions leads to a description of context, but a description is not enough. Just as a description of language forms is only the beginning of a linguistic theory of why the forms are as they are and of the relationships that exist among them, a description of context is only the first step in understanding how context influences how people use language and how people employ linguistic resources to construct context. What is needed in addition to description is a way of relating language to context and a way of explaining the relationship. In this book, I have adopted Practice Theory to make and to explain those connections.

With origins in social theory and anthropology, Practice Theory recognizes that human agents do what they do in the context of social forces that impinge upon them. The dilemma for previous theories of social action was whether individual actions are determined by social forces that transcend the individual or whether human will is sufficient to allow freedom of action. Practice Theory resolves that dilemma by looking long and hard at human action and by considering human action not as an abstraction but by considering particular *practices* in which a person participates. Those practices in which people use language, I have called discursive practices and, in this book, I have described

a number of different individuals participating in discursive practices and argued that their linguistic actions are influenced by the social circumstances in
which they perform those actions. I have also argued that, in some practices,
individuals employ linguistic resources to create a new social context. In this
final chapter, I visit again with some of those individuals in order to consider
how clearly the lines connecting language and context are traced on the map
of human interaction, and where the lines are faint, I consider the prospects for
additional studies that might draw the lines more clearly.

Some of the discursive practices that were reviewed in this book served
as examples of particular connections between certain features of context and
participants' use of language. In the conversation that Block (2006, 2007) reported between the Colombian migrant Carlos and his British workmates Dan
and Bob, Carlos created an identity for himself by participating minimally
in the conversation. Carlos's employment of minimal linguistic resources in
English in that conversation had nothing to do with his ability in English,
which he used effectively in other contexts with immigration authorities, doctors, and lawyers. Instead, the connection that can be made between Carlos's
linguistic performance and social context is with Carlos's positioning himself
as a middle-class intellectual, an identity in which others had altercast him
in Colombia but one that he struggled against losing in London. In contrast,
Carlos's workmate Dan positioned himself as a working-class, White male,
an identity that he constructed through his talk of powerlessness, the fate of
his football team, and his use of the f-word. However, this was an identity
that Carlos rejected with a shrug. Their conversation illustrates the connection
between Dan's use (and Carlos's strategic not-use) of language and the identities that these two individuals create. It illustrates the influence of historical
context on local action. We observe, however, only a single conversation, and
without further information, we do not know whether Carlos has successfully
reacquired his identity as a middle-class intellectual or whether he has become
permanently declassed in London. That is the problem with a data snapshot
like this, which, at best, illustrates a connection between features of conversation and social context but which cannot show how that connection develops
in the lives of participants or how it relates to the development of Carlos's
English.

A second example illustrating the connections between context and language use is the comparison that Baquedano-López (1997/2001) made between
stories told by teachers in a catechism class and in a *doctrina* class at the same
Catholic church in Southern California. The Spanish-speaking children in the
doctrina class were told in Spanish a story of the apparition of *Nuestra Señora*

de Guadalupe to the Aztec craftsman Juan Diego, a story in which the Virgin's skin color was the same as that of the teacher and children of Mexican descent— *morenita como nosotros*. The children in the mixed-background catechism class were told in English the story of the apparitions of the Virgin Mary in many guises in many different places. Clearly, not only the language to which the two groups of children were exposed in the two classes differed, but they were also exposed to different ideologies of ethnicity. The ethnic identity of the children in the *doctrina* class as indexed by their skin color was stressed by the teacher, whereas the multiethnic composition of the catechism class was stressed by their teacher. The connection between ethnic identity and language in the stories told by the two teachers is clear, as is the accommodation of the teachers to the children in their classes. What effect did those two lessons have on the children's sense of their own ethnic identities? We do not know. Although a Mexican American community in Southern California exists in which members share a sense of ethnic identity, construction of that identity for Mexican American children almost certainly requires more than a single hearing of the story of the apparition of the Virgin Mary in a Sunday school class. The connection that the research of Baquedano-López illustrates between language and ideology is clear and, framed within Language Socialization theory, her illustration of ways that talk influences development of identity is persuasive. What still needs to be done is to understand the processes by which ideologies created in different languages create different identities and the degree to which individuals can resist the power of ideology over their cognition or can reject the languages in which they are expressed.

A more dynamic picture of the relation between language and context is provided by the longitudinal studies by Toohey of the minority language children in Canada, by Garret and Young of Garret's affective reactions to her intensive Portuguese course, and by Nguyen of a pharmacist's development of communicative skills in patient consultations. In Toohey's (1998, 2000) longitudinal ethnographic study of six minority-language children in English-medium classrooms in Canada, she described three practices in which the children participated in the Grade 1 classroom that contributed to "breaking them up"—to differentiating children one from another and, eventually, to interpellating some children as "ESL," who required further specialized instruction in English. The practices that Toohey identified are so commonplace in elementary school classrooms as to be almost invisible: sitting at your own desk, using your own things, and using your own words and ideas. Yet it was the differential performances of children in these practices that contributed to their future status in the school. It was not their performance as English language learners alone that constructed children as differentially able, but how that performance overlapped with their physical and social behavior in classroom practices.

Toohey's description of the context in which the children learned to use English is very rich. She observed and recorded classroom interactions among the children and between their teacher and her class. She also conducted interviews with the children's families at their homes and with the classroom teacher. Other studies that include rich descriptions of context are Shameem's (2007) research on multilingual classrooms in Fiji and Gebhard's (2002/2004, 2005) study of literacy practices in schools in California. Gebhard's summary of data sources for investigating contextual influences on language learning reproduced in chapter 3 is particularly complete. Because of the resources necessary for the complete description of context in these studies, however, there is comparatively little attention paid to the language that the children produced. In a vein similar to the illustrative studies of Block and Baquedano-López, these rich descriptions of context trace only a few connecting lines between context and language.

Garret and Young's (2009) report of Garrett's emotional responses to her experiences in an intensive Portuguese class, although rich in the description of the learner's emotions, also lacks a close analysis of the language that Garrett learned and used in the class and a description of her developing knowledge of Portuguese. This imbalance between the description of context and the analysis of language seems to be common in studies of discursive practice. In studies such as these, rich descriptions of context are illustrated with superficial analyses of language, whereas in other studies, a close analysis of a newcomer's developing utilization of verbal, nonverbal, and interactional skills is explained by a rather thin description of context.

Two studies of this latter kind are Nguyen's (2006, 2008) reports of the development of communicative skills in patient consultations by the two pharmacy interns Jim and Mai. These two studies are longitudinal and focus on changes of participation as Jim and Mai performed repeated instances of a discursive practice that was initially unfamiliar to them. In Nguyen's analysis of Jim's development of expertise in patient consultations, she described how Jim's initial display of expertise in pharmacology was insensitive to context. In later consultations, however, he employed a different interactional style in which his expertise was displayed only at appropriate moments in consultations with particular patients. As his experience of patient consultations increased, Jim was also able to display greater alignment with his patients. In her analysis of the performance of the other intern, Mai, in the same discursive practice, Nguyen also observed a change in the novice pharmacist's interactional style over time. In the early patient consultations that Nguyen observed, Mai gave the patient her own advice prior to the doctor's prescription, which gave rise to interactional trouble. In later consultations, Mai reversed the sequence, specifically invoking the doctor as author before providing her own advice, a sequence that she maintained throughout the remaining observations. In addition to maintaining a fixed sequence of actions in her later consultations, Mai also managed smoother transitions between them. The descriptions of topics, sequences, and transitions between actions in this discursive practice that Nguyen described provide considerable detail about Jim's and Mai's utilization of verbal, nonverbal, and interactional resources. Nguyen's description of the context of the practice of patient consultation is also quite detailed. It is an institutional practice with a history that is continually reconstructed by practicing pharmacists and maintained by overt instruction in schools of pharmacy. What Jim and Mai do in each performance of the practice is not to repeat their own performance, but, by recreating the context, they extend the history of the practice.

A well-defined institutional practice is also described by Young and Miller (2004) in their analysis of the co-development of skills in one-on-one revision talk by an ESL student and his writing tutor. Young and Miller remarked how the student participated more fully in the practice by performing more of the actions and how his fuller participation was co-constructed by his tutor as she gradually withdrew her own participation. Their report described the sequence of linguistic actions in the practice and how those actions were performed by the two participants. In both the practice of pharmacy consultation and the practice of revision talk, participants' language use in well-defined institutional practices is described in detail, but, in both cases, the context is assumed to be fixed. By maintaining a relatively fixed context in these studies, the researchers were able describe how participants alter their deployment of linguistic resources in changes of participation that, I have argued, index learning. Perhaps, at the present stage of our understanding of the nexus between language and context, that is as close as we can come to tracing a connecting line between local action and global societal context.

Just as future work in discursive practice will, I hope, trace the connections between language and context more clearly, so it will be necessary to evaluate the relative contributions to L2 use and L2 learning of practice and of language. In other words, what does Practice Theory tell us about the *practical* construction of talk-in-interaction and what does linguistic theory tell us about participants' employment of verbal, nonverbal, and interactional resources in talk-in-interaction? Participants' performance in discursive practices as envisioned by Practice Theory cannot be the whole story. Although I maintained in chapter 6 that what is learned of a discursive practice is not the language but the practice, nonetheless the verbal, nonverbal, and interactional resources employed by participants in discursive practice are certainly part of the practice. Every grammatical theory including Systemic Functional Grammar (SFG) admits of constraints on language, constraints of grammaticality and appropriateness in conventional grammar, and the limited systemic choices in SFG. So, what is the relationship between linguistic constraints and practical action?

The social theorist Michel de Certeau provided an image of the relationship between practice as lived experience and universal linguistic constraints in his essay "Walking in the City" (de Certeau, 1984). De Certeau imagined the activity of a person walking through the streets of a city and contrasted it with a view of the walker's route from a very high vantage point such as the top of a skyscraper. He recognized the practical activity of a person walking the streets of the city, who, at a particular time, is in a particular place and is walking in a particular way—fast or slow, running or dawdling—with a particular goal in mind—a goal of arriving somewhere or of just window shopping. The view from the top of a skyscraper is a map of the walker's route, a map that is an abstraction from the person's practice of walking, an image that has a context of its own but is not a representation of the who, where, when, how, and why of the walker. It is a representation only of the route that the walker takes—the what. As de Certeau wrote, the lines on the map "only refer, like words, to the absence of what has passed by" (p. 97). However, the walker is not a superhero, free to go wherever he or she likes. There are streets in the city that can be taken or not, there are high walls that cannot be surmounted, and intersections that must be crossed. These can be seen from on high and can be represented on the map as constraints that describe a limited number of routes, but to the walker they are affordances and impedances, environments that allow the walker to go in one direction and not in another and environments that the walker negotiates tactically and on the fly. The practice of walking, like an individual's performance in a discursive practice, is situated and ongoing; it is a lived experience within an environment. The map, the bird's-eye view of the route, like lexicogrammatical constraints on practice, is a different representation entirely, located nowhere and nowhen. As de Certeau wrote, "The long poem of walking manipulates spatial organizations . . . : it is neither foreign to them . . . nor in conformity with them . . . . It creates shadows and ambiguities within them" (p. 101).

In presenting discursive practice, I have avoided a discussion of linguistic constraints on participants' actions for two reasons: first, because I believe that there is already a vast literature on the ways that language is used in interaction to which I have little to add and, second, because I have preferred to frame the discussion of the language of practice in terms of resources. In doing so, my emphasis is on a repertoire that participants employ to achieve their goals in interaction, goals that may include a conscious desire to persuade or resist another participant, or to accept or reject a proposed action. In some practices, participants are actors with strategies developed to achieve their goals, but, in other practices, participants' act without conscious awareness, such as when they employ a particular register in a particular context or how they sequence actions in a conversation. Recognizing the limitations of that repertoire is a matter of what de Certeau (1984) called strategy, a reflection on what has been done from a distant vantage point, whereas employing that repertoire is the actuality of an action of a person who acknowledges affordances and impedances. It is a matter of what de Certeau called tactics.

This book has focused on tactics rather than strategy, on the practice of walking rather than the map of a route once taken. The city in which de Certeau imagined his walker was New York and the vantage point from which he began his essay was the 110th floor of the World Trade Center. Today, there are still walkers in the city, but, alas, the vantage point is no more.

Language Learning   ISSN 0023-8333

APPENDIX

Transcription Conventions

Transcription conventions are adapted from Jefferson (2004), with additions by Ford and Thompson (1996), and are as follows:

⌐	Point of onset of overlapping talk.
|	Point of onset of overlapping talk.
∟	Point of onset of overlapping talk.
⌐	Point at which overlapping talk terminates.
|	Point at which overlapping talk terminates.
⌐	Point at which overlapping talk terminates.
=	Paired equals signs connect two adjacent lines to indicate that the second is "latched" to the first; that is, it follows the first with no discernable silence between them.
(0.4)	The number in parentheses indicates the duration of silence measured in tenths of a second.
(.)	A hearable silence less than two tenths of a second.
word	Underscoring indicates some form of stress, usually a combination of loudness and pitch movement.
I-	A dash in the transcript indicates an abruptly cutoff sound.
., ?	Punctuation marks are not used to indicate grammar but are instead used to indicate the nuclear tone on a pitch unit. A period "." indicates falling tone, a question mark "?" indicates rising tone, and a comma "," indicates a slight rise or level tone.
::	Colons are used to indicate the prolongation or stretching of the preceding sound. More colons indicate a longer sound.
°°	Degree signs are used to indicate the onset and termination of a stretch of speech that is quieter than the surrounding speech.
> <	A "greater than" followed by a "less than" symbol indicates the onset and termination of speech that is faster than the surrounding speech.

>	A "greater than" symbol on its own indicates the boundary of a pragmatic unit.
/	A slash character indicates the boundary of a syntactic unit.
hhhh	Laughter or hearable out-breaths are indicated by a sequence of "h"s.
°hh	A raised dot preceding "h" indicates a hearable in-breath: the more "h"s, the longer the in-breath.
xxx	Indicates that something was said, but that the transcriber cannot recognize what it was.
↑↓	Up and down arrows indicate a hearably greater range of pitch movement.
((comment))	Double parentheses indicate a comment made by the transcriber.
((gesture))	Italics indicate a description of nonverbal actions.

References

Agar, M. (1994). *Language shock: Understanding the culture of conversation*. New York: Morrow.

Alim, H. S. (2004). Hip Hop Nation. In E. Finegan & J. R. Rickford (Eds.), *Language in the USA: Themes for the twenty-first century* (pp. 387–409). Cambridge: Cambridge University Press.

Althusser, L. (1972). Ideology and ideological state apparatuses (Notes towards an investigation) (B. Brewster, Trans.). In his *Lenin and philosophy, and other essays* (pp. 127–186). New York: Monthly Review Press.

Anastasi, A. (1989). Ability testing in the 1980's and beyond: Some major trends. *Public Personnel Management, 18*(4), 471–484.

Androutsopoulos, J. (2006). Introduction: Sociolinguistics and computer-mediated communication. *Journal of Sociolinguistics, 10*(4), 419–438.

Apple, M. W. (2000). *Official knowledge: Democratic education in a conservative age* (2nd ed.). New York: Routledge.

Arievitch, I. M., & Stetsenko, A. (2000). The quality of cultural tools and cognitive development: Gal'perin's perspective and its implications. *Human Development, 43*(2), 69–92.

Austin, J. L. (1962). *How to do things with words*. Cambridge, MA: Harvard University Press.

Bachman, L. F. (1990). *Fundamental considerations in language testing*. New York: Oxford University Press.

Back, M. P. (2009). *"We did the wrong dance": Ecuadorian musicians negotiating language and identity in a transnational context*. Unpublished Ph.D. dissertation, University of Wisconsin-Madison.

Bailey, K. M. (1983). Competitiveness and anxiety in adult second language learning: Looking *at* and *through* the diary studies. In H. W. Seliger & M. H. Long (Eds.), *Classroom oriented research in second language acquisition* (pp. 67–102). Rowley, MA: Newbury House.

Bailey, K. M. (1985). Classroom-centered research on language teaching and learning. In M. Celce-Murcia (Ed.), *Beyond basics: Issues and research in TESOL* (pp. 96–121). Rowley, MA: Newbury House.

Bailey, K. M. (1991). Diary studies of classroom language learning: The doubting game and the believing game. In E. Sadtono (Ed.), *Language acquisition and the second/foreign language classroom* (pp. 60–102). Singapore: SEAMEO Regional Language Centre.

Bailey, K. M., & Ochsner, R. (1983). A methodological review of the diary studies: Windmill tilting or social science? In K. M. Bailey, M. H. Long, & S. Peck (Eds.), *Second language acquisition studies* (pp. 188–198). Rowley, MA: Newbury House.

Bakhtin, M. M. (1981). Discourse in the novel (C. Emerson & M. Holquist, Trans.). In M. Holquist (Ed.), *The dialogic imagination: Four essays by M. M. Bakhtin* (pp. 259–422). Austin: University of Texas Press.

Bakhtin, M. M. (1986). The problem of speech genres (V. W. McGee, Trans.). In C. Emerson & M. Holquist (Eds.), *Speech genres and other late essays* (pp. 60–102). Austin: University of Texas Press.

Baquedano-López, P. (1997/2001). Creating social identities through *doctrina* narratives. *Issues in Applied Linguistics, 8*(1), 27–45. Reprinted in A. Duranti (Ed.) (2001), *Linguistic anthropology: A reader* (pp. 343–358). Malden: Blackwell.

Barnes, D. (1976). *From communication to curriculum.* Harmondsworth, UK: Penguin.

Bassok, M., & Holyoak, K. J. (1993). Pragmatic knowledge and conceptual structure: Determinants of transfer between quantitative domains. In D. K. Detterman & R. J. Sternberg (Eds.), *Transfer on trial: Intelligence, cognition, and instruction* (pp. 68–98). Norwood, NJ: Ablex.

Bauman, R. (1992). Contextualization, tradition, and the dialogue of genres: Icelandic legends of the *kraftaskáld*. In A. Duranti & C. Goodwin (Eds.), *Rethinking context: Language as an interactive phenomenon* (pp. 125–145). Cambridge: Cambridge University Press.

Bauman, R. (2000). Genre. *Journal of Linguistic Anthropology, 9*(1–2), 84–87.

Bauman, Z. (1992). *Intimations of postmodernity.* London: Routledge.

Bayley, R., & Schecter, S. R. (Eds.). (2003). *Language socialization in bilingual and multilingual societies.* Clevedon, UK, & Buffalo, NY: Multilingual Matters.

Bell, A. (1984). Language style as audience design. *Language in Society, 13*(2), 145–204.

Benesch, S. (1999). Thinking critically, thinking dialogically. *TESOL Quarterly, 33*(3), 573–580.

Benner, P. E. (1984). *From novice to expert: Excellence and power in clinical nursing practice.* Menlo Park, CA: Addison-Wesley.

Birch, D., & O'Toole, M. (Eds.). (1988). *Functions of style.* London: Pinter.

Block, D. (2006). *Multilingual identities in a global city: London stories.* Basingstoke, UK: Palgrave Macmillan.

Block, D. (2007). Socialising second language acquisition. In Z. Hua, P. Seedhouse, L. Wei, & V. Cook (Eds.), *Language learning and teaching as social interaction* (pp. 89–102). Basingstoke, UK: Palgrave Macmillan.

Bloomfield, L. (1933). *Language.* New York: H. Holt and Company.

Bogdan, R., & Biklen, S. K. (1992). *Qualitative research for education: An introduction to theory and methods* (2nd ed.). Boston: Allyn and Bacon.

Bourdieu, P. (1977). *Outline of a theory of practice* (R. Nice, Trans.). New York: Cambridge University Press.

Bourdieu, P. (1984). *Distinction: A social critique of the judgment of taste* (R. Nice, Trans.). Cambridge, MA: Harvard University Press.

Bourdieu, P. (1986). The forms of capital. In J. Richardson (Ed.), *Handbook of theory and research for the sociology of education* (pp. 241–258). New York: Greenwood Press.

Bourdieu, P. (1990). *The logic of practice* (R. Nice, Trans.). Stanford, CA: Stanford University Press.

Bourdieu, P. (1991). *Language and symbolic power* (G. Raymondson & M. Adamson, Trans.). Cambridge, MA: Harvard University Press.

Bourdieu, P., & Wacquant, L. J. D. (1992). *An invitation to reflexive sociology.* Chicago: University of Chicago Press.

Brandt, D. (1998). Sponsors of literacy. *College Composition and Communication, 49*(2), 165–185.

Breen, M. P. (1987). Learner contributions to task design. In C. N. Candlin & D. Murphy (Eds.), *Language learning tasks* (pp. 23–46). Englewood Cliffs, NJ: Prentice-Hall International.

Brouwer, C. E., & Wagner, J. (2004). Developmental issues in second language conversation. *Journal of Applied Linguistics, 1*(1), 29–47.

Butler, C. (1993). Systemic grammar in applied language studies. In R. E. Asher & J. M. Y. Simpson (Eds.), *The encyclopedia of language and linguistics* (Vol. 8, pp. 4500–4504). Oxford: Pergamon.

Butt, D., Fahey, R., Feez, S., Spinks, S., & Yallop, C. (2000). *Using functional grammar: An explorer's guide* (2nd ed.). Sydney: National Centre for English Language Teaching & Research, Macquarie University.

Butterworth, G. (1992). Context and cognition in models of cognitive growth. In P. Light & G. Butterworth (Eds.), *Context and cognition: Ways of learning and knowing* (pp. 1–13). Hillsdale, NJ: Erlbaum.

Cain, C. (1991). Personal stories: Identity acquisition and self-understanding in Alcoholics Anonymous. *Ethos, 19*(2), 210–253.

Canagarajah, A. S. (1997). Safe houses in the contact zone: Coping strategies of African-American students in the academy. *College Composition and Communication, 48*(2), 173–196.

Canagarajah, S. (2004). Subversive identities, pedagogical safe houses, and critical learning. In B. Norton & K. Toohey (Eds.), *Critical pedagogies and language learning* (pp. 116–137). Cambridge: Cambridge University Press.

Carr, D. (1986). Narrative and the real world: An argument for continuity. *History and Theory, 25*(2), 117–131.

Carter, R., & Stockwell, P. (Eds.). (2008). *The language and literature reader.* New York: Routledge.

Cathcart, R. (1986). Situational differences and the sampling of young children's school language. In R. R. Day (Ed.), *Talking to learn: Conversation in second language acquisition* (pp. 118–140). Rowley, MA: Newbury House.

Chaiklin, S., & Lave, J. (Eds.). (1993). *Understanding practice: Perspectives on activity and context.* Cambridge: Cambridge University Press.

Chalhoub-Deville, M. (2003). Second language interaction: Current perspectives and future trends. *Language Testing, 20*(4), 369–383.

Chalhoub-Deville, M., & Deville, C. (2005). A look back at and forward to what language testers measure. In E. Hinkel (Ed.), *Handbook of research in second language teaching and learning* (pp. 815–832). Mahway, NJ: Erlbaum.

Chapelle, C. A. (1998). Construct definition and validity inquiry in SLA research. In L. F. Bachman & A. D. Cohen (Eds.), *Interfaces between second language acquisition and language testing research* (pp. 32–70). New York: Cambridge University Press.

Charmaz, K. (2006). *Constructing grounded theory: A practical guide through qualitative analysis.* London & Thousand Oaks, CA: Sage.

Chatman, S. B. (Ed.). (1971). *Literary style: A symposium.* London: Oxford University Press.

Chomsky, N. (1965). *Aspects of the theory of syntax.* Cambridge, MA: MIT Press.

Chomsky, N. (1986). *Knowledge of language: Its nature, origin, and use.* New York: Praeger.

Cicourel, A. V. (1983). Hearing is not believing: Language and the structure of belief in medical communication. In S. Fisher & A. D. Todd (Eds.), *The social organization of doctor-patient communication* (pp. 221–239). Washington, DC: Center for Applied Linguistics.

Cicourel, A. V. (1992). The interpenetration of communicative contexts: Examples from medical encounters. In A. Duranti & C. Goodwin (Eds.), *Rethinking context: Language as an interactive phenomenon* (pp. 293–310). New York: Cambridge University Press.

Cicourel, A. V. (1995). Medical speech events as resources for inferring differences in expert-novice diagnostic reasoning. In U. M. Quasthoff (Ed.), *Aspects of oral communication* (pp. 364–387). Berlin: W. de Gruyter.

Cicourel, A. V. (2000). Expert. *Journal of Linguistic Anthropology, 9*(1–2), 72–75.

Clancy, P. M. (1986). The acquisition of communicative style in Japanese. In B. B. Schieffelin & E. Ochs (Eds.), *Language socialization across cultures* (pp. 213–250). New York: Cambridge University Press.

Cole, M. (1995). The supra-individual envelope of development: Activity and practice, situation and context. In J. J. Goodnow, P. J. Miller, & F. S. Kessel (Eds.), *Cultural practices as contexts for development* (pp. 105–118). San Francisco: Jossey-Bass.

Conteh, J. (2007). Bilingualism in mainstream primary classrooms. In Z. Hua, P. Seedhouse, L. Wei, & V. Cook (Eds.), *Language learning and teaching as social inter-action* (pp. 185–198). Basingstoke: Palgrave Macmillan.

Council of Europe. (2001). *Common European framework of reference for languages: Learning, teaching, assessment.* Cambridge: Cambridge University Press.

Cran, W., & MacNeil, R. (2005). *Hip hop nation.* Page on the PBS Web site Do you speak American? Retrieved June 10, 2008, from http://www.pbs.org/speak/words/sezwho/hiphop/

Creswell, J. W. (2007). *Qualitative inquiry and research design: Choosing among five approaches* (2nd ed.). Thousand Oaks, CA: Sage.

Daneš, F. (1974a). Functional sentence perspective and the organization of the text. In F. Daneš (Ed.), *Papers on functional sentence perspective* (pp. 106–128). The Hague: Mouton.

Daneš, F. (Ed.). (1974b). *Papers on functional sentence perspective.* The Hague: Mouton.

de Certeau, M. (1984). *The practice of everyday life* (S. Rendall, Trans.). Berkeley: University of California Press.

De Fina, A. (2006). Group identity, narrative and self representations. In A. De Fina, D. Schiffrin, & M. G. W. Bamberg (Eds.), *Discourse and identity* (pp. 351–375). Cambridge: Cambridge University Press.

DeKeyser, R. M. (2007). Introduction: Situating the concept of practice. In R. M. DeKeyser (Ed.), *Practice in a second language: Perspectives from applied linguistics and cognitive psychology* (pp. 1–18). Cambridge: Cambridge University Press.

Detterman, D. K. (1993). The case for the prosecution: Transfer as an epiphenomenon. In D. K. Detterman & R. J. Sternberg (Eds.), *Transfer on trial: Intelligence, cognition, and instruction* (pp. 1–24). Norwood, NJ: Ablex.

Duff, P. A. (1996). Different languages, different practices: Socialization of discourse competence in dual-language school classrooms in Hungary. In K. M. Bailey & D. Nunan (Eds.), *Voices from the classroom: Qualitative research in second language education* (pp. 407–733). Cambridge: Cambridge University Press.

Duff, P. A. (2002). The discursive co-construction of knowledge, identity, and difference: An ethnography of communication in the high school mainstream. *Applied Linguistics, 23*(3), 289–322.

Duff, P. A., & Hornberger, N. H. (Eds.). (2008). *Language socialization* (Vol. 8 of the *Encyclopedia of language and education,* 2nd ed.). New York: Springer.

Durkheim, É. (1966). *The rules of sociological method* (8th ed.). New York: Free Press.

Eggins, S. (2004). *An introduction to systemic functional linguistics* (2nd ed.). New York: Continuum.

Eisenberg, A. R. (1986). Teasing: Verbal play in two Mexicano homes. In B. B. Schieffelin & E. Ochs (Eds.), *Language socialization across cultures* (pp. 182–198). New York: Cambridge University Press.

Eisenhart, M. (1995). The fax, the jazz player, and the self-story teller: How "do" people organize culture? *Anthropology and Education Quarterly, 26*(1), 3–26.

Endo, O. (1999). Endangered system of women's writing from Hunan, China. Retrieved March 28, 2007, from http://www2.ttcn.ne.jp/~orie/aas99.htm

Engels, F., & Marx, K. (1941). *Ludwig Feuerbach and the outcome of classical German philosophy*. New York: International Publishers.

English First. (2008). Official home page of English First. Retrieved August 6, 2008, from http://www.englishfirst.org/index.html

Erickson, F. (1992). They know all the lines: Rhythmic organization and contextualization in a conversational listing routine. In P. Auer & A. Di Luzio (Eds.), *The contextualization of language* (pp. 365–397). Amsterdam: Benjamins.

Erickson, F. (2004). *Talk and social theory: Ecologies of speaking and listening in everyday life*. Cambridge: Polity.

Evans, B. A., & Hornberger, N. H. (2005). No Child Left Behind: Repealing and unpeeling federal language education policy in the United States. *Language Policy, 4*(1), 87–106.

Fairclough, N. (1989). *Language and power*. London: Longman.

Fairclough, N. (1992). Discourse and text: Linguistic intertextual analysis within discourse analysis. *Discourse and Society, 3*(2), 193–217.

Fairclough, N. (2001). *Language and power* (2nd ed.). Harlow, UK: Pearson Education.

Ferguson, C. A. (1977). Baby talk as a simplified register. In C. Snow & C. A. Ferguson (Eds.), *Talking to children: Language input and acquisition* (pp. 209–235). Cambridge, UK: Cambridge University Press.

Fillmore, L. W. (1976). *The second time around: Cognitive and social strategies in second language acquisition*. Unpublished doctoral dissertation, Stanford University. Retrieved August 2, 2008, from Dissertations & Theses: Full Text database. (Publication No. AAT 7707085)

Firbas, J. (1992). *Functional sentence perspective in written and spoken communication*. Cambridge: Cambridge University Press.

Firth, A., & Wagner, J. (1997). On discourse, communication, and (some) fundamental concepts in SLA research. *The Modern Language Journal, 81*(3), 285–300.

Firth, A., & Wagner, J. (1998). SLA property: No trespassing! *The Modern Language Journal, 82*(1), 91–94.

Firth, J. R. (1935). The technique of semantics. *Transactions of the Philological Society, 34*(1), 36–72.

Firth, J. R. (1957). A synopsis of linguistic theory, 1930–1955. In *Studies in linguistic analysis. Special volume of the Philological Society* (pp. 1–32). Oxford: Blackwell.

Ford, C. E. (2004). Contingency and units in interaction. *Discourse Studies, 6*(1), 27–52.

Ford, C. E., & Thompson, S. A. (1996). Interactional units in conversation: Syntactic, intonational, and pragmatic resources for the management of turns. In E. Ochs, E. A. Schegloff, & S. A. Thompson (Eds.), *Interaction and grammar* (pp. 134–184). Cambridge: Cambridge University Press.

Foucault, M. (1978). *The history of sexuality* (R. Hurley, Trans., 1st American ed. Vol. 1: An introduction). New York: Pantheon Books.

Foucault, M. (1995). *Discipline and punish: The birth of the prison* (A. Sheridan, Trans., 2nd Vintage ed.). New York: Vintage Books.

Foucault, M., & Gordon, C. (1980). *Power/knowledge: Selected interviews and other writings, 1972–1977* (C. Gordon, et al., Trans.). New York: Pantheon Books.

Fries, P. H. (1995). A personal view of Theme. In M. Ghadessy (Ed.), *Thematic development in English texts* (pp. 1–19). London: Pinter.

Fulcher, G. (2004). Deluded by artifices? The Common European Framework and harmonization. *Language Assessment Quarterly, 1*(4), 253–266.

Gal'perin, P. Ya. (1969/1989). Study of the intellectual development of the child. *Soviet Psychology, 27*(3), 26–44. (Translation of an article in *Voprosy Psikhologii, 15*(1), 15–25, 1969)

Gal'perin, P. Ya. (1974/1989). Organization of mental activity and the effectiveness of learning. *Soviet Psychology, 27*(3), 65–82. (Translation of a chapter in V. S. Merlin (Ed.), *Vozrastnaya i pedagogicheskaia psikhologiya* [Developmental and pedagogical psychology: Proceedings of an all-union seminar], Perm', pp. 90–103, 1974).

Gal'perin, P. Ya. (1976/1989). The problem of attention. *Soviet Psychology, 27*(3), 83–92. (Translation of a chapter in A. N. Leont'ev, A. A. Puzyrei, & V. Ya. Romanova (Eds.), *Khrestomatiya po vnimaniya* [Selections on attention], pp. 220–228. Moscow: Izd-vo MGU, 1976).

Garfinkel, H. (1967). *Studies in ethnomethodology.* Englewood Cliffs, NJ: Prentice-Hall.

Garfinkel, H., & Sacks, H. (1970). On formal structures of practical actions. In J. C. McKinney & E. A. Tiryakian (Eds.), *Theoretical sociology: Perspectives and developments* (pp. 337–366). New York: Appleton-Century-Crofts.

Garrett, P., & Young, R. F. (2009). Self-discoveries about the language learning process: An analysis of one learner's affective responses to a communicative-based Portuguese course. *The Modern Language Journal, 93*(2).

Gass, S. M., & Selinker, L. (2008). *Second language acquisition: An introductory course* (3rd ed.). London: Routledge.

Gauntlett, D. (2004). *Theory trading cards.* Lanham, MD: Altamira Press.

Gebhard, M. (2002/2004). Fast capitalism, school reform, and second language literacy practices. *The Canadian Modern Language Review/La Revue canadienne des langues vivantes, 59*(1), 15–52. Reprinted in *The Modern Language Journal, 88*(2), 245–264.

Gebhard, M. (2005). School reform, hybrid discourses, and second language literacies. *TESOL Quarterly, 39*(2), 187–210.

Gee, J. P. (1999). *An introduction to discourse analysis: Theory and method.* London: Routledge.

Gee, J. P. (2007). *Social linguistics and literacies: Ideology in discourses* (3rd ed.). Abingdon, UK: Routledge.

Geertz, C. (1973). Thick description: Toward an interpretive theory of culture. In *The interpretation of culture: Selected essays* (pp. 3–30). New York: Basic Books.

Ghadessy, M. (1995). Thematic development and its relationship to registers and genres. In M. Ghadessy (Ed.), *Thematic development in English texts* (pp. 129–148). London: Pinter.

Glaser, B. G. (1978). *Theoretical sensitivity: Advances in the methodology of grounded theory*. Mill Valley, CA: Sociology Press.

Glaser, B. G., & Strauss, A. L. (1967). *The discovery of grounded theory: Strategies for qualitative research*. Chicago: Aldine.

Goffman, E. (1974). *Frame analysis*. New York: Harper and Row.

Goffman, E. (1979). Footing. *Semiotica, 25*(1), 1–29.

Goffman, E. (1981). *Forms of talk*. Philadelphia: University of Pennsylvania Press.

Goodnow, J. J., Miller, P. J., & Kessel, F. S. (Eds.). (1995). *Cultural practices as contexts for development*. San Francisco: Jossey-Bass.

Goodwin, C. (1979). The interactive construction of a sentence in natural conversation. In G. Psathas (Ed.), *Everyday language: Studies in ethnomethodology* (pp. 97–121). New York: Irvington Publishers.

Goodwin, C. (1981). *Conversational organization: Interaction between speakers and hearers*. New York: Academic Press.

Goodwin, C. (1984). Notes on story structure and the organization of participation. In J. M. Atkinson & J. C. Heritage (Eds.), *Structures of social action* (pp. 225–246). Cambridge: Cambridge University Press.

Goodwin, C. (1995). Seeing in depth. *Social Studies of Science, 25*(2), 237–274.

Goodwin, C. (1997). The blackness of black: Color categories as situated practice. In L. B. Resinick, R. Säyö, C. Pontecorvo, & B. Burge (Eds.), *Discourse, tools and reasoning: Essays on situated cognition* (pp. 111–140). New York: Springer.

Goodwin, C. (2000). Action and embodiment within situated human interaction. *Journal of Pragmatics, 32*(10), 1489–1522.

Goodwin, C. (2007). Participation, stance and affect in the organization of activities. *Discourse and Society, 18*(1), 53–73.

Goodwin, C., & Duranti, A. (1992). Rethinking context: An introduction. In A. Duranti & C. Goodwin (Eds.), *Rethinking context: Language as an interactive phenomenon* (pp. 1–42). New York: Cambridge University Press.

Goodwin, M. H. (1990). *He-said-she-said: Talk as social organization among Black children*. Bloomington: Indiana University Press.

Goodwin, M. H. (1997). Byplay: Negotiating evaluation in storytelling. In G. R. Guy, C. Feagein, D. Schiffrin, & J. Baugh (Eds.), *Towards a social science of language: Papers in honor of William Labov* (Vol. 2, pp. 77–102). Amsterdam: Benjamins.

Grin, F. (2005). Linguistic human rights as a source of policy guidelines: A critical assessment. *Journal of Sociolinguistics, 9*(3), 448–460.

Gumperz, J. J. (1992). Contextualization and understanding. In A. Duranti & C. Goodwin (Eds.), *Rethinking context: Language as an interactive phenomenon* (pp. 230–252). New York: Cambridge University Press.

Gumperz, J. J. (2000). Inference. *Journal of Linguistic Anthropology, 9*(1–2), 131–133.

Haenen, J. (1996). *Piotr Gal'perin: Psychologist in Vygotsky's footsteps*. Commack, NY: Nova Science Publishers.

Haenen, J. (2001). Outlining the teaching-learning process: Piotr Gal'perin's contribution. *Learning and Instruction, 11*(2), 157–170.

Hall, J. K. (1993). The role of oral practices in the accomplishment of our everyday lives: The sociocultural dimension of interaction with implications for the learning of another language. *Applied Linguistics, 14*(2), 145–166.

Hall, J. K. (1999). A prosaics of interaction: The development of interactional competence in another language. In E. Hinkel (Ed.), *Culture in second language teaching and learning* (pp. 137–151). New York: Cambridge University Press.

Hall, J. K. (2004). "Practicing speaking" in Spanish: Lessons from a high school foreign language classroom. In D. Boxer & A. D. Cohen (Eds.), *Studying speaking to inform second language learning* (pp. 68–87). Clevedon, UK: Multilingual Matters.

Halliday, M. A. K. (1978). *Language as social semiotic: The social interpretation of language and meaning*. London: Edward Arnold.

Halliday, M. A. K. (1989). *Spoken and written language*. Oxford: Oxford University Press. (Original work published 1985).

Halliday, M. A. K. (1994). Systemic theory. In R. E. Asher & J. M. Y. Simpson (Eds.), *The encyclopedia of language and linguistics* (Vol. 8, pp. 4505–4508). New York: Pergamon.

Halliday, M. A. K., & Martin, J. R. (1993). *Writing science: Literacy and discursive power*. Pittsburgh, PA: University of Pittsburgh Press.

Halliday, M. A. K., & Matthiessen, C. M. I. M. (2004). *An introduction to functional grammar* (3rd ed.). London: Arnold.

Hanks, W. F. (1991). Foreword by William F. Hanks. In J. Lave & E. Wenger (Eds.), *Situated learning: Legitimate peripheral participation* (pp. 13–24). New York: Cambridge University Press.

Hanks, W. F. (1996a). Exorcism and the description of participant roles. In M. Silverstein & G. Urban (Eds.), *Natural histories of discourse* (pp. 160–200). Chicago: University of Chicago Press.

Hanks, W. F. (1996b). *Language and communicative practices*. Boulder, CO: Westview.

Harklau, L. (2003). Representational practices and multi-modal communication in US high schools: Implications for adolescent immigrants. In R. Bayley & S. R. Schecter (Eds.), *Language socialization in bilingual and multilingual societies* (pp. 83–97). Clevedon, UK: Multilingual Matters.

Harkness, S., Super, C., & Keefer, C. (1992). Learning to be an American parent: How cultural models gain directive force. In R. G. D'Andrade & C. Strauss (Eds.),

Human motives and cultural models (pp. 163–178). Cambridge: Cambridge University Press.

Hayes, E. R. (2006). *Situated learning in virtual worlds: The learning ecology of Second Life*. Paper presented at the Adult Education Research Conference.

He, A. W. (2003). Novices and their speech roles in Chinese heritage language classes. In R. Bayley & S. R. Schecter (Eds.), *Language socialization in bilingual and multilingual societies* (pp. 128–146). Clevedon, UK: Multilingual Matters.

He, A. W., & Young, R. (1998). Language proficiency interviews: A discourse approach. In R. Young & A. W. He (Eds.), *Talking and testing: Discourse approaches to the assessment of oral proficiency* (pp. 1–24). Amsterdam: John Benjamins.

Headland, T. N. (1990). Introduction: A dialogue between Kenneth Pike and Marvin Harris on emics and etics. In T. N. Headland, K. L. Pike, & M. Harris (Eds.), *Emics and etics: The insider/outsider debate* (pp. 13–27). Beverly Hills, CA: Sage.

Hellermann, J. (2006). Classroom interactive practices for literacy: A microethnographic study of two beginning adult learners of English. *Applied Linguistics, 27*(3), 377–404.

Hellermann, J. (2007). The development of practices for action in classroom dyadic interaction: Focus on task openings. *The Modern Language Journal, 91*(1), 83–96.

Hellermann, J. (2008). *Social actions for classroom language learning*. Clevedon, UK: Multilingual Matters.

Hewitt, P. G. (1992). *Conceptual physics: The high school science program* (2nd ed.). Menlo Park, CA: Addison-Wesley.

Holland, D. C., & Eisenhart, M. A. (1990). *Educated in romance: Women, achievement, and college culture*. Chicago: University of Chicago Press.

Hutchby, I., & Wooffitt, R. (1998). *Conversation analysis: Principles, practices and applications*. Cambridge, UK: Polity.

Hymes, D. (1962/1974). The ethnography of speaking. In T. Gladwin & W. Sturtevant (Eds.), *Anthropology and human behavior* (pp. 15–53). Washington, DC: Anthropological Society of Washington. Reprinted in B. G. Blount (Ed.). (1974). *Language, culture, and society: A book of readings* (pp. 189–223). Cambridge, MA: Winthrop.

Hymes, D. (1972). Models of the interaction of language and social life. In J. J. Gumperz & D. Hymes (Eds.), *Directions in sociolinguistics: The ethnography of communication* (pp. 35–71). New York: Holt, Rinehart and Winston.

Hymes, D. (1974). *Foundations in sociolinguistics: An ethnographic approach*. Philadelphia: University of Pennsylvania Press.

Iwai, T., Kondo, K., Lim, D. S. J., Ray, G. E., Shimizu, H., & Brown, J. D. (1998–1999). *Japanese language needs analysis*. Mānoa: Department of East Asian languages and literatures at the University of Hawai‘i.

Jakobson, R. (1960). Closing statement: Linguistics and poetics. In T. A. Sebeok (Ed.), *Style in language* (pp. 350–377). Cambridge, MA: MIT Press.

Jefferson, G. (2004). Glossary of transcript symbols with an introduction. In G. H. Lerner (Ed.), *Conversation analysis: Studies from the first generation* (pp. 13–23). Amsterdam: Benjamins.

Jenkins, R., & Johnson, S. S. (2002). *Stand out: Standards-based English*. Boston: Heinle & Heinle.

Johns, A. M. (1991). English for specific purposes (ESP): Its history and contributions. In M. Celce-Murcia (Ed.), *Teaching English as a second or foreign language* (2nd ed., pp. 67–77). New York: Newbury House.

Johnson, M. (2001). *The art of non-conversation: A re-examination of the validity of the oral proficiency interview*. New Haven, CT: Yale University Press.

Kanagy, R. (1999). Interactional routines as a mechanism for L2 acquisition and socialization in an immersion context. *Journal of Pragmatics, 31*, 1467–1492.

Kane, M. T. (1992). An argument-based approach to validity. *Psychological Bulletin, 112*(3), 527–535.

Kaplan, A. (1993). *French lessons: A memoir*. Chicago: University of Chicago Press.

Kasper, G. (1997). "A" stands for acquisition: A response to Firth and Wagner. *The Modern Language Journal, 81*(3), 307–312.

Kasper, G., & Rose, K. R. (2002). *Pragmatic development in a second language*. Malden, MA: Blackwell.

Keenan, E. (1989). Norm-makers, norm-breakers: Uses of speech by men and women in a Malagasy community. In R. Bauman & J. Sherzer (Eds.), *Explorations in the ethnography of speaking* (2nd ed., pp. 125–143). New York: Cambridge University Press.

Kendon, A. (1980). Gesticulation and speech: Two aspects of the process of utterance. In M. R. Key (Ed.), *The relationship of verbal and nonverbal communication* (pp. 207–227). The Hague: Mouton.

Kendon, A. (1990). *Conducting interaction: Patterns of behavior in focused encounters*. Cambridge: Cambridge University Press.

Kinginger, C. (2008). *Language learning in study abroad: Case studies of Americans in France*. Malden, MA: Wiley-Blackwell.

Koshik, I. (2002). Designedly incomplete utterances: A pedagogical practice for eliciting knowledge displays in error correction sequences. *Research on Language and Social Interaction, 23*(3), 277–309.

Kramsch, C. (1996). Stylistic choice and cultural awareness. In L. Bredella & W. Delanoy (Eds.), *Challenges of literary texts in the foreign language classroom* (pp. 162–184). Tübingen: Gunter Narr.

Kramsch, C. (1997). Rhetorical models of understanding. In T. Miller (Ed.), *Functional approaches to written texts: Classroom applications* (pp. 50–63). Washington, DC: United States Information Agency.

Kramsch, C., & Nolden, T. (1994). Redefining literacy in a foreign language. *Die Unterrichtspraxis, 27*(1), 28–35.

Krashen, S. D. (1982). *Principles and practice in second language acquisition*. New York: Pergamon.

Kristeva, J. (1974). *La révolution du langage poétique: l'avant-garde à la fin du XIXe siècle, Lautréamont et Mallarmé*. Paris: Éditions du Seuil.

Kristeva, J. (1980). Word, dialogue and novel (T. Gora, A. Jardine & L. S. Roudiez, Trans.). In L. S. Roudiez (Ed.), *Desire in language: A semiotic approach to literature and art* (pp. 64–91). New York: Columbia University Press.

Kulick, D. (1992). *Language shift and cultural reproduction: Socialization, self, and syncretism in a Papua New Guinean village*. Cambridge: Cambridge University Press.

Lafford, B. A. (2007). Second language acquisition reconceptualized? The impact of Firth and Wagner (1997). *The Modern Language Journal, 91*(Focus Issue), 735–756.

Lantolf, J. P., & Thorne, S. L. (2006). *Sociocultural theory and the genesis of second language development*. New York: Oxford University Press.

Larsen-Freeman, D. (2008). *Having and doing, or is it doing and having? Neither. Learning is about both at the same time.* Paper presented at the seminar on Conceptualising Learning in Applied Linguistics held at Newcastle University, June 19–20.

Larsen-Freeman, D., & Cameron, L. (2008). *Complex systems and applied linguistics*. New York: Oxford University Press.

Lave, J. (1988). *Cognition in practice: Mind, mathematics, and culture in everyday life*. Cambridge: Cambridge University Press.

Lave, J. (1992). Word problems: A microcosm of theories of learning. In P. Light & G. Butterworth (Eds.), *Context and cognition: Ways of learning and knowing* (pp. 74–92). Hillsdale, NJ: Erlbaum.

Lave, J., & Wenger, E. (1991). *Situated learning: Legitimate peripheral participation*. Cambridge: Cambridge University Press.

Lazaraton, A. (2002). *A qualitative approach to the validation of oral language tests*. Cambridge: Cambridge University Press.

Leopold, W. F. (1939, 1947, 1949). *Speech development of a bilingual child: A linguist's record* (Vol. 1–4). Evanston, IL: Northwestern University Press.

Leung, C. (2005). Classroom teacher assessment of second language development: Construct as practice. In E. Hinkel (Ed.), *Handbook of research in second language teaching and learning* (pp. 869–888). Mahway, NJ: Erlbaum.

Leung, C., & Lewkowicz, J. (2006). Expanding horizons and unresolved conundrums: Language testing and assessment. *TESOL Quarterly, 40*(1), 211–234.

Leventhal, H., & Scherer, K. (1987). The relationship of emotion to cognition: A functional approach to a semantic controversy. *Cognition & Emotion, 1*(1), 3–28.

Levinson, S. C. (1992). Activity types and language. In P. Drew & J. Heritage (Eds.), *Talk at work: Interaction in institutional settings* (pp. 66–100). New York: Cambridge University Press.

Light, P., & Butterworth, G. (Eds.). (1992). *Context and cognition: Ways of learning and knowing*. Hillsdale, NJ: Erlbaum.

Linder, D. O. (2007). State v. John Scopes: A final word. Retrieved March 23, 2007, from http://www.law.umkc.edu/faculty/projects/ftrials/scopes/finalword.html

Linell, P. (2005). *The written language bias in linguistics: Its nature, origins and transformations*. London: Routledge.

Liu, G.-q. (2000). *Interaction and second language acquisition: A longitudinal study of a child's acquisition of English as a second language*. Beijing: Beijing Language and Culture University Press.

Long, M. H., & Doughty, C. J. (2003). SLA and cognitive science. In C. J. Doughty & M. H. Long (Eds.), *The handbook of second language acquisition* (pp. 866–870). Malden, MA: Blackwell.

Magnan, S. S. (Ed.). (2008). *Mediating discourse online*. Amsterdam: Benjamins.

Malinowski, B. (1923). The problem of meaning in primitive languages. In C. K. Ogden, I. A. Richards, B. Malinowski, F. G. Crookshank & J. P. Postgate, *The meaning of meaning: A study of the influence of language upon thought and of the science of symbolism* (pp. 296–336). London: Kegan Paul, Trench, Trubner & Co.

Malinowski, B. (1935). *Coral gardens and their magic: A study of the methods of tilling the soil and of agricultural rites in the Trobriand Islands*. New York: American Book Co.

Mannheim, K. (1952/1971). On the interpretation of *Weltanschauung*. In K. Mannheim (Ed.), *Essays on the sociology of knowledge* (pp. 33–83). New York: Oxford University Press. Reprinted in K. Mannheim & K. H. Wolff (1971), *From Karl Mannheim* (pp. 8–58). New York: Oxford University Press.

Markee, N., & Stansell, J. (2007). Using electronic publishing as a resource for increasing empirical and interpretive accountability in conversation analysis. *Annual Review of Applied Linguistics, 27*, 24–44.

Marx-Engels-Lenin Institute (Ed.). (1949). *Karl Marx and Frederick Engels: Selected works in two volumes*. Moscow: Foreign Languages Publishing House.

McDermott, R. (1980). Profile: Ray Birdwhistell. *The Kinesis Report, 2*(3), 1–4, 14–16.

McDermott, R. (1993). Acquisition of a child by a learning disability. In S. Chaiklin & J. Lave (Eds.), *Understanding practice: Perspectives on activity and context* (pp. 269–305). Cambridge: Cambridge University Press.

McLaughlin, B. (1990). Restructuring. *Applied Linguistics, 11*(2), 113–127.

McNamara, T. F. (1997). "Interaction" in second language performance assessment: Whose performance? *Applied Linguistics, 18*(4), 446–466.

McNamara, T. F., & Roever, C. (2006). *Language testing: The social dimension*. Malden, MA: Blackwell.

McNeill, D. (1992). *Hand and mind: What gestures reveal about thought*. Chicago: University of Chicago Press.

McNeill, D. (2005). *Gesture and thought*. Chicago: University of Chicago Press.

Messick, S. (1989). Validity. In R. L. Linn (Ed.), *Educational Measurement* (3rd ed., pp. 13–103). New York: American Council on Education and Macmillan Publishing Company.

Messick, S. (1996). Validity of performance assessments. In G. W. Phillips (Ed.), *Technical issues in large-scale performance assessment* (pp. 1–18). Washington, DC: U.S. Department of Education, Office of Educational Research and Improvement.

Mey, J. L. (2001). *Pragmatics: An introduction* (2nd ed.). Malden, MA: Blackwell.

Miller, B. D. (1995). Precepts and practices: Researching identity formation and among Indian Hindu adolescents in the United States. In J. J. Goodnow, P. J. Miller, & F. S. Kessel (Eds.), *Cultural practices as contexts for development* (pp. 67–85). San Francisco: Jossey-Bass.

Miller, E. R. (2006). *The discursive construction of subject positioning, power, and language ideologies among adult immigrant learners of English*. Unpublished doctoral dissertation, University of Wisconsin-Madison. Retrieved August 4, 2008, from Dissertations & Theses @ CIC Institutions database. (Publication No. AAT 3222847)

Miller, E. R. (2009). Orienting to "being ordinary": The (re)construction of hegemonic ideologies in interactions among adult immigrant learners of English. *Critical Inquiry in Language Studies*, *6*(4).

Miller, P. J. (1982). *Amy, Wendy, and Beth: Learning language in South Baltimore*. Austin: University of Texas Press.

Miller, P. J., & Goodnow, J. J. (1995). Cultural practices: Toward an integration of culture and development. In J. J. Goodnow, P. J. Miller, & F. S. Kessel (Eds.), *Cultural practices as contexts for development* (pp. 5–16). San Francisco: Jossey-Bass.

Mislevy, R. J., Steinberg, L. S., & Almond, R. G. (2003). On the structure of educational assessments. *Measurement: Interdisciplinary Research and Perspectives*, *1*(1), 3–67.

Mitchell, T. F. (1957/1975). The language of buying and selling in Cyrenaica. *Hespéris, 44*, 31–71. (Reprinted as The language of buying and selling in Cyrenaica: A situational statement. In T. F. Mitchell (Ed.), *Principles of Firthian linguistics* (pp. 167–200). London: Longman)

Moore, L. C. (1999). Language socialisation research and French language education in Africa: A Cameroonian case study. *The Canadian Modern Language Review/ LaRevue canadienne des langues vivantes, 56*(2), 329–350.

Morgan, M. (2004). Speech community. In A. Duranti (Ed.), *A companion to linguistic anthropology* (pp. 3–22). Malden, MA: Blackwell.

Mori, J. (2004). Negotiating sequential boundaries and learning opportunities: A case from a Japanese language classroom. *The Modern Language Journal, 88*(4), 536–550.

Morson, G. S., & Emerson, C. (1990). *Mikhail Bakhtin: Creation of a prosaics.* Stanford, CA: Stanford University Press.

Munby, J. (1978). *Communicative syllabus design: A sociolinguistic model for defining the content of purpose-specific language programmes.* Cambridge: Cambridge University Press.

Negueruela, E. (2003). *A sociocultural approach to teaching and researching second languages: Systemic-theoretical instruction and second language development.* Unpublished doctoral dissertation, The Pennsylvania State University. Retrieved August 2, 2008, from Dissertations & Theses @ CIC Institutions database. (Publication No. AAT 3106296)

Negueruela, E., & Lantolf, J. P. (2006). Concept-based instruction and the acquisition of L2 Spanish. In R. A. Salaberry & B. A. Lafford (Eds.), *The art of teaching Spanish: Second language acquisition from research to praxis* (pp. 79–102). Washington, DC: Georgetown University Press.

Nelson, C. D. (1999). Sexual identities in ESL: Queer theory and classroom inquiry. *TESOL Quarterly, 33*(3), 371–391.

Nelson, C. D. (2004). Beyond straight grammar: Using lesbian/gay themes to explore cultural meanings. In B. Norton, A. Pavlenko, & J. Burton (Eds.), *Gender and English language learners* (pp. 15–28). Alexandria, VA: Teachers of English to Speakers of Other Languages.

Nelson, C. D. (2008). *Sexual identities in English language education: Classroom conversations.* New York: Routledge.

Nemoianu, A. M. (1980). *The boat's gonna leave: A study of children learning a second language from conversations with other children.* Amsterdam: Benjamins.

Nguyen, H. T. (2003). *The development of communication skills in the practice of patient consultation among pharmacy students.* Unpublished doctoral dissertation, The University of Wisconsin-Madison. Retrieved August 2, 2008, from Dissertations & Theses @ CIC Institutions database. (Publication No. AAT 3113624)

Nguyen, H. T. (2005). *Talking about drugs: The interactional patterns of the pharmacy patient consultation.* Unpublished manuscript.

Nguyen, H. T. (2006). Constructing "expertness": A novice pharmacist's development of interactional competence in patient consultations. *Communication and Medication, 3*(2), 147–160.

Nguyen, H. T. (2008). Sequence organization as local and longitudinal achievement. *Text and Talk, 28*(4), 523–550.

Nicholas, H. (1987). *A comparative study of the acquisition of German as a first and second language.* Unpublished doctoral dissertation, Monash University, Australia.

No Child Left Behind Act of 2001, 20 U.S.C. 70 § 6301 et seq. (2002).

Norton, B. (2000). *Identity and language learning: Gender, ethnicity and educational change.* Harlow, UK: Longman.

Nunes, T. (1995). Cultural practices and the conception of individual differences: Theoretical and empirical considerations. In J. J. Goodnow, P. J. Miller, & F. S. Kessel (Eds.), *Cultural practices as contexts for development* (pp. 91–103). San Francisco: Jossey-Bass.

Nunes, T., Schliemann, A. D., & Carraher, D. W. (1993). *Street mathematics and school mathematics*. Cambridge: Cambridge University Press.

Ochs, E. (1979). Transcription as theory. In E. Ochs & B. B. Schieffelin (Eds.), *Developmental pragmatics* (pp. 43–72). New York: Academic Press.

Ochs, E. (1986). Introduction. In B. B. Schieffelin & E. Ochs (Eds.), *Language socialization across cultures* (pp. 1–13). Cambridge: Cambridge University Press.

Ochs, E. (1996). Linguistic resources for socializing humanity. In J. J. Gumperz & S. C. Levinson (Eds.), *Rethinking linguistic relativity* (pp. 407–437). Cambridge: Cambridge University Press.

Ochs, E. (2002). Becoming a speaker of culture. In C. J. Kramsch (Ed.), *Language acquisition and language socialization: Ecological perspectives* (pp. 99–120). London: Continuum.

Ochs, E., Gonzalez, P., & Jacoby, S. (1996). "When I come down I'm in the domain state": Grammar and graphic representation in the interpretive activity of physicists. In E. Ochs, E. A. Schegloff, & S. A. Thompson (Eds.), *Interaction and grammar* (pp. 328–369). New York: Cambridge University Press.

Ochs, E., & Schieffelin, B. B. (1984). Language acquisition and socialization: Three developmental stories and their implications. In R. A. Shweder & R. A. LeVine (Eds.), *Culture theory: Essays on mind, self, and emotion* (pp. 276–320). New York: Cambridge University Press.

Ogden, C. K., Richards, I. A., Malinowski, B., Crookshank, F. G., & Postgate, J. P. (1923). *The meaning of meaning: A study of the influence of language upon thought and of the science of symbolism*. London: Kegan Paul, Trench, Trubner & Co.

Ong, W. J. (1981). *Fighting for life: Contest, sexuality, and consciousness*. Ithaca, NY: Cornell University Press.

Ortner, S. B. (1984). Theory in anthropology since the sixties. *Comparative Studies in Society and History, 126*(1), 126–166.

Patrick, P. J. (2002). The speech community. In J. K. Chambers, P. Trudgill, & N. Schilling-Estes (Eds.), *Handbook of language variation and change* (pp. 573–597). Oxford: Blackwell.

Pavlenko, A. (2001a). "How am I to become a woman in an American vein?": Negotiation of gender in second language learning. In A. Pavlenko, A. Blackledge, I. Piller, & M. Teutsch-Dwyer (Eds.), *Multilingualism, second language learning, and gender* (pp. 133–174). Berlin: Mouton de Gruyter.

Pavlenko, A. (2001b). Language learning memoirs as a gendered genre. *Applied Linguistics, 22*(2), 213–240.

Pavlenko, A., & Lantolf, J. P. (2000). Second language learning as participation and the (re)construction of selves. In J. P. Lantolf (Ed.), *Sociocultural theory and second language learning* (pp. 155–177). New York: Oxford University Press.

Peirce, C. S., Hartshorne, C., & Weiss, P. (1933). *Collected papers of Charles Sanders Peirce*. Cambridge, MA: Harvard University Press.

Pennycook, A. (2001). *Critical applied linguistics: A critical introduction*. Mahwah, NJ: Erlbaum.

Philips, S. U. (1985). Indian children in Anglo classrooms. In N. Wolfson & J. Manes (Eds.), *Language of inequality* (pp. 311–323). Berlin: Mouton.

Pienemann, M. (1984). Psychological constraints on the teachability of languages. *Studies in Second Language Acquisition, 6*(2), 186–214.

Pienemann, M. (1998). *Language processing and second language development: Processability theory*. Amsterdam: Benjamins.

Pienemann, M., & Johnston, M. (1987). Factors influencing the development of language proficiency. In D. Nunan (Ed.), *Applying second language acquisition research* (pp. 45–141). Adelaide, Australia: National Curriculum Resource Centre.

Pienemann, M., Johnston, M., & Brindley, G. (1988). Constructing an acquisition-based procedure for second language assessment. *Studies in Second Language Acquisition, 10*(2), 217–243.

Pike, K. L. (1967). *Language in relation to a unified theory of the structure of human behavior* (2nd rev. ed.). The Hague: Mouton.

Pomerantz, A., & Fehr, B. J. (1997). Conversation analysis: An approach to the study of social action as sense making practices. In T. A. van Dijk (Ed.), *Discourse studies: A multidisciplinary introduction* (Vol. 2, pp. 64–91). Thousand Oaks, CA: Sage.

Pratt, M. L. (1999). Arts of the contact zone. *Profession, 91*, 33–40.

Propp, V. (1968). *Morphology of the folktale* (L. Scott, Trans.). Austin: University of Texas Press.

Rampton, B. (1995). Language crossing and the problematisation of ethnicity and socialisation. *Pragmatics, 5*(4), 485–515.

Ranney, S. (1992). Learning a new script: An exploration of sociolinguistic competence. *Applied Linguistics, 13*(1), 25–50.

Reisman, K. (1989). Contrapuntal conversations in an Antiguan village. In R. Bauman & J. Sherzer (Eds.), *Explorations in the ethnography of speaking* (2nd ed., pp. 100–124). New York: Cambridge University Press.

Roberts, C. (2001). Language acquisition or language socialisation in and through discourse? Towards a redefinition of the domain of SLA. In C. N. Candlin & N. Mercer (Eds.), *English language teaching in its social context: A reader* (pp. 108–121). London: Routledge in association with Macquarie University and the Open University.

Robins, R. H. (1971). Malinowski, Firth, and the "context of situation." In E. Ardener (Ed.), *Social anthropology and language* (pp. 33–46). London: Tavistock Publications.

Rogoff, B. (1995). Observing sociocultural activity on three planes: Participatory appropriation, guided participation, apprenticeship. In J. V. Wertsch, P. del Río, & A. Alvarez (Eds.), *Sociocultural studies of mind* (pp. 139–164). Cambridge: Cambridge University Press.

Rogoff, B. (2003). *The cultural nature of human development*. Oxford: Oxford University Press.

Rogoff, B., Baker-Sennett, J., Lacasa, P., & Goldsmith, D. (1995). Development through participation in sociocultural activity. In J. J. Goodnow, P. J. Miller, & F. S. Kessel (Eds.), *Cultural practices as contexts for development* (pp. 45–65). San Francisco: Jossey-Bass.

Romaine, S. (2000). *Language in society: An introduction to sociolinguistics* (2nd ed.). Oxford: Oxford University Press.

Rosenbusch, M. H. (2005). The No Child Left Behind Act and teaching and learning languages in U.S. schools. *The Modern Language Journal, 89*(2), 250–261.

Rosenwald, G. C., & Ochberg, R. L. (1992). Introduction: Life stories, cultural politics, and self-understanding. In G. C. Rosenwald & R. L. Ochberg (Eds.), *Storied lives: The cultural politics of self-understanding* (pp. 1–18). New Haven: Yale University Press.

Rousseau, J.-J. (1766). *Contrat social, ou, Principes du droit politique*. Genève: Chez Marc-Michel Bousquet.

Röver, C. (2005). *Testing ESL pragmatics: Development and validation of a web-based assessment battery*. Frankfurt am Main: Peter Lang.

Rymes, B. (2001). *Conversational borderlands: Language and identity in an alternative urban high school*. New York: Teachers College Press.

Sacks, H., Schegloff, E. A., & Jefferson, G. (1974). A simplest systematics for the organization of turn-taking for conversation. *Language, 50*, 696–735.

Sahlins, M. D. (1981). *Historical metaphors and mythical realities: Structure in the early history of the Sandwich Islands kingdom*. Ann Arbor: University of Michigan Press.

Sahlins, M. D. (1985). *Islands of history*. Chicago: University of Chicago Press.

Salomon, G. (1993). Editor's introduction. In G. Salomon (Ed.), *Distributed cognitions: Psychological and educational considerations* (pp. xi–xxi). Cambridge: Cambridge University Press.

Saslow, J. M., & Collins, T. (2001). *Workplace plus: Living and working in English*. New York: Longman.

Saussure, F. de, Bally, C., Sechehaye, A., Riedlinger, A., & Baskin, W. (1966). *Course in general linguistics* (1st McGraw-Hill paperback ed.). New York: McGraw-Hill Book Co.

Schank, R. C., & Abelson, R. (1977). *Scripts, plans, goals and understanding*. Hillsdale, NJ: Erlbaum.

Schegloff, E. A. (1978). On some questions and ambiguities in conversation. In W. U. Dressler (Ed.), *Current trends in textlinguistics* (pp. 81–102). New York: Walter de Gruyter.

Schegloff, E. A. (1982). Discourse as an interactional achievement: Some uses of "uh huh" and other things that come between sentences. In D. Tannen (Ed.), *Georgetown University Roundtable on Languages and Linguistics 1981. Analyzing discourse: Text and talk* (pp. 71–93). Washington, DC: Georgetown University Press.

Schegloff, E. A., & Sacks, H. (1973). Opening up closings. *Semiotica, 8,* 289–327.

Scherer, K. R. (1984a). Emotion as a multi-component process: A model and some cross-cultural data. *Review of Personality and Social Psychology, 5,* 37–63.

Scherer, K. R. (1984b). On the nature and function of emotion: A component process approach. In K. R. Scherer & P. Ekman (Eds.), *Approaches to emotion* (pp. 293–317). Hillsdale, NJ: Erlbaum.

Schieffelin, B. B. (1979). *Adɛ*: A sociolinguistic analysis of a relationship. *Sociolinguistic Working Paper, 69,* 1–22.

Schieffelin, B. B. (1990). *The give and take of everyday life: Language socialization of Kaluli children.* Cambridge: Cambridge University Press.

Schieffelin, B. B., & Ochs, E. (Eds.). (1986). *Language socialization across cultures.* Cambridge: Cambridge University Press.

Schmidt, R. W. (1983). Interaction, acculturation, and the acquisition of communicative competence: A case study of an adult. In N. Wolfson & E. Judd (Eds.), *Sociolinguistics and language acquisition* (pp. 137–174). Rowley, MA: Newbury House.

Schmidt, R. W. (1990). The role of consciousness in second language learning. *Applied Linguistics, 11*(2), 129–158.

Schmidt, R. W., & Frota, S. N. (1986). Developing basic conversational ability in a second language: A case study of an adult learner of Portuguese. In R. R. Day (Ed.), *Talking to learn: Conversation in second language acquisition* (pp. 237–326). Rowley, MA: Newbury House.

Schumann, F. M., & Schumann, J. H. (1977). Diary of a language learner: An introspective study of second language learning. In H. D. Brown, C. A. Yorio, & R. H. Crymes (Eds.), *On TESOL '77—Teaching and learning English as a second language: Trends in research and practice* (pp. 241–249). Washington, DC: Teachers of English to Speakers of Other Languages.

Schumann, J. H. (1998). *The neurobiology of affect in language.* Malden, MA: Blackwell.

Schweder, R. A., Jensen, L. A., & Goldstein, W. M. (1995). Who sleeps by whom revisited: A method for extracting the moral goods implicit in a practice. In J. J. Goodnow, P. J. Miller, & F. S. Kessel (Eds.), *Cultural practices as contexts for development* (pp. 17–39). San Francisco: Jossey-Bass.

Scopes v. State, 152 Tenn. 424, 278 S.W. 57 (Tenn. 1925).

Scribner, S., & Cole, M. (1981). *The psychology of literacy*. Cambridge, MA: Harvard University Press.

Searle, J. R. (1969). *Speech acts: An essay in the philosophy of language*. London: Cambridge University Press.

Seedhouse, P. (2004). *The interactional architecture of the language classroom: A conversation analysis perspective*. Malden, MA: Blackwell.

Seidlhofer, B., Breiteneder, A., & Pitzl, M.-L. (2006). English as a lingua franca in Europe: Challenges for applied linguists. *Annual Review of Applied Linguistics, 26*, 3–4.

Sfard, A. (1998). On two metaphors for learning and on the dangers of choosing just one. *Educational Researcher, 27*(2), 4–13.

Shameem, N. (2007). Social interaction in multilingual classrooms. In Z. Hua, P. Seedhouse, L. Wei, & V. Cook (Eds.), *Language learning and teaching as social inter-action* (pp. 199–217). Basingstoke, UK: Palgrave Macmillan.

Shohamy, E. (1998). Critical language testing and beyond. *Studies in Educational Evaluation, 24*(4), 331–345.

Shohamy, E. (2001a). Democratic assessment as an alternative. *Language Testing, 18*(4), 373–391.

Shohamy, E. G. (2001b). *The power of tests: A critical perspective on the uses of language tests*. Harlow, UK: Longman.Shohamy, E. (2004). Assessment in multicultural societies. In B. Norton & K. Toohey (Eds.), *Critical pedagogies and language learning* (pp. 72–92). Cambridge: Cambridge University Press.

Siegal, M. (1994). *Looking East: Learning Japanese as a second language in Japan and the interaction of race, gender and social context*. Unpublished doctoral dissertation, University of California, Berkeley. Retrieved June 7, 2008, from Dissertations & Theses: Full Text database. (Publication No. AAT 9529497)

Siegal, M. (1996). The role of learner subjectivity in second language sociolinguistic competency: Western women learning Japanese. *Applied Linguistics, 17*(3), 356–382.

Smith, A. D. (1987). *The ethnic origins of nations*. Oxford: Blackwell.

Snicket, L. (1999). *The bad beginning*. New York: HarperCollins.

Steiner, E. (1983). *Die Entwicklung des britischen Kontextualismus*. Heidelberg: Julius Groos.

Stok, D. (Ed.). (1993). *Kieślowski on Kieślowski*. London: Faber and Faber.

Strauss, A. L. (1987). *Qualitative analysis for social scientists*. Cambridge, UK, & New York: Cambridge University Press.

Strauss, A. L., & Corbin, J. M. (1990). *Basics of qualitative research: Grounded theory procedures and techniques*. Newbury Park, CA: Sage.

Strauss, A. L., & Corbin, J. M. (1998). *Basics of qualitative research: Techniques and procedures for developing grounded theory* (2nd ed.). Thousand Oaks, CA: Sage.

Strauss, C. (1992). Models and motives. In R. G. D'Andrade & C. Strauss (Eds.), *Human motives and cultural models* (pp. 1–20). Cambridge: Cambridge University Press.

Streeck, J. (1995). On projection. In Wissenschaftskolleg zu Berlin & E. N. Goody (Eds.), *Social intelligence and interaction: Expressions and implications of the social bias in human intelligence* (pp. 87–110). Cambridge: Cambridge University Press.

Sunaoshi, Y. (2005). Historical context and intercultural communication: Interactions between Japanese and American factory workers in the American South. *Language in Society, 34*(2), 185–217.

Swales, J. M. (1990). *Genre analysis: English in academic and research settings.* Cambridge: Cambridge University Press.

Tannen, D. (2004). Talking the dog: Framing pets as interactional resources in family discourse. *Research on Language and Social Interaction, 37*(4), 399–420.

Tarone, E., & Liu, G.-q. (1995). Situational context, variation, and second language acquisition theory. In G. Cook & B. Seidlhofer (Eds.), *Principle and practice in applied linguistics: Studies in honour of H. G. Widdowson* (pp. 107–124). Oxford: Oxford University Press.

Toohey, K. (1998). "Breaking them up, taking them away": ESL students in grade 1. *TESOL Quarterly, 32*(1), 61–84.

Toohey, K. (2000). *Learning English at school: Identity, social relations, and classroom practice.* Clevedon, UK: Multilingual Matters.

Tracy, K. (2002). *Everyday talk: Building and reflecting identities.* New York: Guilford.

Traweek, S. (1988). *Beamtimes and lifetimes: The world of high energy physicists.* Cambridge, MA: Harvard University Press.

U. S. Congressional Budget Office. (2006). *Immigration policy in the United States.* Retrieved August 5, 2008, from http://www.cbo.gov/ftpdocs/70xx/doc7051/02-28-Immigration.pdf

Urban, G. (1996). Entextualization, replication, and power. In M. Silverstein & G. Urban (Eds.), *Natural histories of discourse* (pp. 21–44). Chicago: University of Chicago Press.

Vachek, J. (1964). *A Prague school reader in linguistics.* Bloomington: Indiana University Press.

Voloshinov, V. N. (1973). *Marxism and the philosophy of language* (L. Matejka & I. R. Titunik, Trans.). New York: Seminar Press.

Wagner, J. (2008). *Whose language? Whose learning? And whose participation?* Paper presented at AILA 2008: The 15th World Congress of Applied Linguistics.

Watson-Gegeo, K. A., & Gegeo, D. W. (1986). The social world of Kwara'ae children: Acquisition of language and values. In J. Cook-Gumperz, W. A. Corsaro, & J. Streek (Eds.), *Children's worlds and children's language* (pp. 109–128). Berlin: Mouton.

Watson-Gegeo, K. A., & Nielsen, S. (2003). Language socialization in SLA. In C. J. Doughty & M. H. Long (Eds.), *The handbook of second language acquisition* (pp. 155–177). Malden, MA: Blackwell.

Weber, M. (1957). *The theory of social and economic organization* (A. M. Henderson & T. Parsons, Trans.). Glencoe, IL: Free Press.

Weedon, C. (1997). *Feminist practice and poststructuralist theory* (2nd ed.). Oxford: Blackwell.

Wei, S. S. (1978). *A practical dictionary of Chinese idioms, English idioms, English synonyms*. Hong Kong: The Practical English Press.

Wenger, E. (1998). *Communities of practice: Learning, meaning, and identity*. Cambridge: Cambridge University Press.

White, H. (1980). The value of narrativity in the representation of reality. *Critical Inquiry, 7*(1), 5–27.

Willett, J. (1995). Becoming first graders in an L2: An ethnographic study of L2 socialization. *TESOL Quarterly, 29*(3), 473–503.

Willis, P. (1977). *Learning to labour: How working class kids get working class jobs*. Farnborough, UK: Saxon House.

Wittgenstein, L. (1933). *Tractatus logico-philosophicus*. New York: Harcourt, Brace.

Wittgenstein, L. (1969). *Preliminary studies for the "Philosophical investigations" generally known as The Blue and Brown Books* (2nd ed.). Oxford: Blackwell.

Wittgenstein, L. (2001). *Philosophical investigations: The German text, with a revised English translation* (G. E. M. Anscombe, Trans., 3rd ed.). Malden, MA: Blackwell.

Worth, R. (2006). *Learner resistance in the university foreign language classroom*. Unpublished doctoral dissertation, University of Wisconsin-Madison. Retrieved August 6, 2008, from Dissertations & Theses @ CIC Institutions database. (Publication No. AAT 3245650)

Worth, R. (2008). Foreign language resistance: Discourse analysis of online classroom peer interaction. In S. S. Magnan (Ed.), *Mediating discourse online* (pp. 245–271). Amsterdam: Benjamins.

Wortham, S. (2001). Language ideology and educational research. *Linguistics and Education, 12*(3), 253–259.

Wu, C., & Matthiessen, C. M. I. M. (2007). SysFan (Version 1.0) [Computer program]. Sydney: Department of Linguistics, Macquarie University.

Ye, V. Z. (2003). "La double vie de Veronica": Reflections on my life as a Chinese migrant in Australia [Electronic Version]. *Mots Pluriel, 23*. Retrieved July 10, 2008, from http://www.arts.uwa.edu.au/MotsPluriels/MP2303vzy.html

Young, R. (1999). Sociolinguistic approaches to SLA. *Annual Review of Applied Linguistics, 19*, 105–132.

Young, R. (2003). Learning to talk the talk and walk the walk: Interactional competence in academic spoken English. *North Eastern Illinois University Working Papers in Linguistics, 2*, 26–44.

Young, R., & Halleck, G. B. (1998). "Let them eat cake!" or how to avoid losing your head in cross-cultural conversations. In R. Young & A. W. He (Eds.), *Talking and testing: Discourse approaches to the assessment of oral proficiency* (pp. 355–382). Amsterdam: Benjamins.

Young, R., & He, A. W. (Eds.). (1998). *Talking and testing: Discourse approaches to the assessment of oral proficiency.* Amsterdam: Benjamins.

Young, R. F. (2002). Discourse approaches to oral language assessment. *Annual Review of Applied Linguistics, 22,* 243–262.

Young, R. F. (2007). Language learning and teaching as discursive practice. In Z. Hua, P. Seedhouse, L. Wei, & V. Cook (Eds.), *Language learning and teaching as social inter-action* (pp. 251–271). Basingstoke, UK: Palgrave Macmillan.

Young, R. F. (2008a). *Language and interaction: An advanced resource book.* Abingdon, UK: Routledge.

Young, R. F. (2008b). Second language acquisition as changing participation. In G. Bernini, L. Spreafico, & A. Valentini (Eds.), *Competenze lessicali e discorsive nell'acquisizione di lingue seconde: Atti del convegno Bergamo, 8–10 giugno 2006* (pp. 407–435). Perugia: Guerra Edizioni.

Young, R. F., & Lee, J. (2004). Identifying units in interaction: Reactive tokens in Korean and English conversations. *Journal of Sociolinguistics, 8*(3), 380–407.

Young, R. F., & Miller, E. R. (2004). Learning as changing participation: Negotiating discourse roles in the ESL writing conference. *The Modern Language Journal, 88*(4), 519–535.

Young, R. F., & Nguyen, H. T. (2002). Modes of meaning in high school science. *Applied Linguistics, 23*(3), 348–372.

Zhao, Y. (1996). Language learning on the world wide web: Toward a framework of network based CALL. *CALICO Journal, 14*(1), 37–51.

Zuengler, J., & Cole, K. (2005). Language socialization and second language learning. In E. Hinkel (Ed.), *Handbook of research in second language teaching and learning* (pp. 301–316). Mahwah, NJ: Erlbaum.

Index

Index